Perspectives in Asian History

No. 3
STUDIES IN EARLY CHINESE CULTURE

STUDIES IN
EARLY CHINESE CULTURE

FIRST SERIES

BY
HERRLEE GLESSNER CREEL
Assistant Professor of Chinese Literature and Institutions at the
University of Chicago

PORCUPINE PRESS
Philadelphia

First edition 1937
(Baltimore: Waverly Press, 1937)

Reprinted 1978 by
PORCUPINE PRESS, INC.
Philadelphia, Pennsylvania 19107

Library of Congress Cataloging in Publication Data

Creel, Herrlee Glessner, 1905-
    Studies in early Chinese culture, first series.

    (Perspectives in Asian history ; no. 3)
    Reprint of the 1937 ed. published by Waverly Press,
Baltimore, which was issued as no. 3 of the American
Council of Learned Societies' Studies in Chinese and related
civilizations.
    Bibliography: p.
    Includes index.
    1.   China—Civilization.   2.   China—Antiquities.
I.   Title.   2.   Series.   III.   Series: American
Council of Learned Societies Devoted to Humanistic
Studies.   Studies in Chinese and related civilizations ; no. 3.
DS723.C73   1978   951   78-14504
ISBN 0-87991-601-X

Manufactured in the United States of America

TABLE OF CONTENTS

Preface.. v
Special Note concerning Dates.......................... xvi

I. Source Materials for the History of the Shang Period
1. The Inscribed Bones................................. 1
2. Excavation... 16
3. Books of the Shang Period.......................... 21
   Books and writing in ancient China................. 21
   Shang Sung.. 49
   T'ang Shih.. 55
   Pan Kêng.. 64
   Kao Tsung Yung Jih................................ 69
   Hsi Po K'an Li.................................... 76
   Wei Tzŭ... 81
   Summary... 93

II. Was there a Hsia Dynasty?
1. Traditions of pre-Hsia China........................ 97
2. Hsia traditions..................................... 100
3. The location of the Hsia state..................... 120
   Summary... 129

III. Who were the Shangs?
1. The period of Shang residence at Anyang............ 133
2. Racial origins...................................... 140
3. Geographical origins................................ 152
4. Origins of Shang culture............................ 168
   Neolithic cultures in North China.................. 170
   A northeastern culture area........................ 194
   The manufacture of bronze.......................... 218
   Shang decorative art............................... 234
   Foreign parallels to Shang design.................. 245
   Summary... 253
Books and articles cited................................ 255
Bibliographical abbreviations........................... 261

Index... 263

TO CARL WHITING BISHOP

PREFACE

"Of all the numerous problems with which the scientific research of China is concerned, the problem of the early origin and development of Chinese civilization is the most important, and at the same time the most fascinating."—Berthold Laufer[1].

For the past nine years it has been my intention to make a study of the origins of Chinese culture, and its development during the earliest known periods, on the basis of first-hand examination of all the contemporary documents and other data which are now available. During four of those years I have spent my entire time in realizing this aim. The papers included in this volume are the first of the results of this investigation.

It was first necessary to delimit the field of investigation. From the cultural point of view I set the limit of "Chinese culture", and have arbitrarily defined Chinese culture as the culture of people using the Chinese written language. But it was necessary to investigate not only these people, but others who may have influenced them directly. In this latter category the Neolithic inhabitants of North China are most important, and it has been necessary to study all available data concerning them. These are almost exclusively the results of excavation, both artifacts and publications in Chinese and European languages. While my study of these materials has been as thorough as I could make it, it has not been as exhaustive, or as first-hand, as my study of the Chinese materials, which fall within my proper field.

Definition of chronological limits was less simple. History, and especially Chinese history, is a continuum. To demarcate is

1. *The Journal of Race Development*, 1914, 5.2.160.

to some extent to distort, but in practice is inevitable. It was only gradually, in the course of the actual investigation, that I was able to mark out a period which at the same time lent itself to the practical necessities of investigation, and corresponded in considerable measure to the realities of political, social, and cultural history.

The present starting-point for the history of Chinese culture as such is determined by our materials. As is shown in the following papers, the earliest contemporary materials, and the earliest completely reliable information which we have concerning Chinese culture, come from some time in the fourteenth century B.C.[2] From exactly when in that century they come we can not say, but it seems probable that they come early rather than late. It has been necessary, of course, in the investigation, to go back of this time to study the Neolithic materials. But they have been studied only as throwing light on the nature and origins of the Chinese culture which succeeded them. The proper period of this investigation begins, therefore, with the fourteenth century B.C.

A priori it might seem that from this time to the end of the Shang period provided ample field for study. But unfortunately it is not possible to study the Shang period by itself, as a single fact will demonstrate. There are several documents in the transmitted literature which have been considered to be of Shang date; at least two of them have been pronounced so even by the most critical scholars. A specialist in the Shang period exclusively would consider, and indeed some of them have considered, these documents to be fundamental materials to be used in the study of that period. But I have shown in the first of these papers that there is conclusive evidence that these documents are not really Shang; on the contrary every one of them is a production of Chou date. But this can be determined only by careful study of these documents in comparison with Shang and early Chou literature, especially the *Shang Shu* and the bronze inscriptions. The student who limited himself to Shang mate-

---

2. According to the traditional chronology, which is used throughout these papers; see "Special Note Concerning Dates," p. xvi.

rials alone would utilize these documents and distort his conclusions, as specialists not infrequently do, because of an unsuitably narrow limitation of his field of study.

This is only one of a number of such instances which could be drawn. There is the further fact that our present knowledge of the Shang period is very meager, and stands in need of all the supplementation possible. We know from many facts that Chou culture was in many respects a continuation of Shang culture; the recent excavation of the 衞 Wei tombs in Hsün Hsien has emphasized this. There were also, as will be brought out in these papers, great and significant differences between Shang and Chou culture, so that it is impossible to suppose ipso facto that what we find in the Chou period was true in the Shang. But it is no less true that, since our Shang material is so little, we can form an adequate conception of conditions in the Shang period only by projecting our known Shang materials against a background of perception formed by intimate acquaintance with the relatively knowable early Chou civilization, and making due allowance for problematic variations and the lacunae in our information.

The late Shang and early Chou periods do form a single epoch in one sense. This is the epoch in which Chinese culture was assuming its definitive form. I do not mean in any sense to suggest that it ceased to change, or to grow and develop, after that time. I object strongly to such statements as that Chinese culture has been "petrified" for more than two thousand years. But it is true that Chinese culture "came of age", as it were, much earlier than our own. The Chinese worked out for themselves, a very long time ago, patterns of social, political, and economic life which were relatively satisfactory, and since that time they have found far less occasion to make drastic changes in them than have most other cultured peoples within the same period. The bases of those patterns were very nearly completed by the Han period; their foundations had been laid, in many important respects, by middle Chou times.

The history of ideas is the heart of the history of culture. Just as Christianity, itself a product of many thought-currents, is the key to much of the social and political structure of medieval

Europe, so the distinctive world-conception of the Chinese is the pattern on which the social and political organization of China during the last two thousand years was formed. That conception was to a very large extent the product of the stirring events of late Shang and early Chou China. And it probably underwent more fundamental change during the millenium from the Shang king Pan Kêng to Confucius than it did during the twenty-five hundred years from Confucius to Sun Yat-sen.

From some points of view the time of Confucius would seem the logical terminus of this period for investigation. I have not chosen it as such, for several reasons. One of these is purely practical. I wished to limit the field of study to a time within which the contemporary materials, and especially documents, still preserved to us, were sufficiently few in number so that I could, within a few years' time, make a thorough first-hand investigation of every one of them in its most original form. If one consider the many thousands of bone inscriptions and the hundreds of important bronze inscriptions, as well as the several classics, it is apparent that the materials from Shang and very early Chou times are not slight in sum. But those which emanate from a period ending shortly before the time of Confucius are much less, and much more homogeneous, than those which must be included if his period is taken in.

Another year or less might have served, however, to include the time of Confucius, and I would have taken it if it had seemed intrinsically suitable. It did not. Confucius, like many such figures, sums up the past and forecasts the future. As he himself insists, he was not very original, and I believe that it is possible to find almost every important tenet of his philosophy stated before his time. None the less, Confucius and his contemporaries belong to the times which succeeded them, rather than to those which came before.

Confucius and his philosophic contemporaries are engaged, for the first time, primarily in constructing theories about social relations and political action, rather than in meeting social and political problems and letting theories result incidentally from their solution. As a result of this fact thought and even modes of action are beginning to become formalized and schematized. Chinese culture has already passed the stage of most rapid change, and is nearing maturity, entering a phase when great alterations are accomplished much more slowly. But it is with the earlier, undeveloped, more raw and more creative period that this investigation is concerned. I hope in later years to make a study, along similar lines, of the period which includes Confucius. But before that can be done it is necessary to trace, as adequately as possible, the development which preceded and prepared the Confucian era.

I have not chosen to stop with the end of the Western Chou period for two reasons. First, without in any way denying the importance of the change which took place at that time, one must grant that the final collapse of the Chou royal power, and the coming of the Chou kings under the tutelage of the powerful feudatories, was only the culmination of a process which had been long in preparation, and entailed comparatively little in the way of abrupt and absolute change. In the second place, we know comparatively little of the Western Chou period, and need the greater knowledge of early Eastern Chou times to throw light on that, just as we need the Western Chou for the Shang.

I have chosen the approximate date of 600 B.C. as the latter termination of this period, for several reasons. The latest genuine document of the *Shu Ching* and the latest poems in the *Shih Ching* are commonly dated at around that time. This makes it convenient from the point of view of material. This date is also about the end of period of the *"pa"*. Most important of all, it brings us down to a time close to that of Confucius, in which the pending tendencies to formalism had not yet, apparently, made themselves manifest.

In the actual investigation the first task, formally, was to establish a corpus of genuine, contemporary materials from this period, as a basis for research. Actually, this task had to wait until work was well advanced. As a result of comparative study of the bone and bronze inscriptions, archeological evidence, and transmitted books which have been supposed to come from this time, I was able to determine that certain materials could be used as sources of basic evidence, and certain other materials as sources of corroborative evidence. Among the basic materials the published squeezes of Shang oracle bone inscriptions, numbering above ten thousand, and published squeezes of Chou bronze inscriptions long enough to yield important information, have occupied a prominent place. All of the published bone inscriptions have been examined in the original[3]. All of the current authenticated bronze inscriptions, of length and importance, numbering more than three hundred, have been studied in the original, character by character. Many hundreds of others, consisting of one or a few characters, have been examined in the original with less care. In every case, great care has been taken to eliminate forged or dubious material.

The original text of the *I Ching* has been studied with care. A disproportionately great amount of time has been expended on the *chin wên* text of the *Shu Ching*. The principal works in the *chin wên ku wên* controversy, and all of the principal commentators, have been studied to some extent. Every book of the *chin wên* text has been analyzed, compared with bone and bronze inscriptions and other material, and assigned to at least a tentative date. The entire *Shih Ching* has been studied.

In addition to these fundamental bodies of literature, of which at least parts are contemporary documents from this period, other works of a corroborative nature have been studied. The *Tso Chuan* and the *Kuo Yü*, while they were edited and in large part composed after the end of this period, contain materials which date from it and information which bears on it. The same

3. By the term "original", as applied to a bone or bronze inscription, I do not mean examination of the piece of bone or bronze itself. I mean, rather, examination of a squeeze or a photographic facsimile of a squeeze, as contrasted with a transcription of the characters into their hypothetical modern forms. Persons unacquainted with such inscriptions sometimes suppose that to work with squeezes is to work at second hand, with materials which are not thoroughly reliable. On the contrary, an expert, confronted by such an inscription, wishes first of all to make a squeeze of it, so that he can study it clearly. It is true, of course, that the published squeezes sometimes fail of clarity, but even the Chinese experts work with them primarily. The bones are too fragile and too widely distributed to be worked with directly.

is probably true in lesser degree of the *I Li*. As will be seen in the course of these papers, these works are not used as sources of basic evidence. But since our contemporary evidence is so scant, they cannot be ignored as sources of corroborative testimony. These works also have been studied in detail.

All texts have of course been studied in the Chinese and in the best text available, going back where possible to the Han stone classics. In all of this study, I have made detailed notes on every matter, however slight, which seemed to bear on the history of culture. Those notes, on some ten thousand cards, form the basic material of these papers.

In addition to these documentary materials I have studied the results of archeology, primarily the published results of excavations both in Neolithic and in historic sites. I have also seen a great deal of the actual materials excavated, made two visits to the Anyang site while excavation was in progress, and talked with various excavators themselves about their problems on a great many occasions. In May, 1935, I made a trip through northern Honan, Shensi, and Shansi, in the course of which I visited Anyang, saw the early Chou materials from Hsün Hsien at Kaifêng, and visited every one of the spots most important in the history of the period under investigation.

In addition I have tried to familiarize myself with all of the most important results of current Chinese scholarship in this field. This has involved the reading of books and periodicals and very frequent conferences and conversations with many Chinese scholars.

Translations from bone and bronze inscriptions, and from untranslated works, are my own. Where I have used the work of a translator, I have given his name in the footnote. But reference, for instance, to one of Legge's translations does not mean that the translated passage in the text necessarily reproduces Legge's rendering. For the *Shu Ching*, in particular, Legge used a poor text. I have not hesitated to make changes in translations wherever they seemed warranted, either on textual or other grounds. For the *Shu*, where the textual problem is especially complicated, I have in general held to the *chin wên* text. But there is, of course, no single standard even for this, and I have followed the opinions of no single scholar exclusively; on some occasions I have even preferred what is usually considered the *ku wên* reading, giving my reasons in footnotes. My own study, and my working notes, have been based in every case on Chinese texts, with the classics usually the *Shih San Ching*. But for the convenience of Western readers I have reduced these in the footnotes, where it was feasible, to terms of generally available translations. But these references are to be considered as referring primarily to the Chinese text, and only secondarily to the translation.

The papers in this first series are preliminary, defining the extent of the valid materials for Shang history and describing, in so far as can be done at this time, the antecedents of the period which is the proper subject of this investigation. Future series will be devoted to papers dealing with various aspects of Chinese culture during that period.

The way to be infallible in a field like this one is to say and write nothing. I have endeavored in these papers to state fact as fact and hypothesis as hypothesis. I have spared neither time nor effort in the attempt to make them as accurate as possible. Every statement which they contain is one which I had reason to believe true at the time of the final revision. But I have no doubt that the time will come, possibly soon, when due either to new material or to a better understanding of old material I will have to recognize that some of them are mistaken. That fact does not worry me. In my opinion it is relatively unimportant whether or not a scholarly work possesses the formal and sometimes negative virtue of impeccability. The vital question is "Does it contribute to the advance of knowledge? Does it continue the process, and can it in turn be built on?" If it has been produced carelessly, so that it cannot be relied upon, it obviously fails to meet the test. But an unduly timid straining after infallibility may be as fatal.

The most pleasant aspect of these years of work has been the association which they have brought with many Chinese scholars. In seeking to express my gratitude for their friendly helpfulness and magnificent generosity I find myself at a loss for words. It must suffice to say, loath as I am to say it, that I do not believe that any scholar, of any race, would have met in my own country or in Europe with the warm, open-handed, and often self-sacrificing coöperation which has been extended to me in China. Thousands of items of not yet published information and many unpublished results of laborious research have been vouchsafed to me. Not once but on several occasions I have been allowed to read and to make notes from manuscripts of important monographs which were sometimes not published until a year later. At the same time they have heard my own small theories always with respect and sometimes with acclaim. Such an attitude and such generosity can be maintained only by scholars of such abundant creativeness, and such assurance of the ultimate value of their work, that they do not feel it necessary to hoard its results to themselves. I wish to state my conviction that that assurance is completely justified. Chinese archeologists have needed the scientific methods of the West to supplement their own techniques. But they are mastering, and some have already mastered them. In addition they are creating methods of their own, more applicable to the Chinese materials than either traditional Chinese or traditional Western methods. The decipherment of the Shang oracle bones, to mention only one instance, is among the major achievements of scholarship, of whatever nation, during the past century. Chinese archeologists and historians have already attained distinction; they are destined to occupy a ranking place among the scholars of the world.

It is impossible to mention more than a few of the Chinese scholars who have assisted me. Professor Mei Kuang-ti helped me, with the expenditure of an incalculable amount of his time, through the perplexities of the critical literature on the history of the various classical texts. Professor Liu Chieh has given me the benefit of his broad knowledge of paleography in semi-weekly conferences during two years, dealing with problems which arose in my study of bone and bronze inscriptions. Both Professor Mei and Professor Liu did this out of pure kindness, with no return whatsoever. Mr. Chang Tsung-ch'ien assisted me by expounding the classics studied, and in various other ways, with purely nominal remuneration, until patriotism called him to the service of his country.

The various officials of the National Research Institute, and especially Dr. Fu Ssŭ-nien, Dr. Li Chi, Mr. Tung Tso-pin, Mr. Liang Ssŭ-yung, Mr. Kuo Pao-chün, and Mr. Hsü Chung-shu have assisted me immeasurably. Mr. Tung and Mr. Liang have entertained me on visits to Anyang, and answered my numerous questions with unfailing patience and courtesy.

Among the many Chinese scholars who have aided me with very material assistance are Mr. Chang P'êng-i, Chairman of the Shensi Archeological Association; Professor Ch'ên Yin-k'ê of National Tsinghua University; Professor Hu Kuang-wei of National Central University; Professor Jung Kêng of Yenching University; Professor Ku Chieh-kang of Yenching University; Mr. Kuan Pai-i, Director of the Honan Provincial Museum; Professor Li I-shao of National Central University; Mr. Liu I-chêng, Director of the Kiangsu Provincial Sinological Library; Mr. Lo Mou-tê of the Shensi Archeological Association; Professor Miu Fêng-lin of National Central University; Professor Shang Ch'êng-tso of Chinling University; Mr. Sun Hai-po, author of the *Chia Ku Wên Pien*; Professor T'ang Lan of the National University of Peking and National Tsinghua University; Professor T'ang Yung-t'ung of the National University of Peking; Dr. C. C. Young of the Geological Survey of China; and Mr. T. L. Yuan, Director of the National Library of Peiping. To all these, and to the many others from whom I have received information and assistance, either through personal kindness or through their writings, I wish to acknowledge my profound indebtedness and express my deep appreciation.

Mr. Carl W. Bishop, Associate Curator and Chief Field Archeologist of the Freer Gallery of Art, Smithsonian Institution, has allowed me to consult with him constantly on problems which arose in the course of the investigation, particularly those concerning the Neolithic period, in person while he was in China and through the medium of a voluminous correspondence afterward. It is only fair to him to state that some of the opinions expressed herein do not coincide with his own. But he has saved me from many mistakes, and given me a great deal of very valuable material. Mr. Mortimer Graves, of the American Council of Learned Societies, has helped me in so many ways that it is impossible to enumerate them. Professor Paul Pelliot, of the Collège de France, kindly examined a bibliography on the *Shu Ching* and suggested some additions to it. Dr. Nils Palmgren, Curator of H. R. H. the Crown Prince of Sweden's Collections, has kindly discussed with me his research on the Neolithic materials from north China, and given me information additional to that which he has published. Mr. Laurence C. S. Sickman, Curator of Far Eastern Art in the Nelson Gallery of Art, Kansas City; Mr. Orvar Karlbeck of the Museum of Far Eastern Antiquities, Stockholm; H. E. Dr. Oskar P. Trautmann, German Ambassador to China; and Dr. Otto Burchard have made it possible for me to see many ancient objects, and especially bronzes, which have come onto the antique market. This has been of great value in this study. Professor Lewis Hodous, of Hartford Seminary Foundation, suggested a correction which has been embodied in the manuscript.

The American Council of Learned Societies and the Harvard-Yenching Institute have made it possible, through research fellowships, for me to devote my whole time to this investigation.

Last but not least, I am glad to acknowledge my obligation to a scholar whose aid, due first to distance and later to his untimely death, it has not been possible to seek in connection with this particular investigation, but without whose early encouragement and interest I should never have been given the opportunity to make it—Dr. Berthold Laufer, whose unusual breadth of vision, no less than the profundity of his scholarship, will be missed as an irreparable loss for many years to come.

HERRLEE GLESSNER CREEL

Chicago
July 17, 1936

SPECIAL NOTE CONCERNING DATES

All authorities on the chronology of ancient China are in general agreement concerning both the relative and the absolute dating of events later than 841 B.C. But for the period earlier than this, in which the greater part of the span covered by these papers falls, there is very great difference of opinion both as to relative and as to absolute chronology. The diversity between the dates set by various systems of reckoning increases in proportion to the remoteness of the events in question.

The ideal manner in which to cope with this difficulty would be to devote an initial paper to the problem, assemble all of the evidence, determine scientifically which of the various systems is correct or if necessary construct a new one, and thereafter adhere to it rigidly. Unfortunately this is impossible, since the materials on which to base such a paper do not exist. That the various chronologies differ interposes a difficulty, but that no one of them can be shown to rest on a basis of assured authenticity brings us to something very close to an impasse.

The traditional chronology, and the one most usually encountered, is based upon the chronological table given in the second part of the twenty-first chapter of the *Han Shu*. Various expansions and revisions of this have been published at different times. A Chinese Jesuit, Père Mathias Tchang, made an exhaustive study of various Chinese works on chronology and published his results in 1905 under the title *Synchronismes Chinois*[1]. Based on the traditional chronology, this volume has the great advantage that it not only gives a system of dates for the kings but also includes, in relation to this and to the Christian era, chronologies for a number of the most important of the feudal states during the Chou period. This work is eminently

1. Published in Shanghai, as No. 24 of the *Variétés Sinologiques*.

convenient for the Occidental and even for the Chinese scholar, and among the former at least it has come to be used very widely as a standard.

Yet despite their convenience such works, which depend upon the traditional chronology, almost certainly include considerable errors, and it is only natural that the search for a more satisfactory criterion should be prosecuted. Bishop, in a paper dealing with various aspects of the subject [2], has championed the chronology found in the *Chu Shu Chi Nien*, or Bamboo Books [3], as being more nearly accurate than the traditional chronology. In the table below are set forth three different schemes of chronology, showing respective dates which they assign to the beginning of the reigns of the three so-called dynasties of Chinese antiquity. The first is the traditional scheme as given by Père Tchang, and the second is the chronology of the current text of the Bamboo Books according to Bishop [4]. The third scheme is based on Wang Kuo-wei's partial reconstitution of what he considered to be the genuine text of the Bamboo Books, in contradistinction to the current text which he considered a late fabrication.

	Traditional Chronology (Tchang)	Current Bamboo Books (Bishop) [5]	Ancient Bamboo Books (Wang Kuo-wei) [6]
HSIA	2205 B.C.	1989 B.C.	1994 B.C.
SHANG	1765 B.C.	1558 B.C.	1523 B.C.
CHOU	1122 B.C.	1050 B.C.	1027 B.C.

2. Carl W. Bishop, "The Chronology of Ancient China," *Journal of the American Oriental Society* (referred to hereafter as *JAOS*) (1932) 52.232–47.

3. Cf. p. 25, below, note 5.

4. Mr. Bishop's reckoning of dates from the current Bamboo Books differs slightly from my own reckoning, probably due to differences in the method of calculation. But since the variations are a matter of only a few years, and this whole subject is fraught with such uncertainty, it is not worth while to go into mathematical details.

5. *JAOS* 52.232.

6. Based on *Wang Chung-ch'io Kung I Shu* (1927–28; referred to hereafter as Wang, *I Shu*) III, *Ku Pên Chu Shu Chi Nien Chi Chiao* 3b, 6b, and 9a. The reduction of these dates to terms of the Christian era is my own; Wang gives no such figures.

Bishop has shown, in the paper cited, that if the length of time allowed to each dynasty in the traditional chronology be divided by the number of rulers, we get an average length of reign which is too long, whether judged by averages drawn from European or from later Chinese records. From this and other criteria he draws the sound conclusion that the chronology of the Bamboo Books is probably more nearly correct, in the periods of time which it allots to the dynasties, than is the traditional chronology.

It does not immediately follow, however, that one is to cast away the traditional chronology and substitute for it that of the Bamboo Books, in preparing a series of papers like the present one. Both practical and theoretical difficulties stand in the way of such a course. The very fact that a system of chronology has been used, as a convention, for many centuries, and that it is in general use in literature, forbids us to abandon it hastily unless we can substitute for it a chronology which has more than a probability of genuine accuracy. But the chronology of the Bamboo Books has hardly even a probability of genuine, absolute accuracy.

Bishop says, "The 'Bamboo Books'... are in a measure confirmed by Ssŭ-ma Ch'ien's *Shih chi* (ca. 100 B.C.). These two, in turn are supported in certain respects by the inscriptions on bone and tortoise-shell, of late Shang date (i.e., latter part of the second millenium B.C.), which have been unearthed during recent years near An-yang, in Honan. The correspondence between these three entirely independent sources is too close not to have had a documentary basis of some kind[7]." He recognizes, however, that the bone inscriptions have not as yet yielded any definite information as to the length of the Shang period or the length of reigns[8]. It is in fact very unlikely that they ever will give us any connected absolute chronology for the Shang period. They do give us the genealogy; the names and the order of the Shang kings, and in this they agree fairly well with the Bamboo Books. But in this they also agree about equally well with the traditional chronology, which leaves us almost where we started.

7. *JAOS* 52.233.
8. *JAOS* 52.241.

To state impossibilities is not the part of the wise man. But it is improbable in the highest degree that the Shang bone inscriptions, as we now have them, will ever yield any information on chronology past setting certain minimal lengths for the reigns of certain kings. Very rarely we find inscriptions which give the date in terms of the reign, as "In the twentieth year of the King."[9] We know, then, that this king must have reigned at least twenty years—but the inscription does not tell us who he is. In some cases we are able, by criteria which will be described later, to assign particular inscriptions to the reign of specific kings. But it is still an open question whether we shall ever be able to do this for every king—certainly such definiteness is far from possible at present. And even if we should be able to name the king under which every single inscription had been carved, we should still be far from assured of complete material for a Shang chronology. As has been said, inscriptions giving the year are rare, and from what we know of such things it is likely that the affixing of such dates was a practice peculiar to certain periods only. Still more discouraging is the fact that even when we do know that a particular inscription was made in the twentieth year of the reign of a particular king, that is no proof at all that he did not rule for fifty. And it is distinctly improbable that our material is complete enough to allow us to infer that these minimal dates are also maximal. Nevertheless, when students have searched out and placed side by side all of the inscriptions having year dates, and when if ever we are able to assign each of these to its proper reign, it will be possible to derive a certain amount of information regarding chronology from the oracle bones. But such a time is well in the future.

With the chronology of the Bamboo Books there are two difficulties. In the first place, even if we could be sure of possessing the whole of the true text of the Bamboo Books, we should still have no assurance that the chronology contained therein is fully reliable. The genuine text tells us of various prodigies; for instance one event was presaged by these: "the heavens rained blood, there was ice in summer... the sun came forth in the

9. Cf. *Yin Hsü Shu Ch'i Ch'ien Pien* 3.28.4.

night and failed to come forth by day"[10]. The current text, which is usually considered a forgery, says that Yao occupied the throne a hundred years[11]. Both the genuine text and the reputed forgery give detailed information concerning ancient rulers who have been shown pretty clearly, by recent research, to be legendary figures only. Neither can be considered a contemporary chronicle of high antiquity.

The Bamboo Books and the traditional chronology differ widely with regard to the dates of rulers prior to 841 B.C., but very little with regard to their order. This seems to indicate that in this early time a great deal of attention was paid to genealogy[12] but relatively little to dates. And this accords precisely with what we are able to observe in early documents. In the Shang bone inscriptions, early Chou bronze inscriptions, and the genuine documents of the *Shu Ching* we commonly find meticulous statement of the day, according to the cyclical system. Frequently the month and sometimes the phase of the moon is given. The year is more rare, but sometimes we do find the year within the reign specified. But an explicit statement of *what* reign the document was produced in is so rare that it could almost be said not to occur[13].

It is quite arguable, then, that the concept of dating as a matter of making possible long-term chronology had not yet come into being in China at this time. And if this be so we can hardly feel more certain of the accuracy of the Bamboo Books' chronology than of the traditional one. The last entry in the Bamboo Books is dated 295 B.C.[14]; this work, then, while it was compiled some four hundred years earlier than the *Han Shu*, is by no means contemporary with the Shang or even early Chou events which it records.

10. Wang, *I Shu*, III, *Ku Pên Chu Shu Chi Nien Chi Chiao* (referred to hereafter as *Ku Chu Shu*) 1ab.

11. *Chu Shu Chi Nien T'ung Chien* (Chêkiang Shu Chü, 1877; referred to hereafter as *Chu Shu*) 2.12a.

12. Which, as Bishop points out, we should expect because of the ancestor cult.

13. The name of the reigning king may be mentioned incidentally in the document, but it is rarely if ever made a part of the date.

14. I.e., the twentieth year of Chou Nan Wang.

All of the above is posited on the supposition that we had the complete, genuine text of the Bamboo Books. But we do not. Chinese scholars have long since pointed out that quotations in old books do not tally, at all points, with the text now current, and have very generally considered the current text to be a document fabricated after the original had been lost. Wang Kuo-wei gathered together quotations of the original text, thus reconstituting fragments of it [15]. Also, in order to prove beyond question the falsity of the current text, he compiled an analysis of it seeking to show, by quoting various works, exactly where the forger of the current text obtained his material. After completing this task Wang declared that the material in the current Bamboo Books was virtually all borrowed from other works. He asserted that the information appearing in this work "which is not found in other books does not exceed one per cent," [16] and he has published in full detail the evidence on which this statement is based [17]. Even more important for our present purpose, he says that "that which was added was only the dates" [18]. But if, as he holds and has gone far to prove, the dates in this work were a more or less arbitrary addition of a time later than the third century [19] we can not suppose that they have any more claim to authenticity than the chronology of the *Han Shu*; on the contrary they would seem to have for our era much less. Yet this criticism does not apply to certain dates found in the genuine document and included in the later one, and Bishop has shown that in some respects the Bamboo Books chronology seems more acceptable, in regard to the number of years it assigns to long periods, than the traditional chronology. But if we take only the genuine text, in the fragmentary state in

15. Cf. Wang, *I Shu* III, *Ku Chu Shu*.
16. *I Shu*, III, *Chin Pên Ku Shu Chi Nien* (referred to hereafter as *Chin Chu Shu*). Preface.
17. Ibid.
18. Ibid.
19. If his contention is correct they must be so, since these books were found in opening a tomb during that century (cf. *Chin Shu, Lieh Chuan* 21, *Shu Hsi Chuan*), after which they became current; it was only after this text was lost that the forgery would have been possible.

which it is preserved to us, we have too little material for use as a full and detailed chronology.

There are difficulties inherent in every scheme of dates for Chinese history prior to 841 B.C. It is a question whether the material for an exact chronology has been preserved—it may never be possible to construct one. Nevertheless we are compelled, in studying and writing history, to adhere to some chronological system if only to place events in relation to each other. For this practical purpose the traditional chronology has many advantages, not the least of which is that it is in general use. And Tchang's *Synchronismes Chinois* provides tables correlating the chronology of the various states, according to the traditional system, which could be duplicated for another system only by means of an amount of labor which the result would scarcely justify. Throughout these papers dates will be given according to Tchang's tables. It is to be understood, however, that these dates are purely conventional and do not necessarily imply that events thus dated have been definitely located with relation to world chronology; they are only relatively located in Chinese chronology.

I. THE SOURCE MATERIALS FOR THE HISTORY OF THE SHANG PERIOD

1. THE INSCRIBED BONES

During the present century, and especially during the last decade, historical research has been able to remove the closing centuries of the Shang state[1] from the realm of legend and to bring many of its aspects into the clear light of history. This achievement has been made possible by a large body of newly discovered material, and all of that material has come to us as a direct or indirect result of the discovery of the Shang oracle bones.

For some decades during the last century farmers tilling their fields north of the tiny village of Hsiao T'un, near Anyang city,[2]

---

1. Usually referred to, of course, as the Shang dynasty, and also as the Yin dynasty, the latter especially as referring to the period after Pan Kêng is reputed to have moved the capital, sometime after 1401 B.C. The genuine Bamboo Books (not the modern forgery) says that Pan Kêng moved his capital to a place called Yin (see *Ku Chu Shu* 5a). Wang cites the *T'ai P'ing Yü Lan* and other works which quote this passage. Ssŭ-Ma Chên, in his *So Yin* commentary on the *Shih Chi* (at the beginning of the *Yin Pên Chi*) says "'P'an Kêng moved to Yin." It has therefore been generally supposed that Yin was the name of the capital of the Shang people after the time of Pan Kêng, and that the name of the state was changed to Yin for this reason.

But it is fairly evident from the oracle bones that the name of the capital was not Yin, but Shang. Furthermore, the character Yin seems to be entirely lacking in the bone inscriptions. This does not necessarily mean that it was unknown to the Shang people, for the range of the content of these inscriptions is narrow. None the less, the most plausible explanation of the name Yin, in the light of our present knowledge, is that it was a name of the Chou people for the Shangs. If so, it has little to recommend it for present scholarly usage. Throughout this book the name Shang will be used exclusively, save in quotations.

2. 安陽 Anyang is the name of the *hsien*, and the city is sometimes called Anyang, sometimes called 彰德府 Changtêfu.

in the northern tip of Honan Province, had noticed that very odd pieces of bone sometimes came to the surface. These were bought up by a man of the village, who sold them as "dragon bones" to drugstores, for medicine. A Shantung buyer of antiques, Fan Wei-ch'ing by name, is said to have been the first to make them known as objects of archeological interest[3]. He discovered them as such in 1899, and in the same year offered some to the famous connoisseur Tuan Fang, who was delighted and purchased a number. In the next year, 1900, he took more than a hundred pieces to Peking, where the official Wang I-jung bought them eagerly. Wang bought several hundred more pieces of inscribed bone from another dealer, but his activities as a collector were cut short by his execution in connection with the Boxer troubles.

In the same year an Englishman and an American, Couling and Chalfant, bought a number of pieces of inscribed bone in Shantung. Some of these went subsequently to the British Museum, the Royal Scottish Museum, the Field Museum in Chicago, and the Carnegie Museum in Pittsburg[4].

Some of the pieces they acquired, especially those carved in the shapes of tortoises, swords, etc., were forgeries. The carving of forged inscriptions on oracle bones undoubtedly began very early. One often hears it said that the bones in certain collections must be genuine because "they were bought very early, before they began making fakes". But a little consideration of the circumstances will show the absurdity of this. In the first place, the subsequent excavations of the National Research Institute have shown that about ninety per cent of the pieces of genuine, ancient divination bone found have no characters[5].

3. The present account of the history of the discovery of the bones is based chiefly on Tung Tso-pin's 甲骨年表 *Chia Ku Nien Piao*, published in the *Bulletin of the National Research Institute of History and Philology* (referred to hereafter, as *Bull. Nat. Res. Inst.*) (1930) 2.2.241–260.

4. See J. M. Menzies, *Oracle Records from the Waste of Yin* (Shanghai, 1917) 2–3; R. S. Britton, *The Couling-Chalfant Collection of Inscribed Oracle Bone* (Shanghai, 1935).

5. See *Preliminary Reports of Excavations at Anyang*, p. 575 (published in Chinese by the National Research Institute of History

These, then, provide the forger with unlimited ancient raw material on which to work. And in the early years there was a good demand at very high prices, with a small supply, since large scale digging for them had not yet flooded the market. Add to that the fact that, since nobody could read the inscriptions, nobody could very well be sure what was genuine and what was not, and one has a faker's paradise. And the things were faked. I have seen a large collection of supposed oracle bones, bought for several thousand dollars by a museum, which consisted in large part of forgeries. They even included the little circles used in modern Chinese for punctuation[6]! Yet these were secured relatively early.

Mr. James M. Menzies, a Canadian missionary stationed at Anyang, lived near the site from which the inscribed bones came. He went frequently to the spot from which the bones came and watched them being dug out of the ground. One would suppose that he would have got only genuine pieces. But he writes: "Many spurious specimens purporting to come from this site are on the market. Many of these are actual bones and objects exhumed, or manufactured from exhumed bones which are afterwards skilfully engraved with copies of other inscriptions. These are to be found in abundance in Changtefu, and even in the village of Hsiao Tun near the Waste of Yin. The first large objects the writer secured were all false."[7]

There are, in collections of supposedly Shang material made by foreigners, a number of pieces of malachite, of various shapes, inscribed with characters. Some, perhaps all, of these are definitely forgeries. And it is interesting to note that the National Research Institute has never, in all its years of excavation, uncovered such a piece. Some Chinese experts say that all such objects are false.

In 1902 the collections of Wang I-jung and Fan Wei-ch'ing were purchased by Mr. Liu Ê. The same collector also bought a

---

and Philology, in four parts paged consecutively, Peiping 1929, 1931, Shanghai 1933; hereafter referred to as *Anyang Pao Kao*).

6. This particular collection has never, in so far as I know, been placed on exhibition.

7. *Oracle Records from the Waste of Yin*, p. 4.

number of other pieces from other sources, bringing his collection to a total of about five thousand pieces. In this same year they were examined for the first time by the archeologist Lo Chên-yü, who immediately saw their significance for philological study, declaring them to be such materials as no scholars since the beginning of the Han period had possessed. In 1903 Liu published the first volume of squeezes of bone inscriptions, a lithographed work reproducing one thousand fifty-eight pieces, entitled 鐵雲藏龜 *T'ieh-yün Ts'ang Kuei*[8]. Lo Chên-yü wrote a preface discussing the bones, and Liu in his preface discussed the history of the discovery, etc.

In 1904 Sun I-jang published his 契文舉例 *Ch'i Wên Chü Li*, which was the first published attempt at deciphering the oracle bone inscriptions. Sun brought to this task the indispensable preparation, a knowledge of ancient bronze inscriptions. His work may seem primitive if viewed from the vantage-point of thirty years of further study, but it gives him undisputed right to the title of founder of this branch of research. In the same year the task of digging for inscribed bones was organized on a large scale by one of the residents of the village of Hsiao T'un, which actually stands on the site of the Shang capital. As a result of this enterprise several cartloads of oracle bones are said to have been excavated. This led to disputes among the villagers, however, and as a result the digging was forbidden by the district officials.

In 1909 two articles on the Anyang discoveries were published in Japan. In 1910 Lo Chên-yü published his 殷商貞卜文字攷 *Yin Shang Chên Pu Wên Tzŭ K'ao*, a brief but important contribution to the literature of interpretation. In the preface to this work he made the statement, on the basis of the occurrence of the names of the Shang kings on the bones, that these were "relics of the royal court of Yin". This same year Lo hired men to dig for him at Anyang, which undertaking netted him some twenty thousand pieces of divination bone. A certain amount of digging by the villagers had been going on almost constantly, of course, with the products trickling into the hands of collectors.

8. This work will be referred to hereafter as *T'ieh Kuei*. Its name comes, of course, from Liu's *tzŭ*.

In 1911 squeezes of some of Lo Chên-yü's bones were published lithographically in the 國學叢刊 *Kuo Hsüeh Ts'ung K'an*. Lo has always been a staunch royalist, and when the revolution came he fled to Japan, taking his oracle bones with him in many boxes. The rigors of transportation and the enthusiastic curiosity of naïve customs examiners resulted in serious injury to more than half of his collection. Despite this he made 1912 a memorable year in the history of this research by publishing his 殷虛書契前編 *Yin Hsü Shu Ch'i Ch'ien Pien*. This great collection of squeezes, two thousand two hundred twenty-nine in number, still stands as the most important single work of its sort. And it set a new standard of excellence in printing, which was done by the collotype process. Lo's publications are expensive, and their occasional duplication of materials in successive works is sometimes annoying, but the scholarly world owes him a debt of gratitude for presenting these materials in the most usable form possible. It is with relief that one turns to his books after poring over some of the impossibly obscure reproductions of squeezes which have been published. In 1914 Lo published his 殷虛書契菁華 *Yin Hsü Shu Ch'i Ching Hua*, consisting chiefly of large divination bones, the scapulae of cattle. Due to the dating criteria recently established we now know that most of the contents of this work are inscriptions from the time of the Shang king Wu Ting. In the same year Lo published the first edition of his 殷虛書契考釋 *Yin Hsü Shu Ch'i K'ao Shih*.

In 1914 Menzies, riding his horse outside the Anyang city walls, accidentally came across some villagers in the process of digging for oracle bones. This was the beginning of what became at first a hobby and later his profession. He bought large numbers of the bones, many of them false at first, but soon became able to distinguish.

In 1915 Lo Chên-yü published 鐵雲藏龜之餘 *T'ieh-yün Ts'ang Kuei Chih Yü*, adding forty pieces to the number of published squeezes. In the following year his 殷虛書契後編 *Yin Hsü Shu Ch'i Hou Pien* was issued, adding another one thousand one hundred four pieces. His 殷虛書契待問編 *Yin Hsü Shu Ch'i Tai Wên Pien*, on bone characters "awaiting further investigation", not yet deciphered, also appeared in 1916, as did his 殷虛古器物圖錄 *Yin Hsü Ku Ch'i Wu T'u Lu*. In the latter volume he published illustrations of fifty-five objects of various sorts, dug up at Anyang and presumably of Shang date. Without calling in question the period of any of the objects here illustrated, it must be pointed out that only the most careful of scientific archeological method can serve to make certain the date of uninscribed objects which are excavated. I once bought, in a very reputable Peiping antique shop, a number of articles from Anyang, supposedly from the Shang ruins, including a piece of carved marble with inlaid lines of cinnabar which looked much like a Shang piece. Because the things were bought so very cheaply they were not examined closely until they had been taken home, when the sides of the piece of marble proved to be inscribed—with characters which could not be older than the Ch'un Ch'iu period! Yet the piece probably did come from Anyang, and perhaps from the very site of the Shang ruins. The excavators of the National Research Institute have found the mixing of objects of various periods at Anyang to be very complex. We can not, therefore, be sure that an uninscribed object is of Shang date merely because it comes from the Anyang site; it must have been excavated under scientific conditions, or have been checked by comparison with objects which have been so excavated.

In 1917 Menzies published his *Oracle Records from the Waste of Yin*, containing drawings of two thousand three hundred sixty-nine inscribed bones selected from a collection of some fifty thousand[9]. He wrote a preface for the book in Shanghai while on his way to Canada for war service.

This is an appropriate place to discuss the widely used translation "the waste of Yin" for the term 殷虛 *Yin hsü*. Who started this translation is not clear, but it seems to be quite

9. In the copy of this work in the Library of the College of Chinese Studies (formerly North China Union Language School), Peiping, there is the following handwritten note under drawing no. 758:

"This bone fragment I am now convinced is false, the only one in the collection to my knowledge.

James M. Menzies

Pekin, July 20, 1926."

erroneous, based merely on the inadequate definitions of Chinese-English dictionaries. The noun "waste" as meaning a place is defined in *Webster's Collegiate Dictionary* as "That which is waste, or desolate; devastated or uncultivated region; desert; wilderness", and by the *Concise Oxford Dictionary* as "Desert, waste region, dreary scene". But this does not at all cover the meaning of *hsü* in this expression. Although it is now often written 墟, the original, ancient form of this word evidently lacked the "earth" determinative[10], since the *Shuo Wên* does not have the character with this element, but defines 虛 *hsü* as "a large hill"[11]. The now common sense of "emptiness" attached to this character, from which the translation of "waste" comes, seems therefore to be a late development. The term *Yin hsü* is quite early[12]. The real meaning of this expression is evident from its use in ancient books. The K'ang Hsi Dictionary defines 墟 as "an ancient city", and quotes various

10. The common practise of calling such elements in a character "radicals" is erroneous, since they are actually the last part of the character to be added to it and therefore the least radical.
11. Bernhard Karlgren, *Bulletin of the Museum of Far Eastern Antiquities,* Stockholm (referred to hereafter as *BMFEA*) (1930), 2.17, writes 殷虛書契前編 as *Yin k'ü shu k'i ts'ien pien*, and says, in a footnote on the same page, "Western scholars regularly transcribe *Yin hü shu k'i* etc.; but *hü* here stands for [墟], which is correctly read *k'ü* ... "
The error here is Karlgren's. The title of Lo Chên-yü's book reads 虛, not 墟, and Lo is not, as Karlgren seems to think, mistaken. 虛 was the original, proper character, as is shown by the genuine Bamboc Books (*Ku Chu Shu* 5a.10), the *Tso Chuan* (Legge, *Chinese Classics*, Vol. V, London, 1872; referred to hereafter as *Tso Chuan*) 750.7–10, and the *Shih Chi* (Chin Ling Shu Chü, 1870) 7.10b (cf. both text and commentaries), as well as by the *Shuo Wên*. The *Tso Chuan* does not contain the character 墟, according to Fraser's *Index* (Oxford Press, 1930). This is a late character, made up by the addition of a determinative, and it is an error to substitute it, as Karlgren does, for the original character in texts where the latter occurs.
As for pronunciation, I have heard many Chinese specialists in this material speak of "*Yin hsü*," but never once of "*Yin k'ü*" or "*Yin ch'ü*."
12. It probably occurred in the genuine Bamboo Books; see *Ku Chu Shu* 5a.

ancient works including the *Tso Chuan* and even the Bamboo Books passage referring to the *Yin hsü* as evidence. *Hsü* in this connection does not, then, mean "waste", but rather "ruins" in the sense of "the remains of a ruined city". *Yin hsü* should therefore be translated as "the Yin ruins".

It was in 1917 that Wang Kuo-wei, one of the greatest of interpreters of the oracle bone materials, published his 殷卜辭中所見先公先王考 *Yin Pu Tz'ŭ Chung So Chien Hsien Kung Hsien Wang K'ao*, and 續考 *Hsü K'ao*, and his 殷周制度論 *Yin Chou Chih Tu Lun*[13]. In 1918 Chi Fo-t'o published another collection of squeezes, entitled 戩壽堂所藏殷虛文字 *Chien Shou T'ang So Ts'ang Yin Hsü Wên Tzŭ*, in the 藝術叢編 *I Shu Ts'ung Pien*. In 1919 Wang Kuo-wei published the *Chien Shou T'ang So Ts'ang Yin Hsü Wên Tzŭ K'ao Shih* in the same periodical. In 1920 Wang Hsiang published the 簠室殷契類纂 *Fu Shih Yin Ch'i Lei Tsuan*, a large work of interpretation. A Japanese scholar, Dr. Taisuke Hayashi, brought together squeezes of one thousand twenty-three pieces of inscribed bone, from three collections, and published them in 1921 under the title 龜甲獸骨文字 *Kuei Chia Shou Ku Wên Tzŭ*. In the same year K'ê Ch'ang-chi published the 殷虛書契補釋 *Yin Hsü Shu Ch'i Pu Shih*.

Beginning with the year 1923 books and articles on the oracle bones multiplied rapidly. A large number of Chinese scholars had begun to do serious work in this field, and it is their coöperative research which has changed these materials, in a few years, from objects of interesting speculation into documents of basic historical value. From this time forward it is not possible, in this historical sketch, to list any but the largest or most important publications. A somewhat more complete list is given in Tung Tso-pin's *Chia Ku Nien Piao*[14] for the years up to and including 1930.

A most valuable aid to research in the bone inscriptions was given to scholars by the publication of Shang Ch'êng-tso's

---

13. Originally published in the 學術叢書 *Hsüeh Shu Ts'ung Shu*. Now in his collected works, Wang, *I Shu*, I, 9 and 10.

14. Published in *Bull. Nat. Res. Inst.*, 1930, 2.2.241–260.

殷虛文字類編 *Yin Hsü Wên Tzǔ Lei Pien*, in 1923[15]. This work had an index in which the modern forms of characters were arranged by strokes, by reference to which it was possible to find actual occurrences of a given character in the various books of squeezes. It was not a complete index, but gave specimen forms of each of the characters which were considered to have been deciphered. It also included quotations from Lo Chên-yü's discussions of the characters, with occasional remarks by Shang. Together with this in a single series was printed Lo Chên-yü's *Yin Hsü Shu Ch'i K'ao Shih*, and Shang Ch'êng-tso's 殷虛文字待問編 *Yin Hsü Wên Tzǔ Tai Wên Pien*.

In 1923 Yeh Yü-shên published 殷契鉤沈 *Yin Ch'i Kou Ch'ên* as an article in the 學衡 *Critical Review*, No. 24. Two papers, entitled 說契 *Shuo Ch'i* and 擘契枝譚 *Yen Ch'i Chih T'an* were contributed by the same author to No. 31 of the same journal in 1924[16].

In 1925 Yeh published the 鐵雲藏龜拾遺 *T'ieh-yün Ts'ang Kuei Shih I*, including two hundred forty squeezes, with an appended transliteration of each into modern characters. In the same year Wang Hsiang issued the 簠室殷契徵文 *Fu Shih Yin Ch'i Chêng Wên*.

In 1927 a revised and enlarged edition of Lo Chên-yü's *Yin Hsü Shu Ch'i K'ao Shih* was published. This volume includes a great deal of quotation of the work of Wang Kuo-wei. Three months after it was published Wang committed suicide by drowning as a gesture of despair and protest against the condition of his country. His collected writings, which have been published in four groups, include many important articles on the oracle inscriptions.

In 1928 the National Research Institute[17] had a reconnaissance

---

15. Shang's preface has the cyclical characters *kuei ch'ou*, or 1913. But this must be an error. The book could not have been published so early, for it quotes much later works. Tung Tso-pin places it in 1923, and the title-page of the *Tai Wên Pien*, issued at the same time, has the characters *kuei hai*.

16. These three articles were republished, as two volumes, in Peiping in 1929.

17. 國立中央研究院, also translated as "Academia Sinica." It is a government research institute.

excavation made on the Anyang site, under the direction of Mr. Tung Tso-pin. In the first season's excavation seven hundred seventy-four pieces of inscribed bone were found. In 1929 the work was put on a larger basis, as a coöperative enterprise of the National Research Institute and the Freer Gallery of Art. In 1930 there was no excavation, but each year since that time excavation has been carried on by the National Research Institute. This excavation, under the direction of scientifically trained men, has settled once for all the question of whether all of the oracle bones are forgeries. Many of them are, and some forgeries have been published by scholars as genuine. But as late as 1930 one could hear that it was said by some scholars in Europe that the whole oracle bone business was a myth, made up by one or more Chinese scholars for their own profit. But the many thousands of bones found in situ by the excavators, which tally in every detail with squeezes found in such books as Lo Chên-yü's, make any such contention absurd.

In 1929 the National Research Institute issued the first of the *Preliminary Reports of Excavations at Anyang*, which included two articles by Tung Tso-pin on the bone inscriptions, and drawings of three hundred eighty-one pieces of inscribed bone excavated by the Institute. In 1930 Tung published his *Chia Ku Nien Piao*, giving a brief history and bibliography of the work on the oracle inscriptions up to that date, and an article entitled 殷墟沿革 *Yin Hsü Yen Kê*, "A History of the Yin-hsü Site"[18]. In 1931 the third of the *Preliminary Reports of Excavations at Anyang* appeared, and in 1933 the fourth; both of these contained articles by Tung Tso-pin on the inscriptions and reproductions of excavated inscribed bone.

T'ieh-yün Ts'ang Kuei, the pioneer volume of squeezes of the bone inscriptions, was reprinted in 1931, with transcriptions of the characters into modern forms by Pao Ting.

1933 was a red-letter year. It saw the publication, first of all, of Tung Tso-pin's 甲骨文斷代研究例 *Chia Ku Wên Tuan Tai*

---

18. *Bull. Nat. Res. Inst.*, 1930, 2.2.224–240.

Yen Chiu Li[19], which for the first time laid down principles by which a large portion of the bone inscriptions may be dated within a possible error of decades, rather than of centuries as had been the case[20]. The most important of the dating criteria is that which Tung calls the names of the 貞人 *chên jên*. There is a regular formula on a large number of the bones which may be represented as follows: 甲子卜 X 貞 ... "*Chia tzŭ* (or any other of the sixty possible days) *pu* X *chên*..." In the place of "X" in this formula there occur a number of characters, but only a limited number. And sometimes the character 王 *wang*, "the king", occurs here. Tung decided that these characters, which occurred at point "X", were the names of diviners. Abundant proof supports his theory, and it is now almost universally accepted by scholars. He found, in testing out this theory, that a particular name occurring in this place was ordinarily associated with the same kind of character-cutting, or "hand-writing". He also found that individual names did not occur promiscuously distributed over several hundred years, but were limited to the reign of one or at most two kings[21], exactly as we should expect in the case of a human individual who lived a normal lifetime and then died. These names are very important because once it has been determined that they belong to the period of a certain king, it is then possible to date any inscription in which they occur as belonging to about that same period.

Tung also suggested certain other criteria. He did not present them as more than tentative, and scholars vary in their accept-

19. Published in *Studies Presented to Ts'ai Yuan P'ei on his Sixty-fifth Birthday*, by Fellows and Assistants of the National Research Institute of History and Philology 慶祝蔡元培先生六十五歲論文集 Vol. I (Peiping, 1933; referred to hereafter as *Ts'ai Anniv. Vol.*), 323-424.
20. This means, of course, relative date. The absolute chronology of the Shang period is still an open question.
21. It is possible to determine this because of the fact that a certain number of the bones are quite datable due to the occurrence of the names of kings we can identify. When we find a certain king sacrificed to as "father" and another as "grandfather" we can usually determine the generation which produced the inscription.

ance of them. Tung distinguished five periods, represented by the various inscriptions, as follows:

  I. Period of Wu Ting and earlier (Pan Kêng, Hsiao Hsin, and Hsiao I)[22]
 II. Period of Tsu Kêng and Tsu Chia
III. Period of Lin Hsin and K'ang Ting
 IV. Period of Wu I and Wên Ting[23]
  V. Period of Ti I and Ti Hsin[24]

For the bones of each of these periods he established certain tentative criteria—grammar, phraseology, forms of characters, etc., in addition to the names of diviners which occur. He published a table showing the forms of the twenty-two cyclical characters, the "stems" and "branches", as they appear in the inscriptions of various periods[25]. Some of these criteria will have, no doubt, to be modified. But anyone who studies them carefully will find that they provide a very convenient tool of research for verifying findings reached by other means. We

22. The question of whether we have any bone inscriptions which are as early as the time of Pan Kêng is still being debated.
23. Wên Ting (on the bones called 文武丁 Wên Wu Ting) is the king usually called T'ai Ting. He is called Wên Ting in the genuine Bamboo Books; see *Ku Chu Shu* 6a.
24. Ti Hsin is the last Shang king, ordinarily called simply 紂 Chou. But this practice of calling him by a name, and without a title, is contrary to the Shang practice, and is unquestionably due to the fact that the Chous, having overthrown him, were compelled in self-defence to represent him as wicked and treat his memory with contempt. The name Ti Hsin occurred in the genuine Bamboo Books; see *Ku Chu Shu* 6b.
Whether we have any inscriptions from the time of this last Shang sovereign is an open question. If the capital was removed to Ch'ao Kê in the reign of Ti I and the capital at Anyang was abandoned (cf. quotation from *Ti Wang Shih Chi* in *Chu Shu* 6.11b), then we could hardly have such inscriptions. It has been suggested that Ch'ao Kê, was only an alternative capital. According to the genuine Bamboo Books "From the time when P'an Kêng moved to Yin down to the fall of Chou (i.e., the last Shang king) . . . the capital was not again moved." See *Ku Chu Shu* 5a.
25. *Ts'ai Anniv. Vol.*, chart opp. 410.

shall have further developments in this line, of course, in the way of more extensive and more exact establishment of criteria. But there can be no question that this one paper advanced research on the bone inscriptions an incalculable distance, and increased their availability as historical material by many fold. Tung acknowledges that he received a part of the stimulus to this type of research from Menzies, who constantly urged upon him the importance of seeking dating criteria, so that a part of the credit for this great advance must be given to the Canadian scholar[26].

Chu Fang-p'u brought out his 甲骨學, 文字編 *Chia Ku Hsüeh, Wên Tzŭ Pien*, in 1933. This work reproduces several examples of each character discussed, after the manner of the *Yin Hsü Wên Tzŭ Lei Pien*, and in many cases appends lengthy discussion and quotations from various scholars concerning their interpretation.

Five additional collections of squeezes were published in 1933. Shang Ch'êng-tso called his collection 殷契佚存 *Yin Ch'i I Ts'un*; Jung Kêng and Ch'ü Jun-min published theirs under the title 殷契卜辭 *Yin Ch'i Pu Tz'ŭ*. Both works included transcriptions of the inscriptions into modern characters, with occasional discussion. The former had several prefaces by various scholars, constituting so many papers; the latter included an index of the characters in the inscriptions. Lo Chên-yü brought out the 殷虛書契續編 *Yin Hsü Shu Ch'i Hsü Pien*; along with a great deal of new material, this work included a number of squeezes which had already appeared elsewhere. Squeezes of the oracle bones in the collection of Dr. John C. Ferguson were published with transcription and notes by Shang Ch'êng-tso, under the title 福氏所藏甲骨文字 *Fu Shih So Ts'ang Chia Ku Wên Tzŭ*. The first of several volumes of squeezes of bone inscriptions in the Honan Museum at Kaifêng, with transcriptions and notes by Hsü Ching-ts'an, appeared under the title 殷虛文字存眞 *Yin Hsü Wên Tzŭ Ts'un Chên*.

Another work of great importance appeared in 1933. It came from the hand of Kuo Mo-jo, a Chinese scholar living in

26. See ibid. 412.

Japan. Kuo is at once the admiration and the despair of all scholars working in this field. He is brilliant but erratic. He produces theories of the greatest value, and sets them forth with a carelessness which sometimes defeats his ends. One must read his books, but one cannot rely upon them without checking everything. This work on the bones, called 卜辭通纂 *Pu Tz'ŭ T'ung Tsuan*, is an introductory handbook which includes, in its first volume, reproductions of the squeezes of something like one thousand pieces of bone, drawn from various collections. In the text, under various headings, these inscriptions are translated and discussed. Kuo has succeeded in bringing together, within one brief work, a very large proportion of all the important inscriptions, and in creating a book which is without a rival as an introduction to this field. Anyone who studies through this volume with care can feel himself to have a great deal more than a superficial knowledge of the bone inscriptions, and will find himself able to read most of the inscriptions which he may encounter elsewhere. In addition to its usefulness as an introduction to the field this work has been made a very valuable reference book by the addition of an index under the three heads of "names of men", "names of diviners", and "place names". This makes it a very convenient source of proof references for many points which may arise in research. At the same time that full credit is given to its excellences it must be remembered, however, that this book cannot be used uncritically.

A tool of the greatest service has been given to the worker in this field with the publication, in October of 1934, of Sun Hai-po's 甲骨文編 *Chia Ku Wên Pien*. This work constitutes a complete index of the following collections of squeezes: *T'ieh Yün Ts'ang Kuei, T'ieh Yün Ts'ang Kuei Chih Yü, T'ieh Yün Ts'ang Kuei Shih I, Yin Hsü Shu Ch'i Ch'ien Pien, Yin Hsü Shu Ch'i Hou Pien, Yin Hsü Shu Ch'i Ching Hua, Kuei Chia Shou Ku Wên Tzŭ*, and *Chien Shou T'ang So Ts'ang Yin Hsü Wên Tzŭ*[27]. It represents six years of work and a stupendous amount of

27. Works consisting of drawings rather than squeezes of inscriptions were not included in this index, because they cannot be checked as to exactness. Some collections of squeezes not included here were

labor. For all but the most common characters every single separate occurrence was traced on transparent paper and then reproduced by photography. For the most common characters, several hundred separate forms are given and a list, detailing the place of every occurrence, is appended. The characters are arranged according to the *Shuo Wên* system[28], with an index according to the modern form of the characters, arranged under the number of strokes. There is also an index of compounds made of two or more characters written together. Characters not yet recognized are included in an appendix. It would be easy to point out imperfections in this work; Sun's reading of characters cannot, in the nature of the case, agree with everybody's, and his rendering of the form certainly does, at times, differ to some extent from that found on the original squeeze. But it is much easier to pick flaws in a work of this sort than to produce its like, and the world of scholarship owes Mr. Sun a great debt of gratitude for a book which will do more than any other publication of its type to facilitate progress in this field.

Late in 1935 Dr. Roswell S. Britton of New York University published, as editor, in Shanghai, a volume entitled *The Couling-Chalfant Collection of Inscribed Oracle Bone*. According to his preface "Chalfant's sketch-plates here printed contain his facsimile drawings of 670 mammal bone pieces, 1016 plastron pieces, and one antler, a total of 1687 pieces". He omitted "so-called amulets", "now known to be largely forgeries". The editor later

---

published only after this work had been completed; it is hoped to analyze them in a supplement—see Sun's *Fan Li*.

I am very greatly obliged to Mr. Sun for his kindness in allowing me to examine his manuscript, and to use it for purposes of research, almost a year prior to its publication. This made possible certain results which could not otherwise have been attained.

28. This is on the whole the best system for arranging paleographic material, since any system is all right so long as it has a good index to guide the user, and scholars are more or less familiar with the *Shuo Wên* system. There is a famous scholar in Peiping who has had a manuscript on the bone characters ready for years, and one which everyone wishes to see—but he will not publish it because he has not yet perfected his private system of arrangement.

circulated an *Addendum*[29] listing sixty of the entries as considered wholly spurious, and twenty-three as considered partly spurious by Kuo Mo-jo.

It would be a great mistake to suppose that anything like the last word on the bone inscriptions has been arrived at. But very notable advancements in their decipherment have been made. It is now possible to read most of the characters in almost any inscription and to understand quite adequately the meaning of most inscriptions. We are able to date a very large proportion of the inscriptions within a possible error of decades, so that this material is available as a sound basis for historical research. And we possess, in the *Chia Ku Wên Pien*, an index which makes it possible to use this material effectively.

2. Excavation

The excavations of the National Research Institute of History and Philology, begun in collaboration with the Freer Gallery of Art, from 1928 to the present, have been mentioned. These excavations are still in progress, and it is not known how much longer they may continue. A series of four reports, called *Preliminary Reports of Excavations at Anyang*, was issued from 1929 to 1933. In the fourth volume the work up to that time was summarized, and it was stated that no further report would be issued until the completion of the work, when a final report would be published. All of these reports are entirely in Chinese, with the exception of one very brief paper[1].

These excavations have been and are being conducted along scientific lines. Dr. Li Chi, who has had general charge of the work, is a Doctor of Philosophy of the Department of Anthropology of Harvard University, and Mr. Liang Ssŭ-yung, who has been associated with the work since 1931, was trained in the same Department. Several of the younger scholars aiding in the supervision of field-work have been trained in archeological method in Chinese universities by teachers trained abroad.

29. Tokyo, December 31, 1935.
1. "Preliminary Report on Chinese Bronzes", by H. C. H. Carpenter, *Anyang Pao Kao* 677–680.

The difficulties encountered by the National Research Institute in connection with excavation are very considerable. One of its officials has said that sixty per cent of their time and energy goes into making arrangements to dig unmolested, and only forty per cent into the actual work. The well known prejudice against all digging in China, based on *fêng-shui* and on the feeling against opening graves, has much to do with this. As recently as April, 1934, the Chairman of the Examination Yüan, one of the highest officials in the national government, issued a circular telegram denouncing the excavation of ancient tombs and declaring that instead of paying salaries to excavators the government should punish them.

The fact is, however, that until recently the government excavators at Anyang were given very little opportunity to open tombs. The people of the locality considered grave-robbing to be their exclusive prerogative, in which they would brook no interference. The Institute, in excavating the site of the ancient city, has paid high rents for the land, more than the peasants could hope to make by cultivating it for the same period, yet even there their work has been resented. Notice was served on them that they were to stick to this location and not go outside it—not to bother with tombs, unless they wished to be assassinated. The reason is, of course, that it is from the tombs that the valuable bronzes come, for the most part. These are dug up by countrymen who ruthlessly destroy everything else, skeletons, the wooden parts of chariots, etc., to get the bronze which will sell. Up to the fall of 1934 not a single Shang tomb had been scientifically excavated, and not a single skeleton which was certainly Shang had been preserved to science. The remaining tombs were becoming fewer and fewer. For years digging in the daylight has been taboo, prohibited by an official ban. But it is almost impossible to prevent nocturnal digging; it is done by large bands of heavily armed men who gut a tomb in one night, according to officials of the Institute. Nevertheless, there has been a drastic reduction, amounting to comparative cessation, of the activities of grave robbers in the Anyang area, if one may judge from the sharp drop in the number of bronzes which have come into the Peiping antique shops since the summer of 1934. This is attributed directly to the fact that a strongly-worded telegram from the central government, signed by Chiang Kai-shek and Wang Ching-wei, was despatched to the regional authorities in the early fall of 1934, directing them to give full coöperation to the officials of the National Research Institute in the suppression of private digging.

Backed by this support, the excavators did turn their attention to a grave field north of the Huan River and northeast of the village of Hou Chia Chuang. Their finds there during the fall of 1934 and the spring of 1935 have been epoch-making in the fullest sense of the word. Up to May 2, 1935, the date of my most recent visit to Anyang, more than three hundred tombs had been excavated scientifically. Four of them were huge, the largest thirteen meters deep and twenty meters square[2]; from their size and the nature of the objects found in them, these are believed to be royal. One other large tomb, which has not yet been opened, is also known to the excavators[3].

Probably the most remarkable finds made in these great tombs are the sculptures. It was previously thought that Chinese sculpture did not go back of the Han period, but the finding of a fragment of a stone image of a man in the excavations at Anyang in 1929 showed that this art had been known in the Shang period[4]. But this fragment hardly foreshadowed the many pieces of beautifully sculptured marble, perfect in design, execution, and finish, which were found in one large tomb in 1934 and 1935. Even if we had no other evidence, we could be almost

2. Unlike the Chou tombs northwest of Hsian, Shensi, these Shang tombs were apparently not surmounted by tumuli. This is a conspicuous difference in Shang and Chou customs. It is interesting to note that the tombs, considered to be those of the rulers of the State of 衛 Wei, in 濬 Hsün Hsien, Honan, about twenty miles south of Anyang, apparently had no tumuli. This seems to indicate that the Wei rulers, although scions of the Chou house, followed the custom of their subjects, the former Shang people. The Wei tombs were excavated by the Honan Archeological Association in 1932 and 1933.

3. Verbal communication from Liang Ssŭ-yung, May 2, 1935.

4. See *Anyang Pao Kao* 249-50, and illustration opp. 250.

certain that these sculptures belong to the Shang period from their style alone. In detail and in spirit they belong to the same art which produced the Shang bronzes.

Until autumn, 1934, the excavations of the National Research Institute had not brought to light a single complete bronze vessel which was certainly of Shang date, although many fragments of vessels[5] and copper ore, charcoal, slag, and moulds for bronze vessels proved that such utensils were made at Anyang in Shang times in great numbers[6]. But there is no reason why anything but broken vessels should be found within a city, and most of the excavations had been carried on in the heart of a dwelling area. That such vessels should be found in tombs seems to stand in opposition to the dictum of the *I Li* that "there are no 祭器 sacrificial vessels" among the articles buried with the 士 *shih*[7]. And on the face of the matter there seems little reason why sacrificial vessels should be buried with the dead. Nevertheless, a very great number of bronze vessels, which are identical in type with sacrificial vessels[8], have been found in tombs of the Shang period at Anyang in recent years[9]. And the recent excavation of tombs by the National Research Institute has proved definitely that bronze vessels of such types were buried with the dead in Shang times[10]. Some dozens of bronze

5. See *Anyang Pao Kao* 575.
6. Ibid. 681.
7. *Shih San Ching Chu Su* (Kianghsi ed. 1815; referred to hereafter as *SSC*), *I Li* 38.14a. But the exact meaning of this passage is very hard to determine. The interpretation of the commentators is by no means certainly correct. If by their distinction between "utensils for men" and "utensils for spirits" they mean that the latter are such as are made intentionally unuseable, with holes in the bottoms of vessels, etc., then they are speaking of a practice which seems to have originated later than Shang times. In so far as I know such articles are not found in Shang tombs.
8. I.e., they are identical in type with early Chou vessels bearing inscriptions which prove them to be sacrificial in character.
9. It is the universal testimony of antique dealers and others that these vessels come from tombs.
10. It is sometimes said that these vessels were not buried with the dead directly in ancient China, but in a sort of separate chapel beside

vessels, many of them of the first quality, have now been scientifically excavated. Two of them, found in May 1935, are of unusually large size. As is the case with Shang bronzes generally, they are rarely inscribed, and the inscriptions which have been found do not, I understand, exceed a single character in any case. That these bronze vessels are definitely Shang is proved by two facts. First, they were found in undisturbed tombs in association with typical objects, such as the ceremonial white pottery, identical with objects which are found in the Shang city remains together with the inscribed and datable oracle bones. In the second place, the designs of these bronzes are in the same style as, and in many cases identical with, the designs found on white pottery and carved bones, which are found with the inscribed bones and therefore dated.

There are a great many objects which have been dug up in the Anyang region under anything but scientific conditions—bronzes, some hundred thousand pieces of inscribed bone [11], bone hairpins and other decorative objects, etc.—which can yet be used as materials for research because they can be authenticated either by their inscriptions or by comparison with material which has been excavated. But such things have to be used with the greatest caution, of course. One point which should be made clear is that the scholars of the National Research Institute have paid very careful attention to the problem of distinguishing

---

the tomb. But this was evidently not the case in Shang times. On February 21, 1935, Liang Ssŭ-yung showed me a photograph of a Shang tomb excavated in the fall of 1934, with the objects still in situ; an almost unbelievable profusion of bronze vessels surrounded the skeleton on all sides, although this was not a large tomb and therefore probably not that of a very important individual.

In the Wei tombs excavated in Hsün Hsien ritual vessels were regularly buried, although most of these tombs had been looted. The regular arrangement in the tomb was with ritual vessels on the north, armor on the east, weapons on the west, and chariots on the south. From this it appears that such vessels were buried with the dead in Chou times also. (Verbal communication from Mr. Kuo Pao-chün at Kaifêng, May 6, 1935.)

11. Cf. *Anyang Pao Kao* 44.

genuinely Shang materials—dated by their occurrence together with the inscribed bones—from materials of other date which are sometimes intruded into the Shang culture stratum by burials, etc.

The valid, contemporary materials for the study of Shang history which are now available include the inscribed bones, such relics of the Shang period as have been excavated scientifically and others which can be checked by comparison with them, and the reports of the excavations of the National Research Institute. It remains to examine certain books which have been supposed to fall into this category.

3. BOOKS OF THE SHANG PERIOD

Among transmitted Chinese literature there are a few books, specifically the *Shang Sung* section of the *Shih Ching* and five documents of the *Chin Wên Shang Shu*[1], all or some of which have been considered, even by the most critical scholars, to be actual productions of the Shang period. We must investigate this position. The first question to be asked is whether or not, on the sound basis of our excavated material, it is probable that a literature aside from the bone inscriptions existed in Shang times.

Books and Writing in Ancient China

There is a curious impression, which is quite general among Chinese as well as foreign scholars, to the effect that in China prior to about the time of Confucius books were rare, and the ability to read and write was possessed by only a very small number of individuals and used by them only on occasions of the greatest importance and after much deliberation. Nothing could be farther from the truth. Books in this period were extremely common. The production of documents of some length was a matter of daily, not monthly occurrence. The ability to write was not, to be sure, diffused among the common people even as much as it is today. But on the other hand it is

---

1. I.e., the *chin wên* text of the *Shu Ching*. The term 尚書 *Shang Shu*, as will be shown in a later paper, means "preserved books" or "archives," and is rather older than the term *Shu Ching*. It is the name by which Chinese scholars most usually call the book.

quite certain that those people (and they were not few) who were able to write used that ability with a freedom and a casualness which is denied to a vast number of those who, in Western countries at the present day, figure among the "literate" in our census estimates.

Among foreigners this impression has been associated, no doubt, with the utterly erroneous notion that the Chinese of the centuries before and after 1000 B.C. were "primitive", and therefore must have depended chiefly on oral transmission to preserve such literature as they had. And it has been easy for Chinese scholars, who know that their books of high antiquity have commonly been memorized since the Han dynasty, to suppose that this method of preservation must have been used in earlier periods to an even greater extent. But it is my opinion that the memorization of texts was comparatively rare before the Han dynasty. Poetry was memorized, beyond question, but there is reason to believe that the farther back we go the less there was of memorization of the other materials which have come down to us in documentary form. Let us consider the evidence.

In the first place, why do people memorize? They memorize poetry so that they may be able to recite it on appropriate occasions, and so did the Chinese. Other materials are memorized, it is suggested, for three reasons. First, because the individual memorizing is unable to read. Second, because books are scarce. Third, because the books memorized are regarded with a peculiar veneration, or at any rate are considered of such special importance that frequent and facile quotation from them is considered desirable.

But it is altogether improbable that any person unable to read would have wished to memorize the sort of books which come down to us from very ancient China. Unquestionably there were popular tales which circulated, then as now, by means of storytellers who may well have been illiterate[2]. But the books

2. It is probably from such popular tales that much of the marvelous and legendary element, comparatively rare in quite early books but seeming to appear, as an important factor in literature, rather

which have come down to us have to do almost exclusively with the affairs of the aristocratic class, their ancestors, their ritual, their philosophy. And even had some illiterate individuals wished to memorize these books, it is almost certain that they could not have done so without first learning to read. For the writing of that period was couched in an idiom quite different from the spoken tongue [3].

---

suddenly in the late Eastern Chou period, was taken. It is altogether improbable that the writers of this later date invented these tales; rather, they adopted what was already current in verbal form, no doubt altering or at least choosing between various versions.

If we ask why the books of Western Chou date are comparatively free from the marvelous and incredible, the answer is not difficult. It is not because the writers of that time were less credulous than those of a later date, but rather because writing was at that time primarily a practical instrument, used almost entirely for purposes of communication, giving orders, making records, etc. Save perhaps for some poetry, writing in the sense of belles-lettres had hardly been born.

3. I am well aware that this position is exactly opposed to that of Professor Bernhard Karlgren, who has held that the Chinese in which the old texts are written is "the natural reproduction of the spoken language" (*Philology and Ancient China*, Oslo, 1926, p. 43). This, he says, "is clear from the fact that the language is just as short and concise, with simple words; even when animated conversations, or philosophical discussions were reproduced" (loc. cit.). There is nothing, however, to preclude the possibility that conversations, like everything else, were reduced to the literary style when written. As a matter of fact this is done at the present day, almost every time an interview is published in a Chinese daily newspaper, and there is good evidence to indicate that the same practice was followed long ago. For we find persons of neither birth nor breeding speaking the same kind of polished literary language as that uttered by the most cultivated scholars. Han Kao Tsu, founder of the Former Han dynasty, started as a village headman and rose as a robber chief to the throne. But he remained the burly bandit to his death. Possibly as a result of an inferiority complex he had little use for scholars. The *Shih Chi* tells us that even as Emperor he delighted to humiliate them with vulgar pranks more worthy of a schoolboy. Yet the language of Han Kao Tsu, as recorded in the *Shih Chi* and *Han Shu*, is quite polished. It may be said that this is from a desire to flatter him, but this is not true; Ssŭ-Ma Ch'ien takes delight in revealing his rusticities, and has been reviled

If it be said that the contents of books were memorized for the second reason, namely, because physical books were scarce, that can hardly be proved. On the contrary, as we shall see, there is abundant evidence that they were common. And there is no reason why they should not have been. They were written chiefly on wood or bamboo[4], materials sufficiently plentiful.

---

no little therefor. Evidence of this sort, concerning various persons, is manifold.

There may be room for some possible question as to whether the literary language of Han times was ever a medium of speech. As to that of the Western Chou period, there is none; it could not have been a vehicle of verbal communication. The idiom is too terse, too ambiguous, as Karlgren himself has put it too "lapidarian," for the rapid exchanges of conversation. Chinese scholars who have spent their whole lives in the study of this type of Chinese sometimes differ radically as to the whole purport of the same sentence written in it; are we to suppose that the Chinese of that time were so wonderfully keen that they could grasp its meaning in the moment allowed in talk? As a matter of fact, Chinese scholars find that genuine Western Chou writing, like the text of the *Ta Kao* of the *Shu Ching*, is so terse, so utterly lacking in connectives, etc., that it is almost impossible to repeat from memory. No Chinese scholar, of the number with whom I have discussed this question, has believed that the written style of early Chinese books could represent the spoken language of the time.

4. No bamboo, even decomposed, has yet been identified among the Shang relics to my knowledge. But there is good reason to suppose that it was probably used by the Shang people. Bishop says, "even during the full historical period, beginning in the 9th century B.C., the bamboo is mentioned as growing considerably to the northward of its present limit" (*Antiquity*, 1933, 390). All of the Shang arrowheads known to me, of whatever material, are made with a tang designed to fit into the shaft; this almost certainly presupposes shafts made of reed or, better, bamboo, since a wooden shaft does not lend itself effectively to boring. Bamboo arrows are mentioned in the *Ku Ming* of the *Chin Wên Shang Shu, Shu* (Legge, *Chinese Classics* Vol. III, London, 1865; referred to hereafter as *Shu*) 555. The *I Li* lists a bamboo writing tablet among the articles to be buried with a deceased *shih*, SSC *I Li* 35.14a. In an inscription on a bronze vessel attributed to the reign of Duke Ling of Ch'i (cf. *Liang Chou Chin Wên Tz'ŭ Ta Hsi*, referred to hereafter as *Liang Chou Hsi*, 243–247), 581–554 B.C., we find important evidence of the early use of bamboo for books. The character 典 *tien*,

They were written, from a very early period, with a brush dipped in ink, a tool easily and rapidly used. And there were, in early Chou times at least, numerous officials and clerks whose chief duty consisted in writing and making books; in fact, every aristocratic family seems to have had one or more of such retainers. If these facts are not ample, even quantitative evidence is not lacking for a time shortly after that of Confucius. There has been a general opinion that books were rather rare even down to the Han dynasty. But in the history of the Chin dynasty we read that in the year 281 A.D. an ancient tomb was opened. It proved to be that of Wei Hsiang Wang, who died in 296 B.C. And in this one tomb were found books, all of a date earlier than this, "sufficient to fill several tens of carts"[5].

More than a century earlier, in 408 B.C.[6], the ruler of the state of Wei finally succeeded in conquering the small but powerful state of Chung Shan. The general who carried out the final campaign returned full of swaggering pride, taking all of the credit for the achievement. To humble this bumptious warrior, his ruler had the Keeper of the Archives bring into the court, and show to him, two chests full of books. Each of these books was a special treatise discussing the strategy to be used in attack-

---

used to mean "to record," is normally composed of a book made of wood or bamboo strips standing on a table. In this instance the whole is surmounted by 竹 *chu*, "bamboo," as a determinative; *Li Tai Chung Ting I Ch'i Kuan Shih Fa T'ieh* (Liu Shih ed. 1903; referred to hereafter as *Li Tai T'ieh*) 78a.

5. *Chin Shu* (Chung Hua Shu Chü reprint, 1923, of Wu Lin Chu Chien Chai reprint, 1892, of palace edition of 1739) 51.7a (*Lieh Chuan* 21, *Shu Hsi Chuan*).

Among the books found here were the famous 竹書紀年 *Chu Shu Chi Nien*, or Annals of the Bamboo Books (ordinarily called simply Bamboo Books). The work now current under that name has, of course, long been known to be a forgery, but this does not invalidate the account of their finding. The work which was actually found has long been lost, but Wang Kuo-wei has reconstituted a considerable portion of it from quotations in various works, publishing his results under the title 古本竹書紀年輯校. It is included in his collected works, third series.

6. For this date, cf. *Shih Chi* 44.2b.

ing the state of Chung Shan, which had a territory of only a few square miles[7].

The third reason mentioned for the memorization of material other than poetry is that it is regarded with a peculiar veneration, or at any rate considered of such especial importance that frequent and facile quotation from it is considered desirable. It is true that there was already, in the pre-Confucian period, a great veneration of the ancestors and their writings and sayings, but this extended, in considerable degree, to all of the ancestors and former kings, and the materials preserved from them were, at that time, too many to admit of memorization. The books, for instance, which are preserved to us in the *Shang Shu* are not all really important books. The book called *Wên Hou Chih Ming*[8], the most evidently genuine book (because it agrees perfectly with bronze inscriptions) in the whole *Shu*, is one of a type of which hundreds if not thousands of examples were produced in the Western Chou period. It is simply a little speech of presentation, first read aloud and then handed to a feudal noble along with some gifts from the king. It was so unimportant that we do not even have a record telling us to which noble it was presented[9]. That noble treasured it, as a communication from the king, and put it in his family archives. But no one would have thought of memorizing so usual a writing. It was only after the perishable nature of their materials and the misfortunes of history had made such books rare that they were regarded as exceptionally precious, and worthy of being memorized. The same is true in lesser, but only lesser degree, of most of the other books which have come down to us.

There is no evidence, in the literature of the early Chou period, that any material save poetry was memorized at that

7. *Lü Shih Ch'un Ch'iu*, chap. 16, section 5.
8. *Shu* 613–620.
9. There are, of course, the traditional attributions to Chin Wên Hou and to Chin Wên Kung. But it will be shown in the detailed discussion of this work that neither of these attributions rests on valid evidence. In fact, these variant attributions, and the flimsy foundation of each, themselves indicate that those who put the book into the canon had no real knowledge of its origin.

time. It is only in the post-Confucian period, especially in the works produced by the various philosophic schools, that we begin to find references to such a practice. And here it is clearly as a discipline, rather than as a method of transmitting the literature, that it is recommended. Even in works like *Hsün Tzŭ*, produced around 300 B.C., we cannot be sure that complete memorization of specific works is intended[10]. References to 詩 *shih*, 書 *shu*, and 禮 *li*, such as occur in *Hsün Tzŭ*[11], do not necessarily point to such definite collections of writings as our *Shih Ching*, *Shu Ching*, and *Li Chi* or *I Li*. *Shu* in particular was a term of many meanings in pre-Han times, used to mean merely "writings" in general[12] or even "the study of characters"[13]. In any case, the whole situation which gave rise to these philosophic schools is quite different from that in pre-Confucian times, and it ultimately produced a very different attitude toward documents.

In the *Tso Chuan* we read that in the year 527 B.C., in the midst of a feast, the king had occasion to chide an official of the state of Chin for his lack of knowledge of the history of his own state. He said, in part: " 'Moreover, your ancestor Sun Po-yen had charge of the archives of Chin ... You are the descendant of the superintendent of the archives;—how is it that you are so forgetful of these matters?' Chi T'an could not reply; and when his guests went out the king said, 'Chi Fu will not, we may anticipate, leave any posterity. He must have run through the archives, and yet he has forgotten *the work of* his an-

10. Cf. *Hsün Tzŭ* (Chêkiang Shu Chü, 1876) 1.5b. The exact meaning of the term 誦 *sung* here may be questioned. It evidently could mean "to repeat from memory," to judge from its use in the *Lun Yü*; see Legge, *Confucian Analects* (*Chinese Classics*, vol. I, 2nd ed. 1893, referred to hereafter as *Lun Yü*) 225 and 265. But we can not be certain that it could not also mean merely "to read aloud" from a book, as priests in Buddhist temples do today.
11. Loc. cit.
12. But in the passage in *Hsün Tzŭ* referred to above it has specific reference to government documents, see loc. cit.
13. Cf. *SSC Chou Li* 10.24b.

cestors!' "(14). The matters the king referred to were the sort which are preserved in just such documents as are in our present *Shu Ching*, yet it is evident that there was no idea, at that time, of their being memorized.

In the year 213 B.C. the Ch'in Emperor, Shih Huang Ti, ordered the burning of a number of books, including the *Shih* and the *Shu*, and it was forbidden for a time to possess them, under the most severe penalties. But it was only six years from that time to the end of the Ch'in dynasty, and only a few decades to a time when the utmost energy was expended in the effort to reconstitute these ancient texts. If the practise of memorizing had been in force before the Han dynasty as it was during it and later, it should have been a simple matter for the scholars to write down these books from memory. And a number of Western scholars have said that just this was done (15). But save for one very doubtful case which we shall consider later, they mention no actual instances in which this was done, and it seems probable that they have been misled by the current assumptions in this regard.

The *I Wên Chih* of the *Ch'ien Han Shu*, in its discussion of the *Shih Ching*, includes a most illuminating passage, as follows: 遭秦而全者以其諷誦不獨在竹帛故也 "The reason why it [the *Shih Ching*] was able to pass through *the burning of the books in* the Ch'in period and yet remain complete and intact was that it was recited from memory, and thus was not *dependent* solely on bamboo and silk *for its preservation*." This, then, is a statement of Han date which plainly infers that other books, such as the *Shu Ching*, which did suffer from the destruction by Ch'in, were not recited from memory at that time, but *were* dependent solely on bamboo and silk, i.e., physical books, for their transmission.

14. *Tso Chuan* 660. Legge translates 數典 *shu tien* as "numbered the archives", but this is out of place in the text. It must rather mean "to run over the archives".

15. Cf.: Edouard Chavannes, *Memoires Historiques* cxii–cxiii; Karlgren, *Philology and Ancient China* 90; Leopold de Saussure, "L'Astronomie Chinoise dans l'Antiquité," *Revue Generale des Sciences*, 28 Février, 1907, 135; Walter Gorn Old, *The Shu King*, v.

Three versions of the *Shu Ching* are recorded as having been recovered in Han times. By explicit record, every one of them consisted of a physical, written book; not one of them was written down from memory. The first was that of Fu Shêng, a scholar who had held office under Ch'in and who, when the order went out to destroy the books, hid his copy of the *Shu* in a wall. In the disorders which soon followed he had to flee. Some years later when he went back to look for his hidden books he could find only twenty-nine *p'ien*; these are supposed to be the originals of our present *chin wên* text[16]. The second is the text which is known by the name of K'ung An-kuo, because it is supposed to have been turned over to him for study. It again was found, we are told, in a wall—this time the wall of the house of Confucius, which was being demolished. A number of other books are said to have been found in this same wall[17]. The third copy of the *Shu* did not come to light until the Later Han period, when Tu Lin found what is called a "lacquer book", presumably one written with lacquer[18]. It is obvious, then, that not one of these three books could have owed its preservation to oral transmission, and it is worthy of careful note that the books of the *Chin Wên Shang Shu* (i.e., the only portion of the *Shu Ching* which critical scholars consider as old as the Han dynasty) are just those, no more and no less, which Fu Shêng is said to have recovered as physical books from his wall[19].

The men of early Han times were painfully conscious that they had lost touch with much of the ancient learning of their nation, and many of them directed the most diligent efforts toward recovering as much of the old literature as they could. Perhaps the chief of these was the prince who is known as Hê Chien Hsien Wang, son of Ching Ti (156–129 B.C.). He made it known far and wide that he would pay richly for any old books which were brought to him. But neither he, nor, in so far as I know, any

16. Cf. *Shih Chi* 121.7a; *Ch'ien Han Shu* (Chin Ling Shu Chü, 1869), 30.3a.
17. Loc. cit. There are those who doubt this whole account, but in any case the books, if they existed, were not recovered from memory.
18. *Hou Han Shu* (Chin Ling Shu Chü, 1869), 27.5a.
19. Loc. cit.

other of those engaged in this search, made any effort to find persons who carried on an ancient tradition of oral transmission. We know that the texts which Hsien Wang himself obtained 皆古文先秦舊書 "were all old books of pre-Ch'in date in ancient characters"[20].

There is, I believe, only one account which attributes the recovery of any of the Classics to repetition from memory. In the preface to the *Shu Ching* ascribed to K'ung An-kuo we are told that the scholar "Fu Shêng was more than ninety years old. He had lost his text, but taught, by word of mouth, more than twenty *p'ien*"[21]. Here, then, is a definite statement that Fu Shêng knew the *Shu*, or rather a part of it, and was teaching it from memory. What is this statement worth, as history? Nothing. It occurs in the preface of the *Ku Wên Shang Shu* which critical scholars have long agreed in denouncing as a forgery of the third or fourth century A.D. Chinese scholars long ago pointed out that it is probably a garbled version of a quotation from Wei Hung[22].

It is not hard to understand why this story came into being and why, despite its extremely dubious origin and its contradiction of clearly recorded history[23], it has had much influence on the

20. *Ch'ien Han Shu* 53.1ab.
The *Shih Chi* (121.7a) does say that Han Hsiao Wên Ti 欲求能治尚書者天下無有 "wished to seek out persons who could handle the *Shang Shu*, but in all the empire there were none [save Fu Shêng]". But it by no means follows that to "handle the *Shang Shu*" means to repeat it from memory, and the same passage definitely states that Fu Shêng, the only person found, depended on physical books. If, on the other hand, it does mean to memorize, and yet not a single person who knew it was living only some forty years after the proscription, which was itself of only a few years duration, then the practise could not have been very widespread among scholars.
21. SSC *Shang Shu* 1.10b.
22. Cf. *Shang Shu K'ung Chuan Ts'an Chêng* 36.11a, and *Ch'ien Han Shu, Ju Lin Chuan, Fu Shêng*, commentary of Shih Ku (88.7a.9). It must be noted that this statement of Wei Hung (who lived in the first century of our era) does not at all say that he gave his text orally, but only his teaching, i.e., his explanation of the text.
23. Cf. *Shih Chi* 121.7a; *Ch'ien Han Shu* 30.3a.

opinions of both Chinese and foreign scholars. In the late centuries of what we call the Chou dynasty (though the Chous had almost no power in the Eastern Chou period) there was not a little of memorization of literary materials of various sorts. Perhaps the first material (except poetry) to be memorized on an extensive scale was the sayings of the various philosophical teachers, of whom Confucius is the chief example. The *Lun Yü* is considered not to have been written down, in collected form at least, until many years after his death, and much of it was probably transmitted by word of mouth for a long time. The same is true of other materials of the sort. Perhaps even some portions of the 禮 *li* were committed to memory—I know of no evidence either for or against this possibility. But the archives, the sort of material which is now in our *Shu Ching*, were not memorized on any extensive scale during the pre-Confucian period or even, it would seem, prior to the Han dynasty. If for no other reason, the documents were too numerous.

But the deliberate destruction of these documents by Ch'in, and the unintentional but perhaps more thorough destruction which came in the disorders attending the fall of that dynasty, rendered these works very scarce indeed. When the men of early Han times awakened to realize that they had very nearly lost the birthright of their ancient culture they set to work, with great zeal, to find as many of these books as they could. In the period which followed many were recovered, many were fabricated, nearly all were treasured. The most important of them, those which were felt to be the foundation stones of Chinese culture, became the subject of state professorships. The system whereby down to the present century a knowledge of these works has been the key to rank and position had its beginnings[24].

In these circumstances it was very natural that portions, at least, of these Classics should be committed to memory. By the

24. Cf. for instance *Shih Chi* 121.3-4. Especially interesting is the case here recorded of Kung-Sun Hung who "through *his knowledge of* the *Ch'un Ch'iu*, although a commoner rose to *the high office of* San Kung to the Son of Heaven, and was ennobled as Marquis of P'ing Ching."

third century of our era it must have seemed that they had always been so memorized, at least since the time of their alleged editing by Confucius. That they could have been lost through the mere destruction of physical books must have seemed very strange. Therefore, we get the "correction" of this story in the pseudo-preface. It was not, we are told, because only a portion of the *books* were found that we have only a part of the *Shu*, but rather because Fu Shêng, being more than ninety years old, could *remember* only something more than a score of books.

The Chinese of the pre-Confucian period did not, then, depend upon word of mouth for the transmission of their literature. And if we would understand them we must realize, first of all, that the deeply and fundamentally literate spirit of Chinese culture goes back to an age which has usually been called prehistoric. Western scholars have held that the rapid strides of Greek culture were a direct outcome of the Greek habit of writing things down, taking notes. This same habit is found among the ancient Chinese. They considered history far too important a matter to be left to memory[25].

It is doubtful that any people in the world had more of historical consciousness, more of a sense of the value of history, than did the Chinese of the time of the beginning of the Chou dynasty. The author of the *Chiu Kao* points out that the Chou rulers, having conquered the Shang monarchs, would do well to study their history so as to avoid the mistakes which led to their downfall[26]. In the *Shao Kao* lengthy illustrations are drawn from the history of the two former (so-called) dynasties, to be a warning and a guide to the reigning king[27]. It was because of failure to regard the lessons of history that all of the former kings who lost their thrones came to that end—so runs the speech of a minister of Duke Hsien of Chin (676–652 B.C.)[28]. This exhortation, to look at history and take it as a guide for one's conduct,

25. Cf. *Kuo Yü* (*Tien Shêng Ming Tao Pên*, reprint of 1800) 4.2a.
26. *Shu* 409–10.
27. *Shu* 426–30.
28. *Kuo Yü* 7, 3a.

is in fact a favorite theme[29]. In a warning against the danger of feminine influence, Shih Su of the seventh century B.C. tells in detail how three dynasties have been ruined, all by women[30]. History was taught to young princes "to stimulate them to good conduct, and warn them against evil"[31].

The date of the beginning of writing and books in China we do not know, and doubtless never shall know. The earliest beginnings of writing must have been crude, of a sort which we could hardly read. But the earliest inscriptions which we know at the present time are those of the Shang oracle bones dating from the fourteenth century B.C.[32]; they are readable to a very satisfactory degree, and have some characters identical in form with those of modern Chinese. Tradition tells us that in high antiquity the Chinese made records by means of knotted cords[33] (compare the quipu)[34], and that writing was first invented by an official of the forty-sixth century B.C.[35]. That these are mere legends goes without saying, but worthy of much more credence is the statement in the *Shang Shu* that the people of the Shang period had "books and archives" recording the events of the

29. *Kuo Yü* 3, 7a; 3, 8a; 19, 3b.
30. *Kuo Yü* 7, 2b.
31. *Kuo Yü* 13, 6b; 17, 1ab.
32. We have a great many bones which unquestionably date from the reign of Wu Ting (1324–1266 B.C.). Whether some of our inscriptions go back to the time of Pan Kêng (1401–1374 B.C.) is a question which is still being debated.
33. SSC I *Ching, Hsi Tz'ǔ*, 8.8a.
34. The word "quipu" is of course Peruvian, and it is the Peruvian examples which are most widely known. But in a letter of March 14, 1935, Mr. Bishop writes me that "Dr. Handy, of the Bishop Museum at Honolulu . . . tells me that the Hawaiian ones are much more comparable to those of ancient China, because in that case there seems to be a genetic connection." Mr. Bishop points out that the quipu still occurs in the Liu Ch'iu islands and among the Miao of southwestern China, concluding that "the quipu seems to have been an element of the ancient Neolithic culture of southeastern Asia".
35. *Lü Shih Ch'un Ch'iu* (Chêkiang Shu Chü, 1880) 17.7b; *Shuo Wên Chieh Tzǔ Chu* (*Huang Ch'ing Ching Chieh* 641–655; referred to hereafter as *Shuo Wên Chu*) 15.1b.

beginning of their power[36]. We know from the bone inscriptions that books and writing were not rare in Shang times, and Chou books tell us the same thing, not only of Shang but even of Hsia times[37], to which the years 2205-1784 B.C. are assigned by tradition. We even have quotations from the Writings of Hsia[38], the Instructions of Hsia[39], and the Decrees of Hsia[40], but it is to be feared that all of these are of doubtful age.

Chinese archeologists are searching, with special attention, for traces of primitive Chinese writing, but so far without success. Excavations in Chinese Neolithic sites have so far produced nothing which appears to be writing[41], and this is among facts which have been held to indicate a disparity so great as to reflect a lack of continuity between the full Neolithic culture and that of the Shang people. Be that as it may, the Neolithic remains, especially the painted pottery, do show unmistakably that the people of Neolithic China had a strong liking for drawing, and it is certainly in the drawing of pictures that Chinese writing took its rise. Neolithic pottery shows a wealth of painted and some impressed designs, and even a few pictures appear on pieces which have been found[42].

36. *Shu, To Shih*, 460. That these books contained the particular statements which it is here asserted that they did contain, I do not believe, for reasons which will be stated in the discussion of this work. But that such books did exist is not implausible.

37. *Kuo Yü* 10.15a, 16.5b; 17.10a.

38. *Kuo Yü* 15.8b.

39. *Tso Chuan* 422.4.

40. *Kuo Yü* 2.9a.

41. J. G. Andersson writes: "In all our extensive excavations in the prehistoric sites of Kansu we never saw on any pottery vessel or other object the slightest indication of writing, in spite of the fact that our attention was constantly bent in that direction (the incised bone plates of the Yang Shao time described on page 14 are at the most some kind of primitive record, in no way related to the archaic Chinese script)." *Preliminary Report on Archaeological Research in Kansu* (*Memoirs, Geological Survey* of China, 1925. Hereafter referred to as *Arch. Res. in Kansu*), p. 30.

42. Cf. *Arch. Res. in Kansu*, plates I–XI, and pp. 16–17; cf. also T. J. Arne, *Painted Stone Age Pottery from the Province of Honan, China* (*Palaeontologia Sinica*, Series D, Vol. 1, Fasc. 2; Peking, 1925).

Many have believed that the Chinese system of writing is an importation from elsewhere, and many books and articles have been written purporting to demonstrate that the basis of Chinese came from Egypt, Babylon, or elsewhere [43]. We shall not discuss these theories, for two reasons. First, they lie outside the special field of this study and would require more space than can be devoted to an extraneous subject. In the second place, such theories as have been propounded and such evidence as has been put forward do not merit the time their discussion would require. With few exceptions, those who have tried to show identities in Chinese on the one hand and Egyptian, Babylonian, etc., on the other, have possessed only superficial knowledge of either the one language or the other. And their efforts are not in the least convincing. At present, the issue is a dead one. New evidence may appear, of course, at any time, but as matters stand there is no proof that Chinese writing originated or was developed anywhere save within the limits of what we know as China.

Chinese writing began with the drawing of pictures. Even in the Shang period which we know, when writing was highly sophisticated, the drawing and the conventionalizing of pictures, as decoration, is perhaps the most highly developed technique which appears from the objects preserved to us. And the decorative art of the Shang period is among the finest decorative art which human beings have ever produced. Yet it is a far development from the mere drawing of pictures to a full system for the recording of human ideas, such as we find on the Shang bones. How and why was that development made? This is a most difficult question. It is all very well to say that one man felt the desire to send or leave a message to another, and used pictures for the purpose. But it is hard to conceive of his doing so when the very idea of writing had not been born, and when he could probably have sent or left a spoken message as well. The desire to keep some sort of records is more plausible, and we know of records made with notched sticks, knotted cords, and even pictures, among people who have no proper writing.

43. Andersson seems to take seriously the theory of importation of writing from the west, though he has not, in so far as I know, done special research in this field. Cf. *Arch. Res. in Kansu*, p. 31.

Beyond question not one but many factors contributed to the development, once it had started, of Chinese writing. But it is highly probable that one, and not the least important, of those factors was the desire to communicate with the dead and perhaps with certain deities. One may talk to a living man, or send him a verbal message through another. But this method is not ordinarily available if one wishes to communicate with one's deceased ancestors. And the ancient Chinese did want very much to communicate with them. Over and above the simple human desire to remain in touch with the beloved and needed dead, there was the almost unlimited power which these ancestors had to influence the lives of their descendants for good or for evil, which caused the living to wish to tell them their troubles and to ask for help, to ask for advice, to ask for blessings of various sorts, and to inform the ancestors that their descendants, in making a sacrifice, were providing such and such food for the sustenance of their ancestors. It is due to the desire for advice from the ancestors that the myriads of oracle bones were produced, but sending a message *to* the ancestors was more difficult. At some time some ingenious Chinese conceived that if this message were *written* on inflammable material and burned, like any other burnt sacrifice, the smoke would carry the message to the heavens, dwelling-place of the dead [44]. This custom survives to the present day [45], and it must be very old indeed. In the prayer of Christianity direct verbal communication with Deity is established, but in the current Chinese idea such com-

44. The heavens were not the only dwelling place of the dead in ancient China, of course. There was also the Yellow Springs, under the earth. These two regions of the dead will be discussed later.
45. When the national government of China recently held a financial conference in Nanking, such a "sacrificial message" to the spirit of Sun Yat-sen figured among the opening ceremonies. The full text of this message, asking for aid and direction, is published in the Peiping *Shih Chieh Jih Pao* ("World Daily News") of May 22, 1934, page 2. Although the account does not specify, Mr. Chang Tsung-ch'ien assures me that it is customary to burn such messages after they are read aloud.

merce with spiritual beings seems ordinarily to be considered less effective than a written message. That this idea prevailed also in ancient times is indicated by a story quoted in the *Kuo Yü* from a still older work. Two of the deceased former rulers of the small state of Pao presented themselves, in the form of two dragons, at the court of one of the Hsia kings, and announced their identity. This king seems to have been a churlish fellow where ghosts were concerned, for he immediately wanted to put them to death. Divination told him, however, that this would be unwise, and it was finally decided that the situation would be met by securing some of the dragons' spittle and storing it away. A cloth was spread to receive this substance, but it was still necessary to request the dragons to expectorate. Being spirits, they apparently could not be spoken to. But they could read, and as soon as a letter of request was presented to them they spat and disappeared [46]. Instances of messages addressed to deities and to the dead may be found all through the pre-Confucian period [47]; nobles, on setting out from their capitals, and on their return, made announcement of the fact, of their business, and of its result in the ancestral temple [48]. We have not material to prove that all of these announcements were written, though they probably were. But in many cases we know that they were, beyond the slightest question [49]. Especially interesting is the practise whereby treaties between states or rulers were solemnized. Three copies were made and each was consecrated with a smear of the blood of a victim sacrificed as part of the ceremony. One copy was taken by each of the parties to the agreement; one copy was buried on the spot (burial was one form

46. *Kuo Yü* 16.5ab.
47. For the Shang period, cf. *Pu Tz'ŭ T'ung Tsuan*, nos. 254, 286, discussion. For the Chou period cf. *Kuo Yü* 19.14ab; 19.7b; and other references listed below.
48. Cf. *Tso Chuan* 38.11.
49. Cf. *Shu, Lo Kao* 451 (this book is very early Chou); *Chin T'êng* 353–355 (the style of this book makes it probable that it was edited rather later than the events it portrays, though it may still be a Western Chou production); *Kuo Yü* 11.5b.

of sacrifice), filed, as it were, with the spirits, who were expected to act as guarantors. "Whoever shall violate this covenant", reads one of these documents, "may the bright spirits destroy him, causing his armies to be defeated and his state to be lost to him!"[50]

There is abundant evidence that this practise of using writing in communication with spirits goes back to the Shang period. On the bones which we have there are many occurrences of the character 㗊, which is undoubtedly identical with 詰 *ch'ê* which occurs in the *Shuo Wên Chieh Tzǔ*. This character is composed of a book and a mouth, and means "to tell by means of a book". That this character stands for such communication with spiritual beings, and especially with the former kings, is indicated by the way it is used[51]. We know some two-score occurrences of it. We also have some ten occurrences, in the bone inscriptions, of the character 舁, composed of two hands raising aloft a book; that this also indicates books offered in sacrifice is suggested not only by usage but also by the addition, in one case, of the element 示 (which may stand by itself on the bones for "spirit")[52]. And we have three occurrences of 册, a character which would seem to mean "to communicate with the 示 spirits by means of a 册 book"[53].

What we call religion, then, by positing a situation in which it was essential to communicate with beings who could not ordinarily be reached by speech, must have given a great impetus to the development of writing. At all events, writing had developed to no mean level by the fourteenth century B.C., when the

50. *Tso Chuan* 377.5. For various aspects of this ceremony cf.: *Tso Chuan* 194.11–12, 608.3; *Kuo Yü* 6.10a; *Lü Shih Ch'un Ch'iu* 12.8b.
51. Cf. *Yin Ch'i I Ts'un* (hereafter referred to as *Ch'i Ts'un*) no. 44; *Yin Hsü Shu Ch'i Hou Pien* (hereafter referred to as *Yin Hou Pien*) 1.23.1.
52. *Yin Ch'ien Pien* 4.43.4. Cf. also 2.40.7; 3.28.5; 4.37.5; 7.6.1; etc. A similar character is found on many bronzes; cf. *Yin Wên Ts'un* (1917), shang 11b, 23a; hsia 4b, 28b, 29a, 34a, 34b.
53. *Yin Hou Pien*, 1.24.2, 2.43.4; *T'ieh Yün Ts'ang Kuei Shih I* (hereafter referred to as *T'ieh I*) 3.15.

Shang bones give us our first knowledge of it. More than two thousand different characters appear on the materials we have. The pronouns 我 *wo* and 余 *yü*[54], various prepositions, and numerous other properties of an advanced system of written expression appear among our earliest inscriptions. Completely ideographic characters predominate, but they are usually conventionalized beyond the "pictographic" stage, and the elements are combined variously to represent a wide range of things and ideas. Characters are borrowed on the phonetic principle, to represent spoken words of similar sound but different meaning; the character 來 *lai*, "come", originally a pictograph of a stalk of grain, is a familiar example frequent on the bones. There are also many characters formed of one signific and one phonetic element. In the period of about two centuries covered by the inscriptions we have, we can trace the development of many characters from their fully ideographic state through greater and greater conventionalization and the addition of a phonetic element[55]. It would be erroneous, of course, to say that the writing which we find on the Shang bones is the same complete and facile instrument for the expression of thought that we have in modern Chinese; on the other hand it is no exaggeration to say that there is scarcely a principle of the formation of modern Chinese characters which we do not find utilized, in greater or less degree, in the Shang inscriptions.

Of original written documents from Shang times we have few, aside from the divination bones. There is a very small proportion of this material, indistinguishable from the divination records save for its content, of other sorts. We have a number of "calendar bones", complete and fragmentary, which simply list the sixty possible combinations of the cyclical "stems" and "branches" by which days were named[56]. There are also

54. Cf. *Yin Ch'ien Pien* 5.26.1 (the form of the character 辰 in this inscription indicates that it is probably early); 7.36.1 (the content of this inscription is typical of the period of Wu Ting); etc.
55. Cf. *Ts'ai Anniv. Vol.* 414–415.
56. Cf. *Ch'i Tz'ǔ* no. 165, etc.

some pieces inscribed with characters which do not, if read consecutively, "make sense"; sometimes the same character is repeated over and over. These have been set down, and undoubtedly correctly, as "practise bones", on which novice scribes developed their skill before employing it in the serious and sacred business of divination[57]. And there are a number of examples of a type of inscription which apparently does not have to do with divination, but the nature and meaning of which is still a subject of general debate[58]. Three animal skulls, with inscribed characters, have been excavated[59]. A few pottery vessels with characters, usually single, rather roughly incised *after* baking[60]; a single piece of jade inscribed with eleven characters[61]; a very few pieces of beautifully carved bone bearing somewhat longer inscriptions which do not have to do with divination, but resemble those on bronzes; a piece of a stone vessel with an inscription on the handle; these complete the tale, save for inscriptions on bronze. That inscribed bronze vessels of Shang date do exist is beyond question, but at present it is rather difficult to determine whether certain bronze vessels with relatively long inscriptions are Shang or early Chou. It may be possible to do this when the vessels and designs on bronze moulds excavated at the Shang capital, and other similar materials have been thoroughly studied. But at present we can only say that for the most part inscriptions on Shang bronzes were very brief, commonly of only one or at most a few characters. On the

   57. Cf. *Ch'i Tz'ŭ*, nos. 230 and 231, etc.
   58. Cf. an article on these inscriptions by Tung Tso-pin, *Anyang Pao Kao* 635–676. Tung's interpretation has not won universal acceptance.
   59. Facsimiles of squeezes of these have been published by the National Research Institute, under the title 獸頭刻辭 *Shou T'ou K'ê Tz'ŭ*.
   60. Cf. *Anyang Pao Kao* 574. An interesting book of these characters has been prepared by Mr. Tung Tso-pin, who has kindly allowed me to examine the manuscript, although it has not yet been published.
   61. Cf. *Ch'i T'sun, T'ang Hsü* 3b. This is called 玉 *yü*, which we usually translate as "jade", but the Chinese designate by that term various substances, not all of which are jade in our sense.

bronzes which have been excavated scientifically inscriptions do not exceed a single character.

When we come to the Chou period, however, we are immediately confronted with bronze inscriptions whose characters may run into the hundreds [62], having a range of subject and presenting a wealth of material far beyond that of the Shang oracle bones. But it would be a mistake to suppose that this indicates that the early Chou conquerors were more literate than the men of Shang; there is good reason to suppose that precisely the reverse of this is true. The Shang bones are limited in material because they were merely records of divination, written in a professionally abbreviated style. A literature of quite another sort existed alongside of them; it was written on perishable materials and has vanished. But the Chou people occasionally cast the text of veritable books on their bronzes, and it is for this reason that the regular literary style of the times comes first within our vision on Chou bronzes.

We have not a single physical book from the pre-Confucian period, except those cast on bronze. But although no one living has ever seen one of these books, we can know many things about them. If we leave out of account the inscribed bones and bronzes, books were of three sorts. The most common ancient books were almost identical with books of Han times which have been found preserved in the dry northwest of China and may be seen in museums. These Han books consist of strips of wood perhaps half an inch wide and in the neighborhood of a foot long. Each strip contains a column of characters, running from top to bottom. Two lines of cords hold the strips together, so that the whole resembles a miniature picket fence. Among the earliest Shang bone inscriptions we find the character 冊 which depicts such strips and the binding cords [63]. From its use on the bones and on bronzes there is no possible doubt that this character is the ancient form of 冊 *t'sê* and stands for a written book. By itself and in combinations it occurs more than eighty

62. Cf. for instance *Chên Sung T'ang Chi Ku I Wên* (1931; hereafter referred to as *Chên I Wên*) 4.49–51.
63. It is found in *Yin Ch'ien Pien* 7.19.1; from the name of the diviner this bone can be dated as from the time of Wu Ting.

times in the Shang bone inscriptions which have been published alone. When we remember that there is little reason for such a word to occur in divination formulae it is plain that such books were not rare[64]. This same element appears in the character 典 *tien* which depicts such a book lying on a table, that is, in a place of honor. This character, which is found on bronzes[65] as well as in Chou books, stands for the honored books bequeathed from more or less remote antiquity, whose instructions should be taken as the norm of action, and from this meaning it then comes to be a verb meaning "to regulate"[66]. Some, at least, of such books composed of strips were made from pieces of bamboo. It has a ready-made smooth surface for writing and would split readily into such strips. That such bamboo books existed in Eastern Chou times we know, and that they go back to Shang is quite probable.

Two other materials used for writing upon are mentioned in the *I Li*, and probably go back at least to the Western Chou period. One is the 方 *fang*, literally "square", presumably a rectangular board, on which were indited writings which did not exceed "a hundred characters"[67]. Only one passage records the practise of writing on silk, but it must have been fairly common, for a silk banner bearing his name was prepared for the funeral of every 士 *shih*, or member of the lowest grade of the aristocratic class[68].

The common writing utensil of the pre-Confucian period was a brush, dipped in some sort of ink or writing fluid. It was formerly supposed that the Chinese writing brush was invented during the

    64. It is true that Mr. Tung Tso-pin formerly suggested that this character represented the tortoise shells used for divination, but he has subsequently altered this opinion and is now firmly convinced that there was a very considerable literature, quite aside from the bones, in Shang times (verbal communication of February 10, 1934).

    65. Cf. *Chin Wên Pien* (1925; referred to hereafter as *Chin Pien*) 5.2b.

    66. Cf. *Shu, Lü Hsing* 598.

    67. *SSC I Li* 39.5a; John Steele, *The I-Li* (London, 1917) II.86. *SSC I Li* 24.3a; Steele I.232 (this latter passage is from the "notes" which are later than the body of the text).

    68. *SSC I Li* 35.9a; Steele II.49.

Ch'in dynasty (246–207 B.C.)[69], while the people of earlier periods got along with some much simpler method, possibly mere scratching with a style. That would work on bamboo; it would be slow and unsatisfactory but that would accord precisely with the old idea of the scarcity of books. But this theory does not account for the writing on silk just mentioned. This could hardly be done without some sort of brush and writing fluid.

As a matter of fact it is suggested with reason by Tung Tso-pin that some variety of brush was used already in the Neolithic period, to paint the figures and designs of what is known as "Yang Shao" pottery[70]. And the character for "writing utensil", 聿 *yü* as we find it both in the Shang bone inscriptions, 𦘒 [71], and in bronze inscriptions, 聿 [72], clearly depicts a hand holding a brush. Even more important as evidence is the character 書 *shu*. The earliest meaning of *shu* was not, of course, "book", but rather "to write", "character", "document". And it appears among our earliest bone inscriptions in the form 𢎥 [73], which represents, I suggest, a hand holding a brush with two lines representing that which has been drawn or written.

69. See H. A. Giles, *A History of Chinese Literature* (1901; reprint of 1931), 80.
70. *Ts'ai Anniv. Vol.* 417.
71. *Yin Hou Pien* 2.38.5. This is the only occurrence of the brush-like form listed under this character by the *Chia Ku Wên Pien* (referred to hereafter as *Chia Pien*); the two others given have a straight line, which may be an abbreviated form or may represent a knife or stylus for carving on bone or other material. But in the character *shu* the brush form predominates; see below.
72. Cf. *Chin Pien* 3.19a.
73. *Yin Ch'ien Pien* 7.40.2. This inscription can be dated with certainty, from the names of the two diviners which are found on this piece of bone, in the reign of Wu Ting (a very small fraction of this character, broken off in this inscription, has been completed by analogy). This character is identified by Sun Hai-po as 畫 *hua*, "to draw," and its immediate pictographic signification would seem to be closer to this character. But what we find on the bones is identical with all but the lowest part of *shu* as we find it in the *Shuo Wên*, and with all but the lowest part of *hua* as we find it in bronze inscriptions (cf. *Chin Pien* 3.19b. This character is very similar to all but the lowest part of *shu* as it appears on the bronzes, too; cf. ibid. 3.19a).

What we have, then, is a character in the bone inscriptions which

But that it definitely means "to write" is proved by its use on the oracle bones in the passages 書告曰 *shu kao yüeh*, "wrote to announce saying..."[74], 書呼 *shu hu*, "write commanding" (i.e., "to command in writing")[75], and 書命 *shu ming*, "write ordering"[76]. These phrases are precisely parallel to 聿命 *yü ming* "order with the pen" which occurs once in the bone inscriptions[77], and 冊命 *ts'ê ming*, "order by means of a written document", which is one of the commonest phrases in early Chou bronze inscriptions[78].

It is significant that out of the sixteen occurrences of *shu* in the material covered by the *Chia Ku Wên Pien*[79], all but three show the writing instrument as a very definite and unmistakable brush. We do not, to be sure, have any of the actual brushes used in Shang times, as we do from the Han period, because the climate at Anyang was too damp to allow of their preservation. But we do have some of the writing done by them. In 1929 the National Research Institute excavated, in the Shang culture-bearing stratum at Anyang, three pieces of bone resembling the ordinary oracle bones but with characters written with writing fluid rather than carved into the surface[80]. They were found in two widely separated places, the two discoveries were sepa-

---

could equally well be the ancestral form of either *hua* or *shu*. That it is the latter rather than the former is proved by the way in which it is used; see below.

74. *Yin Ch'ien Pien* 7.40.2 and *Yin Hou Pien* 2.4.11.

75. *Yin Hou Pien* 2.37.2. For the use of *hu* as meaning "to command," cf. *Yin Ch'ien Pien* 7.35.1, 4.31.3 and *Kuei Chia Shou Ku Wên Tzǔ* (hereafter referred to as *Kuei Tzǔ*) 2.27.7.

76. *Yin Ch'ien Pien* 2.28.7. The character *ming* as it appears in the bone inscriptions does not have the "mouth" determinative, so that it is identical with *ling*; the two characters apparently descended from the same ancestral form.

77. *Yin Hou Pien* 2.38.1.

78. Cf. *K'ê Chai Chi Ku Lu* (1896; referred to hereafter as *K'ê Lu*) 4.23b, and passim.

79. One of these occurrences, *Yin Ch'ien Pien* 2.28.8, has been omitted from the *Chia Ku Wên Pien*. All of them are listed there under *hua* rather than *shu*.

80. See *Ts'ai Anniv. Vol.* 417–418.

rated by half a year, and the date of production of the two earlier of the three is placed by Tung Tso-pin as perhaps a century prior to the date of the later one[81]; they can not be ascribed, therefore, to the accidental action of a single individual at a single time and place. And a potsherd, bearing the character 祀 *ssŭ* written with some sort of writing fluid, was excavated in 1932 under the same scientific conditions[82]. I have examined the potsherd itself, and pictures of the bones, and agree with Mr. Tung that they could only have been produced by some variety of brush[83].

Even on the basis of a careful study of the literature which has long been known, but especially on the basis of the new discoveries, it is impossible longer to repeat the traditional formula that when, in the time of Ch'in Shih Huang, "A general, named Mêng T'ien, added to the triumphs of the sword the invention of the camel's-hair brush", then, and not until then, "The clumsy bamboo tablet and stylus were discarded, and strips of cloth or silk came into general use.... Some say that brickdust and water did duty at first for ink. However that may be, the form of the written character underwent a cor-

81. Loc. cit.
82. See *Anyang Pao Kao* 724.
83. Mr. Tung takes the further position that the regular procedure in carving the oracle inscriptions was to write them first with a brush and then to carve (*Ts'ai Anniv. Vol.* 418). Certainly it is true, as he says, that it would have been difficult to do otherwise if, as he holds with some reason, all vertical strokes in the whole inscription were carved first and then the horizontal ones filled in. But if this were the case, we ought to find the horizontal lines inked in in pieces which have only the vertical ones cut, and in so far as I know they have not been so found. It may be said that they have faded out, but why then do we have still these entirely inked pieces—faded, to be sure? Another point: the characters written with the brush seem to be much larger, perhaps almost twice as large, as those found in cut inscriptions of the same period (compare, for instance, the two earlier written pieces, in the natural size drawing given in *Ts'ai Anniv. Vol.* opp. p. 418, with the characters of supposedly the same period found in the first several plates of the *Yin Hsü Shu Ch'i Ching Hua*). This whole subject is one requiring further study.

responding change to suit the materials employed[84]." Among the most remarkable fallacies in Chinese history is that which holds that the type of writing known as *li shu* came in because, the stylus being abandoned and the brush taken up for writing in the Ch'in period, it was difficult to write the round seal characters with the brush but easy to write square characters. Such an idea could only have been originated by Chinese who had for generations been so drilled in the writing of square characters with the brush that they thought it was natural. Since they have maintained it so stoutly, foreigners have repeated the story, supposing with some plausibility that the Chinese ought to know the history of their own writing. But the fact, which it is easy to see now we know that the writing brush was in use a thousand years before the square characters, is the exact reverse of this. With a stylus or an engraving or carving tool of any kind it is easy to draw straight lines and square characters, and hard to make round ones. But with the brush it is easy to draw circles or any other kind of line one wishes; it will go up as well as down, as a pen will not, and the grain of the material written upon does not form an obstacle, as it does with a stylus, to making curved lines. Let any one not accustomed to writing with a Chinese brush try his hand, and he will see that he can much more readily make passable copies of the round, so-called "seal" characters than of the square characters in use today. For the brush is better adapted to writing the former than the latter.

We have seen, then, that the writing brush was used long before the end of the Shang period, that books composed of strips of wood or bamboo were by no means uncommon at that time, and that the Chinese of the oracle bones is a well-developed medium of expression which could not have been called into being by the narrow necessities of the divination formulae. All of these facts point unmistakably to the existence, in Shang times, of a considerable literature. Furthermore, we have seen that in

---

84. Giles, *A History of Chinese Literature*, 80. It is to be noted that Giles sets this down merely as tradition.

very early Chou times there was a great emphasis on, and appreciation of, history. And this, it seems, must have been a heritage from the Shang culture, rather than any independent development of the Chous themselves. For it looks, from such evidence as we have, as if the Chous probably could not even write, to say nothing of having developed an appreciation of historical records, until very shortly before the Chou conquest. It might be said that they appreciated history as an oral tradition, but the fact is that the Chous were remarkably poor in traditions of any variety concerning their own history prior to the conquest.

The language of early Chou books and inscriptions, and the form of characters as we find them in early Chou bronze inscriptions, is entirely a continuation of the writing found on the Shang bone inscriptions. There are differences, but they are unimportant in comparison with the similarities[85]. Tung Tso-pin has published, in his paper on the dating of the oracle inscriptions, material which indicates that the forms of characters used on early Chou bronzes agree chiefly with those used by the Shang people during the last seventy years before the Chou conquest.[86]. Future investigation may or may not substantiate this; if it does, we shall have to conclude that the Chou people probably learned writing from the Shangs only in the course of the last century before the Chou conquest.

This is not at all unlikely. We find, in early Chou literature, a great deal of talk about the Chou ancestors, a great deal of respect for literature, and a great deal of reference to old books. But with the exception of a part of the *I Ching*, not a single book

85. Due allowance must be made, of course, for the brief and formulary nature of the oracle inscriptions, which in itself would account for a considerable degree of difference.
86. In his chart of the cyclical characters (*Ts'ai Anniv. Vol.* opp. 410) the Chou bronze forms of almost every one of the twenty-two agree most closely with the bone forms of the latest period. The evidence with regard to the forms of 夕 *hsi* and 月 *yüeh* is even more important, though final judgment on this point must await further research (cf. ibid. 416).

is attributed by the Chou people to their own ancestors prior to the conquest. With this single exception, all of the pre-Chou books referred to are ascribed, I believe, to the Shangs, Hsias, etc.—none is described as a product of early Chou culture. For all their care in giving themselves a respectable genealogy, the early Chous were pretty frank in admitting that they had been barbarians[87].

Since references to it show clearly that there was not a little literature in the early Chou period, and since much of it was quite apparently not the work of the Chous, a good deal of it at least must have come from Shang times. And the very remarkable consonance between the genealogy of the Shang kings as it is found in Chinese history and on the oracle bones raises a strong probability that written records survived to form the basis of the history.

There was a Shang literature, entirely apart from the bone inscriptions. Does any part of that literature survive to the present day? The *Shang Sung* section of the *Shih Ching* and the *T'ang Shih, Pan*[88] *Kêng, Kao Tsung Yung Jih, Hsi Po K'an Li*, and *Wei Tzŭ* of the *Chin Wên Shang Shu* have all been attributed to the Shang period[89]. Let us examine, one by one, the validity of their claims to Shang date.

87. A later paper in this series will be devoted to the antecedents and traditions of the Chou people.
88. The original form of this character seems to have been 般 *Pan* rather than the now current 盤 *P'an*; cf. *Chin Wên Shang Shu Ching Shuo K'ao* (*Huang Ch'ing Ching Chieh Hsü Pien* 1079–1116; referred to hereafter as *Chin Wên Shu K'ao*) 6.1a.
89. None of the books of the *ku wên* text of the *Shu* is mentioned here simply because it is taken for granted, as has long been agreed by most scholars, that all of them are late forgeries. It would be possible to show by detailed citation of evidence that they could not possibly date from the Shang period, but it would be a waste of time—what the Chinese call "beating a dead tiger."

Shang Sung

First as to the *Shang Sung*. In the now current edition of the *Shih Ching* it is taken for granted that these poems were actually produced in Shang times. But in the last passage of the *Sung Shih Chia* of the *Shih Chi*, beginning "*T'ai Shih Kung yüeh*," it is said that a minister of Duke Hsiang of Sung (650–637 B.C.) was their author. And P'ei Yin, commenting on this passage, says that the now lost Han edition of the *Shih Ching* agreed with this[1]. Wang Kuo-wei went into the whole problem afresh, on the basis of the bone inscriptions, etc. He gives a detailed discussion of the traditions as to its origins which seems hardly worth going into, for such traditions are not very sound evidence even after we have arrived at their original form[2]. But his criticism of the content of these poems, and comparison of it with our available knowledge of the Shang state, is very valuable indeed.

Wang points out that the last poem in the collection, speaking of the building of a temple for one of the ancestral kings, says:

"We ascended the Ching mountain,
Where the pines and cypresses grew symmetrical"[3].

But the poem refers to a king named 武 Wu, and the only Shang kings of that name are Wu Ting and Wu I[4]. These kings lived at Anyang. But the Ching mountain which ancient literature associates with the Shangs is south of the Yellow River, far from Anyang but near to the capital of the State of Sung. This, Wang holds, is one proof that the poems were written during the Chou period. And not a single element of the whole ritual and cultural complex which we find on the oracle bones can be found in the *Shang Sung*, he declares. Names of places, persons, etc.,

1. 集解韓詩商頌章句亦美襄公
2. For this discussion see Wang, *I Shu*, I.2.16–17.
3. *Shih* (Legge, *Chinese Classics*, Vol. IV, 1871; hereafter referred to as *Shih*), 646. Legge translates "the hill of King," but the present rendering seems preferable; cf. Wang, op. cit., 18a.
4. T'ai Ting is also called Wên Wu Ting (cf. *Yin Ch'ien Pien* 1.18.1 and 4) but he also lived at Anyang.

are wholly of the sort we find in Chou literature, not at all what we find in Shang material. As for the language of the poems, it is not even like that of the beginning of the Chou period, but is that of the middle of Western Chou and later. The Shang capital, called Shang on the bones, is referred to as Yin—a word unknown in the bone inscriptions. The reputed founder of the Shang power, known as 大乙 Ta I on the bones, is called 湯 T'ang[5], 烈祖 Lieh Tsu, and 武王 Wu Wang in the *Shang Sung*. Wang gives several specific expressions found in these poems which are also found in poems which are known to be of Chou date[6], especially the *Lu Sung*. It may be held, of course, that these expressions were borrowed by the *Lu Sung* from the *Shang Sung* itself. But Wang points out that since the rulers of Lu were closely related to the Chou kings, we should normally expect their poems to agree most closely with those of the ruling house. That they do not, but are like the *Shang Sung*, he attributes to the fact that Sung and Lu were in like position, states subject to the Chou house, and that the two sets of poems were composed at about the same time. The fact that the *Shang Sung* comes at the end of the entire *Shih*, violating any sort of chronological order if it really emanated from Shang, is still another piece of evidence on which he bases his conclusion, that these poems must have been written not earlier than the middle of the Western Chou period[7].

That the poems are called the *Shang*, rather than the *Sung*, *Sung* means nothing; Shang was frequently used, without explanation, as an alternate name for the State of Sung[8]. One of the best proofs that these poems cannot be from Shang times was not cited by Wang. We find the deity 天 *T'ien* mentioned in them five times, as frequently, in fact, as *Ti* or

---

5. This criticism is weakened, however, by the fact that Wang himself, as well as others, consider that 唐 T'ang on the bones stands for the same individual, and is the original form of the character given in the text (cf. Wang, *I Shu* I.9.9a). Subsequent alteration by editors is always, in such a case, more than possible, judging by what we know of such practises in general.

6. Op. cit., I.18.
7. Op. cit., I.18b.
8. Cf. *Kuo Yü* 19.5b and 9b; *Tso Chuan* 621.2, 855.12.

Shang Ti is mentioned. The Shang genealogy is begun:
"*T'ien* commissioned the swallow,
To descend and give birth to Shang."[9]

But I have shown that the character *T'ien*, as such, does not occur in the Shang bone inscriptions, and that the deity *T'ien* had no part in Shang religion. It apparently originated among the Chou people and was brought east by them at the time of the conquest[10].

It is, in fact, very generally agreed among those who work in ancient Chinese history that the *Shang Sung* cannot at all be considered a piece of Shang literature[11]. But these poems do give us a most interesting picture of the people of the State of Sung when they were as yet only half assimilated to the Chou philosophy of history. They speak of *T'ien*, and they call their ancestors Yin as well as Shang; the former is certainly, and the latter probably, a mark of Chou influence. But they had not yet accepted *in toto* the mythological history which the Chous introduced to rationalize their conquest. The Chous, as unlettered barbarians coming in from the west to over-run the lands of their more civilized neighbors, found themselves in a position almost impossible to maintain unless they could find a formula to reconcile their new subjects, including other peoples as well as the Shangs, to their rule. They could never hope to hold their conquests indefinitely if they based their right to rule on might alone. Out of this situation there grew the fiction that the wide empire, embracing many tribes and states, which was dreamed of for the first time by the Chou chieftains, had actually been in existence for centuries or millenia. They went back to the misty tradition of a cultured Hsia state (which we shall discuss later), and declared that it had been the first dynasty, embracing the whole of the Chinese world. And the Shangs, according to this

9. *Shih* 636.
10. Full evidence on this point will be given in a later paper of this series. See my article entitled 釋天, translated into Chinese by Prof. Liu Chieh, in 燕京學報 *Yenching Journal of Chinese Studies*, No. 18 (Dec. 1935), 59–71.
11. Cf. *Ku Shih Pien* (Peking, 1926 and later) I.68, III. 505-510, etc.

Chou formula, were loyal subjects of the Hsia dynasty. But later the last Hsia sovereign was wicked, and Heaven picked T'ang, ruler of the Shangs, to displace him. He did so, and became Heaven's representative on earth, ruler of the Shang dynasty. And the Chous, according to this formula, were loyal subjects of the Shang dynasty (though as a matter of fact there is no real evidence that they were ever subject to the Shangs). But later the last Shang sovereign was wicked, and Heaven picked Wu Wang, ruler of the Chous, to displace him. He did so, and became Heaven's representative on earth, ruler of the Chou dynasty. Thus, according to this formula, the descendants of the Shangs and all other people should be loyal and submissive subjects to the divinely appointed Chou ruler.

It was obviously to the interest of the Chous to inculcate these ideas as deeply as possible in all their subjects, and especially in the descendants of the Shangs who might, and indeed on one occasion did, rebel, remembering their past glories. The way in which the Chous inculcated these ideas, and the difficulties which they encountered, will be discussed in a later paper. That they ultimately succeeded is shown, for instance, by the speech of his Minister of War, a descendant of the Shang house, to Duke Hsiang of Sung in 638 B.C. He said, "Heaven's rejection of the house of Shang is of long standing. If your Highness attempts to restore it, your offense will be unpardonable."[12] But in the *Shang Sung* we find various things which do not tally at all with the Chou account of history.

In the *Shang Sung* general dominion by the Shang rulers does not begin merely with the conquest of Hsia by T'ang. Before him:

> "Hsiang T'u, the ardent,
> Spread his dominion even beyond the seas."[13]

After Hsiang T'u there were some eleven rulers before we come to T'ang. T'ang, according to the orthodox historical theory

12. *Tso Chuan* 181.15–16. Cf. *SSC Tso Chuan* 15.3a, commentary.
13. *Shih* 640. Legge translates "And all [within] the seas, beyond [the middle region], acknowledged his restraints." This, he explains in a note, means " 'the outside of the four seas,' the 'four seas' being a

which appears to have been started by the Chous, was a vassal of the Hsia sovereign who felt himself called, because of the latter's wickedness, to overthrow him and reëstablish virtuous government. But the *Shang Sung* treats this incident as follows:

> "The favor of *Ti* did not leave [Shang],
> And in T'ang was found the subject for its display...
> He received the tribute *of the States*, large and small
> And he supported them as a strong steed *does its burden*.
> So did he receive the favor of Heaven.
> He displayed everywhere his valour,
> Unshaken, unmoved...
> The nine regions were effectually secured by him.
> Having smitten *the princes of* Wei and Ku
> He dealt with *the prince* of K'un Wu, and with Chieh of Hsia." [14]

It would be exceedingly difficult to discern, from this passage, that Hsia was anything but another state or tribe on a level with the others mentioned, or that Chieh was supposed to be the Heaven-ordained ruler of T'ang. Nor is there any moralizing apology here for T'ang's action. Quite evidently, he was a powerful military chief who found himself in position to acquire some more territory. And following the good old Chinese (and international) custom he went out and acquired it, with explanations to no one.

---

denomination of the kingdom in all its extent, and the 'outside' leading us to conceive of all the feudal States in distinction from the royal domain." Legge explains the passage thus to avoid the conflict with orthodox historical theory, which is actually present in the text, involved in making a Shang ruler lord of the whole Chinese world at a time when the Hsias were supposed to have reigned.

The difficulty is explained by Chêng Hsüan on the basis that Hsiang T'u was appointed by the Hsia sovereign as chief of the feudal lords, thus controlling the world as his deputy. The only trouble with this is that there is no slightest suggestion of it in the poem, which seems, in fact, pretty definitely to contradict it. For the later mention of Hsia does not at all support the theory that the Shangs were conceived of as subject to Hsia.

14. *Shih* 640-642.

Nor does the *Shang Sung* support the orthodox view of Chinese history according to which feudalism in China extends back into the remote ages of Shang and pre-Shang times. We shall see when we come to investigate early Chou institutions that there is good reason to suppose that feudalism on a large scale probably came into being for the first time with the Chou conquest, and the *Shang Sung* corroborates this. According to the orthodox view Heaven appointed the emperor, the "Son of Heaven", and all other earthly rulers were appointed by him. But the *Shang Sung* says:

> "Heaven appointed the many rulers,
> And established their capitals within the sphere of the
>   labors of Yü,
> But for the business of every year they appeared before
>   our king,
> *Saying*, 'Do not punish nor reprove us;
> We have not been remiss in our husbandry'" [15].

Here we quite evidently have a situation, not of feudal rulers established by the sovereign, but of subject states or tribes reduced by conquest, their rulers forced to send tribute and to come and make a yearly accounting to the conqueror.

The *Shang Sung*, then, cannot be used as contemporary evidence of Shang history and institutions. But on the other hand it is not to be discarded entirely as a source of information concerning the Shang state. Where it differs from the orthodox, and especially from the Chou account of Shang history, and where it corroborates and amplifies our knowledge gained from contemporary Shang materials, it must be considered to be a source of some importance.

15. *Shih* 645.

T'ang Shih

Of the five books of the *chin wên* text of the *Shu Ching* which purport to date from the Shang period, the first is the *T'ang Shih*. It is difficult to criticize this book from the point of view of style. Its grammar and vocabulary are not identical with those of the Shang oracle bones, but this is not to be expected, for the oracle bone inscriptions are a specialized sort of matter employing, one might suppose, a style not at all points identical with that of the rest of Shang literature. The style of the *T'ang Shih* is, however, generally similar to the earliest literary style we know, that of Western Chou bronzes. This in itself is perhaps a little suspicious, since this document is supposed to come from the beginning of the Shang period, which must have covered a number of centuries however we reckon. When we can trace great variations of expression in the comparatively simple formulae of the oracle bones in the short space of two centuries, we may wonder if lengthy documents could have been written, in the time of T'ang, in a style so like that of the Chou scribes. But since we lack Shang literature for comparison this point must go, more or less, by default.

When we apply historical criticism, however, we at once find a discrepancy between this book and the *Shang Sung*. The *T'ang Shih* is supposed to be a speech delivered by T'ang, the founder of the Shang dynasty, to his people upon his setting out to conquer the Hsia ruler. And he says, "It is not that I, the little child, dare to undertake rebellion; the ruler of Hsia is full of crimes, and Heaven has given the charge to destroy him."[1] This book, then, clearly represents T'ang as a vassal of the Hsia ruler, who might be charged with rebellion, but who piously justifies his revolt by declaring that "Hsia is an offender, and as I fear *Shang Ti* I dare not but punish him"[2]. All of this is distinctly at variance with the *Shang Sung*. There, as we have seen, the Shang rulers are supposed to have had general dominion

1. *Shu* 173.
2. *Shu* 174.

eleven generations before T'ang⁽³⁾. And the attack by T'ang upon Chieh of Hsia is not at all represented as a revolt raised in fear and trembling by a vassal who claimed that he was appointed by deity to punish the wickedness of his lord. Instead of this it is represented as the simple culmination of a matter-of-fact career of expansion⁽⁴⁾. It may be objected that it has just been shown that the *Shang Sung* is not a genuinely Shang document, from which it might be held that the version of this matter found in the *T'ang Shih* is the correct one. But as we shall see there is great reason to doubt this.

The most serious difficulty with the *T'ang Shih* is that it is permeated, from one end to the other, with the philosophy of the Decree of Heaven, which holds that *T'ien* seeks out, in every age, the most worthy ruler in all of China and appoints him to govern the Chinese world—charging him, if necessary, to oust by force an unworthy possessor of the throne. It is difficult to suppose that this theory could have been in existence much earlier than the Chou period, for the reason that before the Chou conquest there does not seem to have existed any general sway over even a preponderant portion of north China. It would appear that before that time there were numerous states and tribes, some of which exercised hegemony over a greater or smaller number of the others according to their military power at the moment. But a more or less centralized, feudal state such as this conception supposes does not seem to have existed until the Chous created one. And this theory of the Decree of Heaven seems to have been at once an apologia for and a driving force motivating the Chou conquest and the knitting together of the Chou state. This point will be gone into at greater length in another paper.

Furthermore, the deity Heaven is absolutely foreign to Shang culture. The very character *T'ien* does not occur once in the many thousands of bone inscriptions thus far known, although *Ti* (or sometimes called *Shang Ti*) is of frequent occurrence. The

3. *Shih* 640.
4. *Shih* 642.

nature of these inscriptions is such that this character could not fail to occur in them if *T'ien* had been a deity, to say nothing of the chief deity, of the Shang people. Yet in the *T'ang Shih*, a book supposed to date from the beginning of the Shang dynasty, we find the character *T'ien* occurring twice and the deity of that name occupying the center of the stage. Moreover, *T'ien* and *Shang Ti* are used as alternative names of the same deity[5]; this practice did not grow up until after the coalescence of Shang and Chou culture, about the time of the Chou conquest.

We have, as a matter of fact, literary evidence which indicates very strongly that the *T'ang Shih* could not have been in existence at the time of the Chou conquest, and therefore that it was a production of a subsequent date. Whether we take the orthodox version of the establishment of the Shang dynasty as history or as a Chou fiction, there is no avoiding the fact that the Chous were uncommonly well acquainted with it. It is mentioned, in greater or less detail, in four of the eight documents which we can certify as having been produced by the Chous in the first decades after their conquest of the Shang people[6]. But that mention is very brief and passing[7] except in the case of the *To Shih* and the *To Fang*, two documents which are exhortations addressed directly to the conquered Shang people. In these two books the particulars of that alleged history are gone into in great detail[8], which seems rather strange since, if these were the true traditions of the founding of their own dynasty, the Shang people should have needed no instruction in them by the Chous.

The reason for this zeal of the Chou conquerors, in teaching

5. Cf. *Shu* 173 and 174.
6. I.e., in the *Shao Kao*, *To Shih*, *Chün Shih*, and *To Fang* (cf. *Shu* 427, 429–30, 455–8, 460, 477, 495–502). The other four books of the eight are the *Ta Kao*, *K'ang Kao*, *Chiu Kao*, and *Lo Kao*, all, of course, in our present *Shu Ching*. These eight books can be proved, by historical criticism and by the correspondence of their language with that of early Chou bronze inscriptions, to be genuine and to date from the opening years of the Chou dynasty. This proof will be presented in its proper place.
7. Cf. *Shu* 427, 429–30, 477.
8. Cf. *Shu* 455–8, 460, 495–500.

Shang traditions to the Shang people, is at once apparent when we examine the texts in question. Let us consider the text of the *To Fang*. In this document the Duke of Chou, speaking in the name of the king[9], is exhorting the people of Shang to submit to the Chou rule. They have already rebelled, and been transported and forced to build a city at Loyang, but even the punishments which have been meted out to them have apparently not sufficed to make them give up the hope of ousting the conquerors and restoring their former glories. The Duke charges them to abandon all such ideas, and threatens, cajoles, and philosophizes to urge his point. He says:

> "Ti sent down correction[10] on Hsia, but the Hsia sovereign only increased his luxury and sloth, and would not speak kindly to the people. He proved himself on the contrary dissolute and dark, and would not yield for a single day to the leading[11] of *Ti*—this is what you have heard. He kept reckoning upon *his possession of* the Decree of *Ti*, and would not promote the people's welfare. By great inflictions of punishment he heightened the disorder within the domain of Hsia. Having become involved in internal disorders, he was unable to deal well with the multitudes. Nor did he seek at all to employ men whom he could respect, and who might display a generous kindness to the people, but he daily honored the covetous and cruel, who were guilty of cruel

9. The book opens with 周公曰王若曰 "The Duke of Chou says: The King agrees in saying:" or "It is as if the King said:". The phrase *wang jo yüeh* is very familiar on bronze inscriptions, and in some books of the *Shu*. It prefaces statements made by others—officials, secretaries, or in the case of the Duke of Chou the Regent—in the name of the King.

10. It is a moot point what character appeared here in the original, to say nothing of its translation; cf. Legge, *Shu* 495; *Chin Wên Shu K'ao* 25.2b; Chang Kuo-kan, *Han Shih Ching Pei T'u* (Peiping, 1931) 13b.

This point is immaterial to the present purpose, however, and I have preserved Legge's translation in this place, with only this comment.

11. Instead of 廸 *ti* the text of Ma Jung reads 攸 *yu* at this point; cf. *Chin Wên Shu K'ao* 25.2b.

tortures in the city of Hsia[12]. Heaven on this sought a *true* lord for the people, and sent down its bright favoring Decree on T'ang the Successful, who punished and destroyed the sovereign of Hsia. Heaven's decided refusal of its favor *to Hsia* was because the righteous men of your many states[13] were not permitted to continue long in their posts of enjoyment, and the many officers whom Hsia respected were quite unable to maintain an intelligent preservation of the people in the enjoyment *of their lives*, but on the contrary aided one another in oppression, so that of the hundred ways of promoting *prosperity* they could not advance *one*.

"In the case of T'ang the Successful it was because he was the choice of your many states that he superseded Hsia and became the lord of the people. He paid careful attention to the essential virtues *of a sovereign*, in order to stimulate the people, and they on their part imitated him and were stimulated. From him down to Ti I[14] the sovereigns all,

12. I have translated "city" rather than following Legge in "cities" since this seems to me more in conformity with the usage of the time, considering *Shang I* and *Lo I* which are both names of specific cities, as well as *Chou* used as the name of the Chou capital.

This last sentence is very difficult to translate. I have simply reproduced Legge's rendering, though dubious as to its accuracy.

13. 多方 *to fang*, which Legge translates as "many regions". But we know from the Shang bones that *fang*, which does mean "region" in modern Chinese, was used to denote various peoples with whom the Shangs conducted wars and had other relations, as the 土方 (cf. *Yin Hsü Shu Ch'i Ching Hua*, referred to hereafter as *Yin Ching Hua*, 6.1); 夷方 (cf. *Yin Ch'ien Pien* 2.6.6), etc. One would be tempted to call these tribes, if it were not for the definite territorial connotation of the character *fang*. The word seems to have denoted a group of people known by a particular name, occupying a particular territory, and functioning to some extent at least as a political entity. The best that we can do, then, is to translate *fang* as "state", but with the clear understanding that this does not necessarily mean "independent and sovereign state". It seems probable that some of the *fang* were independent states while others were not.

14. I.e., down to the next to the last Shang king. This is a point on which the Chous were always harping—they had no quarrel with, indeed they had the highest respect for, the Shang kings as a group, they tell us. It was only with their last, unworthy successor that they

with illustrious virtue, were careful in the use of punishments, and thus were able to exercise a stimulating influence *over the people*.... But when it came to your *late* ruler, he was not able with your many states to continue to enjoy the Decree of Heaven.

"Oh! the King speaks to the following effect: I announce and declare to you of the many states, Heaven had no set purpose to do away with the sovereign of Hsia, or with the sovereign of Yin. But your ruler, being in possession of your many states, abandoned himself to great excess, reckoning on *his possession of* the Decree of Heaven, and making trifling excuses for his conduct. And so in the case of the sovereign of Hsia—his schemes of government were not of a sort to secure his enjoyment *of the empire*, so that Heaven sent down ruin on him and the ruler of your state[15] entered into the line of his succession. And likewise your last Shang king was luxurious to the extreme of luxury, while his schemes of government showed neither purity nor progress, so that Heaven sent down this ruin *on him*....

"Heaven then sought among your many states, making a great impression by its terrors to stir up one who might look *reverently* to it, but in all your states there was none able to do so[16]. There were, however, our kings of Chou[17], who had any quarrel, and no one, they give us to understand, regretted any more than the Chous the unfortunate necessity which made it inevitable that they cut off this corrupt king in order to keep the former glories of the Shang line from becoming completely obscured.

15. According to the *Han Shih Ching Pei T'u* 12b, this should read 國 *kuo* instead of *pang*.
16. This translation, while at variance with Legge's, accords with the *K'ung Chuan*, and what is more important seems far more reasonable on the basis of the text.
17. Notice that the Duke of Chou here speaks of the Chou rulers prior to the conquest as *wang*, although according to the orthodox theory they were vassals of the Shang house. As a matter of fact it appears that the Chou were never anything more than the most purely nominal vassals of Shang. And *wang* was a title used by more or less petty rulers, loyal feudatories of the "Son of Heaven", even in the Western Chou period, as will be shown later.

treated well the multitudes of the people, and were able to sustain the burden of virtuous *government* and to preside over all services to spirits and to Heaven. Heaven thereupon instructed them and increased their excellence, made choice of them, and gave them the Decree of Yin, to rule over your many states. . . .

"Why do you not cultivate a sincere and liberal *acquiescence in your present condition*[18] in your many states? Why do you not aid and coöperate with and be governed by us the kings of Chou, to secure the enjoyment of the Decree of Heaven?[19] You now still dwell in your dwellings, and cultivate your fields—why do you not obey our kings, and consolidate the Decree of Heaven? Your ways are continually those of disquietude. Your hearts have not yet *learned to* love us, but do you refuse greatly to acquiesce in the Decree of Heaven? Do you *dare to* triflingly reject that Decree?"[20]

We can see plainly why the Duke of Chou insists so warmly upon the wickedness of the last Hsia sovereign and the divinely ordained nature of T'ang's conquest over him. It is because this provides a precedent for the Chou conquest, and leads to the corollary that the Shang people should submit gladly to the reign of the Chous which has been, in its turn, Heaven-appointed. But our present question is whether this was Shang history, or a Chou version. And there is some evidence that it was the latter. The Duke of Chou seems to have had some difficulty in convincing the Shang people that their history was really so. In the

18. I have added the words in italics because they seem to complete the meaning of this difficult passage. Legge's addition of "obedience" seems to go beyond what the text warrants.

19. The intention of this sentence is clear enough—it is to persuade the Shang people to coöperate with instead of resisting the Chou rule, thus helping the Chou kings to enjoy undisturbed the newly formed empire and also, it is implied, conducing to the greatest welfare of the Shang people, since further resistance will bring only punishment. But exactly how each character should be translated is a question. The above rendering is given after careful study of various commentaries, but I am not completely satisfied with it.

20. *Shu* 495–503.

course of the *To Shih,* a harangue very similar to that just quoted from, the Duke says:

> "The thing was from the Decree of Heaven... (21) Do not murmur against me. You know that your ancestors of the Yin dynasty had their books and archives(22) *showing how Yin superseded the Decree of Hsia.*(23)"

The Duke says that their "forefathers of the Yin dynasty" had such books, but apparently at the time he spoke there was not, in spite of his wide knowledge of the subject, a single book of the sort in existence from which he could quote to clinch his case. Why did he not quote from the *T'ang Shih,* which was admirably suited to his purpose? Evidently, I believe, because it had not yet been written. But this lack was not allowed to continue indefinitely, and some obliging Chou scribe wrote a book to fit the purpose—our present *T'ang Shih.*

Let us run briefly over the evidence concerning the *T'ang Shih.* It is supposed to date from the period of T'ang, which can not have been less than some five hundred years prior to the opening of the Chou period. Yet its literary style is that of the Western Chou period, quite unlike what we find on the Shang oracle bones. The account which the *T'ang Shih* gives of the relation of T'ang to the Hsia state is at variance with Shang tradition as found in the *Shang Sung.* Most important of all, the book is built around the deity *T'ien,* which we know from the oracle bones to have had no part in Shang religion. That this book was not in existence at the beginning of the Chou period is indicated by the statement of the Duke of Chou, who would eagerly have welcomed the authority of such a work, but who could only aver that such books had been among the possessions of the "ancestors" of the Shang people.

But if the history of the conquest by T'ang does not tally with Shang traditions, it is identical at every point with the Chou

21. The omitted passage as found in the stone classics is very different from the received text, and both are of dubious meaning; cf. *Han Shih Ching Pei T'u* 13b.
22. Legge says "archives and narratives", but both of these characters denote physical books, and are best rendered as above.
23. *Shu* 459–60.

version of the matter—a version urged by the Chous because it justified their own conquest and did, in fact, in time succeed in reconciling the descendants of the Shangs to bearing the Chou yoke. When we consider this, and the fact that in style, phraseology, and ideas this book is virtually identical with other documents known to be productions of the early Chou period[24], the inescapable conclusion is, in my opinion, that the *T'ang Shih* was a Western Chou forgery concocted for purposes of political propaganda. At any rate, it can not possibly be a Shang production, and therefore is not to be considered among the materials for Shang history.

In a paper in the first volume of the *Ku Shih Pien*, Ku Chiehkang declared the *T'ang Shih* to have been edited, at least, if not written for the first time, in the Eastern Chou period, after the end of Western Chou[25]. In my opinion Professor Ku went too far in this direction, since he did not grant, in this paper, that any one of the forged books of the *Shu* was written as early as Western Chou. It seems to me evident, from comparison of their style with the bronze inscriptions, that some of them were. In this same paper Professor Ku considered the *Pan Kêng*, the second of the documents we must consider, to be the only book of genuinely Shang date in the *Shu Ching*[26]. This represented the general opinion of scholarship at the time.

24. For instance in the *T'ang Shih* the king speaks of himself as 小子 and 一人 (*Shu* 173, 175); cf. the same expressions in the *Lo Kao* and the *To Shih* (*Shu* 443, 459). The similarities in vocabulary and style are apparent the moment one compares this book with the eight early Chou works mentioned above, or with bronze inscriptions of this time.

25. P. 201.

26. Loc. cit. He has subsequently changed this opinion, and now believes its date to be definitely Chou (verbal communication, October, 1933).

Pan Kêng

The *Pan Kêng* is a long and a rather tedious book. It purports to record the speeches of the king, Pan Kêng, who ruled the Shang state, according to the traditional dates, from 1401 to 1374 B.C.[1] The king is first trying to win over the people, and especially the nobles and officers, to his project of moving the capital, and then, in a later section, to reconcile them to the move after it has actually been made. The place to which the move is made is called 殷 Yin. And here, in the fifth character of the text, crops up the first major difficulty with this book.

Yin is the name by which the Shang capital city at Anyang was known during the Chou period. We know that it is this place, and no other, which is designated by that name, for several reasons. The genuine Bamboo Books, as quoted by the *T'ai P'ing Yü Lan*, says that "Pan Kêng... moved to... Yin"[2]. And the same work is quoted in a commentary to the *Shih Chi* as saying that "From Pan Kêng's moving to Yin down to the extinction of *the Shang state under king* Chou... the capital was not moved again"[3]. Furthermore, we can prove by the oracle bone inscriptions that the Shang seat was located at Anyang at least from the time of king Wu Ting down to Ti Hsin, the next to the last Shang king. This point, which has been disputed, will be proved later. The *Hsiang Yü Pên Chi* of the *Shih Chi* gives us geographical data on the point, relating that certain events took place "on the site of the ruins of Yin, south of the Huan River"[4]. The Huan is a small and a short stream, and the city excavated at Anyang is located on its south bank, utilizing a bend of the river for natural protection. There is little doubt, then, that the Yin of the *Pan Kêng* is the Shang capital excavated at Anyang[5].

1. These dates are, of course, nearly a century earlier than would be allowed by those who follow the Bamboo Books' chronology; cf. C. W. Bishop, in *JAOS* 52.232 footnote 3.
2. *Ku Chu Shu* 5a.
3. Loc. cit.
4. *Shih Chi* 7.10b.
5. See pages 133-139, below.

But it is very doubtful that this city was called Yin by the Shang people during the Shang period. The character Yin has not been located in all the many thousands of bone inscriptions which we know. On the other hand, there is very good evidence that the city at Anyang was called not Yin but 商 Shang. We find frequent reference on the oracle bones to a place called 大邑商 ta i Shang, "the great city Shang"[6]. From the way in which it is used this would appear to be the name of their capital city. And we find the same expression used in the *To Shih* of the *Shu Ching* with reference to the Shang capital[7]. In the *Chiu Kao*, where the state is called Yin, the capital of the last Shang king is still called 商邑 Shang i[8]. There is no warrant, therefore, for supposing that the Shang capital was called Yin by the Shang people prior to the Chou conquest, and much evidence that it was not.

This same question extends to the name of the state. The common theory is that the name of the state was changed to Yin in the reign of Pan Kêng, when the capital was moved to a place called Yin. But since the place was called Shang and not Yin, and since the character Yin does not occur in the oracle bones,

6. Cf. *Yin Ch'ien Pien* 3.27.6, 2.3.7 and 4.15.2 (these are one piece, broken); etc. Compare the term *ta i Chou* for the Chou capital, in *Mencius* 273, and *Shu* 314; while the latter passage is in a *ku wên* book, the two are almost identical, and may come from the same ancient document.

7. *Shu* 460. The text of the *Shu* reads 天邑商 *T'ien i Shang*, which Legge translates as "heavenly city of Shang". But *T'ien* and *ta* were the same character in origin. Both depict a man, standing upright, as seen from the front. Ordinarily the head was not added to the character, since it was a needless and troublesome complication. But as *T'ien* and *ta* developed into two separate characters, there grew up the convention of adding a head to *T'ien* while leaving it off of *ta*. The Shang people had neither the deity nor the character *T'ien*, but they sometimes wrote *ta* with the addition of a head. Sometimes we find *ta i Shang* so written on the oracle bones (cf. *Yin Ch'ien Pien* 2.3.7 and 4.15.2, etc.). When Chou scribes read this they naturally considered it to be *T'ien* rather than *ta*. Complete evidence on this point will be given in a later paper.

8. *Shu* 408.

and since we have no valid evidence that the Shang people ever called themselves Yin, it becomes very doubtful whether we should use the name Yin in connection with the Shang state at all. It has been suggested that Yin was originally a Chou name for the Shang state and people, and this seems very plausible. It does not seem, however, that it was a term of contempt, as such names often are. The character 殷 *yin* has, among others, the meaning of "great, flourishing". And it is quite possible that the Chou people, who admired Shang culture, applied this name to the Shang state for that reason, just as some of the barbarians who vanquished the Romans looked upon Rome as the center of all that was civilized.

When we find, then, that the *Pan Kêng* opens with the statement that "Pan Kêng was moving to Yin", this is reason enough to question its authenticity. We must doubt it still more when we find that the character *T'ien*, absent from the oracle bones, occurs in this book no less than five times [9] as a name of the chief Shang deity, while *Shang Ti* (common in the bone inscriptions) is mentioned only once [10]. The familiar phrase of Chou religion, 天命 *T'ien ming*, is found here [11]. Pan Kêng even calls himself 天子 "Son of Heaven" [12], although in all of the hundreds of times the king is mentioned on the oracle bones this title does not occur once.

The discrepancies in this book which have already been mentioned are enough to show that it is a forgery. But even if they did not occur, we could be perfectly sure that it was not genuine merely from an examination of its style. Not only does this style have nothing in common with the bone inscriptions of Shang date; it is, in fact, much more smooth, flowing, and easy to read than any bronze inscriptions or authentic books which we possess from the Western Chou period. While it may certainly be held that Shang literary style may have been more flowing than what we have on the bones, and one might contend, as a

9. *Shu* 222, 223, 234, 238.
10. *Shu* 245.
11. *Shu* 222.
12. *Shu* 238.

matter of argument, that it might have been more graceful than that of Western Chou times, yet we certainly should not expect it to be just that of the Eastern Chou period—and that is what the style of the *Pan Kêng* is.

General statements comparing the style of documents are necessarily subjective and therefore unsatisfactory. Unfortunately very little has been done, as yet, in the way of scientific analysis of Western Chou literary style, so that it is difficult to cite much in the way of objective criteria, but a start can be made in this direction. An idea of the way in which the character 之 *chih* was used in Chou documents may be obtained by an analysis of its use in the bronze inscriptions in Kuo Mo-jo's *Liang Chou Chin Wên Tz'ŭ Ta Hsi*[13], which includes most of the current bronze inscriptions, of Chou date, which are of any considerable length or importance. *Chih* is fairly common among the Eastern Chou inscriptions, occurring eighty-one times in one hundred fourteen inscriptions. But the case is very different with those of Western Chou date; one hundred thirty-eight inscriptions contain only fourteen occurrences of *chih*[14]. I have examined the early Chou books of the *Shu* in this regard, and they are in general very sparing of the use of *chih*, although the *K'ang Kao* has it rather more frequently than the rest.

But in the *Pan Kêng* we find the particle *chih* no less than twenty-two times. More important, we find it used, in some cases, in a manner which is not at all characteristic of Western Chou prose, but is characteristic of that of later periods. In its fourteen occurrences on the Western Chou bronzes mentioned, *chih* is used seven times as a pronoun, four times to connect a preceding adjectival phrase with the following noun it modifies, and three times to connect two nouns as a simple genitive particle. These are, in general, the ways in which it was used in

13. This valuable volume is marred by the well-known carelessness of its brilliant author, who occasionally leaves out several characters of an inscription or makes obvious mistranslations merely for want of sufficient care. It must be checked, therefore, with the original rubbings of inscriptions every time it is used.

14. *Liang Chou Hsi* 39, 40 (twice), 50, 51, 74, 89, 101, 104, 107, 128, 138 (twice), 149.

Western Chou times. In the *Pan Kêng* we find a quite different and much more complicated sort of use of *chih*. Western grammatical terms are seldom fully satisfactory for describing Chinese usage, but in Western terms, *chih* is used to connect a preceding, modifying noun, with a verb or participle of which the verbal function is rendered unmistakable by the fact that it is followed by an object, or in some other manner. This usage is illustrated by the following clauses, which are quoted from the *Pan Kêng*. The translations are as literal as possible, *chih* being rendered in each case by 's in order to make its function clear.

罔知天之斷命
"not know Heaven's cutting short the Decree"[15].
若顛木之有䔄櫱
"like a fallen tree's having sprouting branches"[16].
若火之燎于原
"like a fire's blazing in the plains"[17].
若射之有志
"like an archer's having a mark"[18].
聽予一人之作猷
"listen to me the One Man's making plans"[19].
我先神后之勞爾先
"my ancestral spirit sovereigns's toiling for your ancestors"[20].

Constructions of this type are quite foreign to genuine Western Chou prose, but are common in later periods.

Other discrepancies of style, and late phraseology, could be pointed out in the *Pan Kêng*, but this, with the anachronisms pointed out above, should suffice to show that it certainly does not date from Shang times. In my opinion it can not even be very early Chou. Professor Ku Chieh-kang now considers this book

15. *Shu* 223.
16. *Shu* 223. For this version of the text, cf. *Chin Wên Shu K'ao* 6.6a, and *Han Shih Ching Pei T'u* 11a.
17. *Shu* 229.
18. *Shu* 231.
19. *Shu* 231.
20. *Shu* 238. None of these literal translations would be fully satisfactory as a rendering of the sense of the passages, of course, but from the point of view of grammatical analysis they are fairly accurate.

possibly to have been written in the Western Chou period, but revised in Eastern Chou[21].

The *Pan Kêng* seemed suspicious to me long before any concrete reasons for the suspicion had made themselves known. The book is remarkably vague. The king argues endlessly for his project of moving the capital, but never once tells why he wishes it moved. Looking on the book as a forgery we can understand why this is. The man who wrote it probably did not know the reason for the move himself! If we ask why it was forged, it is more difficult to assign a reason for the writing of this book than for the *T'ang Shih*. But it is devoted, in large measure, to a defense of the royal authority as over against that of the nobles, and it may have been written by one of the supporters of the kings during the time when their power was gradually being usurped by the great feudatories.

Kao Tsung Yung Jih

The book called *Kao Tsung Yung Jih* is the briefest in the *chin wên* text of the *Shu Ching*, consisting of only some eighty characters[1]. It relates that "On the day of the supplementary sacrifice[2] of 高宗 Kao Tsung, there appeared a crowing pheasant. 祖己 Tsu Chi said, 'It is necessary first to correct the king, that this affair may be rectified'." Tsu Chi proceeds to deliver a brief sermon to the king[3].

It is necessary to ask who this Tsu Chi is. He must necessarily have lived after Kao Tsung, who is mentioned as being sacrificed to, but it is not easy to say who this Kao Tsung is[4]. Legge says of Tsu Chi, "Tsoo Ke was evidently a worthy minister

21. Verbal communication, October, 1933.
1. The number varies slightly in different texts.
2. The expression 肜曰 will be discussed later in connection with Shang religion.
3. *Shu* 264-6.
4. In so far as I am aware the term "Kao Tsung" has not turned up in the oracle inscriptions, though it is perfectly possible as a Shang title since we have a reference to 中宗祖乙 Chung Tsung Tsu I; cf. *Chien Shou T'ang So Ts'ang Yin Hsü Wên Tzǔ* (referred to hereafter as *Chien Yin Tzǔ*) 3.4. But even if we found it applied to a particular king we could not be sure that he was the only one to whom this title

of Woo-ting; but we know nothing more of him than is here related. I suppose 祖 to be the surname"⁽⁵⁾. Legge wrote long before the oracle bones were discovered, of course; such a supposition would be impossible in the light of our present knowledge. We know (as, indeed, the *Pai Hu T'ung* related in Han times)⁽⁶⁾ that the Shangs used the ten cyclical "stems", which were the names of the days of the ten-day Shang "week", as names for people. Whether they were named, as the *Pai Hu T'ung* says, after the day on which they were born, or after the day on which they died, or whether the day was chosen in some other fashion, we cannot tell. But that these names had definite connection with days we can prove, as will be shown when we come to speak of Shang sacrificial customs. It seems from the oracle inscriptions that these names were applied only to deceased persons, and were probably sacrificial names. The commonest method of designating a person sacrificed to in the oracle inscriptions is by the name of the relationship in which he stood to the person sacrificing—elder brother, father, mother, grandfather, or grandmother—and the name of a day of the ten-day cycle. The terms 祖 *tsu* "grandfather" and 妣 *pi* "grandmother"⁽⁷⁾ were not restricted to these degrees of relationship; any defunct ancestor prior to the father or mother might be so called.

Tsu Chi, then, is a very common sort of name on the oracle bones, and means "an ancestor of the degree of grandfather or more remote with whom is associated the day *chi*." Furthermore, this kind of name is restricted, on the oracle bones, in so far as I am aware, to members of the royal house, though not

---

was given, for the Shang people had the habit of bestowing the same title on more than one king or queen. For instance both T'ang and Wang Hai were called 高祖 Kao Tsu; cf. *Pu Tz'ŭ T'ung Tsuan* no. 248 and *Chien Yin Tzŭ* 1.4.

5. *Shu* 265, note.
6. See *Chin Wên Shu K'ao* 7.2a.
7. This term is now usually said to denote a deceased mother, based on the statement of the *Li Chi* which makes it equivalent to 母 *mu* (*SSC Li Chi* 5.22b), but we know definitely from the oracle bones that this was not the Shang usage. In Shang times *mu* meant the deceased mother, and *pi* the grandmother.

necessarily to those who have come to the throne. It is, then, essentially improbable that we would have a minister called by such a name.

Furthermore, we do find, on the oracle bones, mention of sacrifices made to ancestors called Tsu Chi. We can not be quite certain how many of these there are, but it appears that there are two and no more, for we know of only two male members of the Shang house who were known by the day *chi*. One is the king 雍己 Yung Chi who is traditionally held to have reigned 1649–1638 B.C.[8]. The other is the son, probably the eldest son, of king Wu Ting who traditionally reigned 1324–1264 B.C.[9]. This Chi apparently did not come to the throne, for he is not mentioned in the *Shih Chi* or in our other Shang genealogies, which in general show a surprising correspondence to the genealogy revealed to us by the oracle bones. That he is later called Tsu Chi does not show that he ruled, for ancestors who did not reign were sacrificed to just as those who did[10].

There was a persistent tradition, however, that Wu Ting had a son called 孝己 Hsiao Chi, and this is undoubtedly the same person[11]. That it is this and not the other Tsu Chi who is spoken of in the *Kao Tsung Yung Jih* is indicated by the fact that virtually all critics place the events of this book either, like the *Shih Chi*, the *Shang Shu Ta Chuan*, and the current Bamboo Books, in the time of Wu Ting[12], or, like Chin Jên-shan, in the reign of Tsu Kêng[13].

Therefore, since this is just the type of name which we find

8. Kuo Mo-jo identifies a number of inscriptions as referring to him; cf. *Pu Tz'ŭ T'ung Tsuan* nos. 206–10. But at least one of these is attributed by Tung Tso-pin to the later Chi; see *Ts'ai Anniv. Vol.* chart 3 opp. p. 344.
9. This Tsu Chi is the son of Wu Ting because we find, in the time of Tsu Chia, who was the son of Wu Ting, repeated divinations mentioning "elder brother Chi and elder brother Kêng". The latter is Tsu Kêng, who did come to the throne. Cf. *Yin Hou Pien* 1.19.14.
10. Cf. Wang, *I Shu*, I.1.5a.
11. Cf. loc. cit.; *Chu Shu* 6.2a.
12. *Shih Chi* 3.7b–8a; *Chin Wên Shu K'ao*, 7.1a; *Chu Shu* 6.2b.
13. Cf. *Chin Jên-shan Hsien Shêng Shang Shu Chu* (1879) 6.32a.

used for royal ancestors, and since there was a scion of the royal house known, subsequently, as Tsu Chi, who lived at just the time at which persistent tradition places this book, it is probable that this is the Tsu Chi mentioned in the *Kao Tsung Yung Jih*[14]. Yet if we understand the book so it is very strange indeed. For no matter who this Tsu Chi may be, if he was, as his name indicates, a royal scion, then the king to whom his preaching is addressed must have been either his father or his elder brother, since he himself was not yet king. But we can hardly suppose a son or a younger brother to have used such strongly didactic language as we find here—especially not in China, where the respect due to elders is so strongly emphasized[15]. And if we take him to be the son of Wu Ting, as he probably was, the difficulty is even greater. For in this case the king in question must be his father. For if the events be said to have taken place in the time of Tsu Kêng, then Tsu Chi was already dead[16]. Wang Kuo-wei quotes the *Ti Wang Shih Chi* and the *Chia Yü* which say that Hsiao Chi's mother died, and his father, Wu Ting, was influenced by a new wife to put him to death (according to the *Chia Yü*), or to banish him as a result of

14. That the *Shih Chi* and commentators call him a minister is sufficiently accounted for by the fact that such explanation is almost necessitated by the awkwardness of considering him a member of the royal house—if we regard the *Kao Tsung Yung Jih* as a genuine book, as the critics of Han times did. The same may be said for the *Ku Chin Jên Piao* of the *Han Shu*, which gives Tsu Chi and Hsiao Chi as two different men, apparently contemporary (cf. *Ch'ien Han Shu* 20.21a); the two names handed down in tradition, and the difficulty of reconciling the two, made this course almost inevitable.

15. That this emphasis went back to Shang times is indicated, if not proved, by the preëminent place of ancestor worship in Shang religion.

16. Since his younger brother had succeeded to the throne. That Tsu Chi or Hsiao Chi was older than Tsu Kêng is indicated by the *Ku Chin Jên Piao* of the *Han Shu* and by the various books quoted by Wang Kuo-wei (*I Shu*, I.1.5a) and is the general opinion of Chinese scholars specializing in this field; cf. *Ts'ai Anniv. Vol.* chart 3 opp. 344. The current Bamboo Books says that Hsiao Chi died in the twenty-fifth year of Wu Ting; *Chu Shu* 6.2a.

which he died (according to the *Ti Wang Shih Chi*)[17]. But according to this Tsu Chi could not have been alive in the time of king Tsu Kêng, when Wang thinks these events took place. Therefore, Wang says, perhaps these books are mistaken, and Tsu Chi was not put to death after all, but only banished. And when his younger brother Tsu Kêng came to the throne he, knowing his elder brother was innocent, recalled him to court although he did not give up his throne to him[18]. This theory of Wang's has no basis even in tradition, much less in history, and it can only be considered a rare and unaccountable excursion into fancy by one who was usually a very critical scholar.

Another difficulty with this book is the fact that Chi is called Tsu Chi in the relation of events occurring in his own lifetime. The term 祖 *tsu* in the bone inscriptions seems to be restricted entirely to the names of deceased ancestors, never used for living persons, just as its female counterpart, *pi*, is similarly restricted. Unlike the latter, *tsu* has come later to be used of the living as well as the dead grandfather, but that it specially denoted the deceased is indicated by the presence of the "spirit" determinative[19]. The origin of this character has been discussed at great length, without bringing us to any particular conclusions. Bernhard Karlgren has argued, without bringing any real proof, that its original form is designed to represent a phallus[20]. He gives a whole page of ancient forms of this and other characters; anyone who thinks that more than one or two of them have any real resemblance to the male organs of generation is a poor anatomist. The fact is that phallic worshippers are not generally afflicted with that false modesty and that desire to conceal the significance of their images which scholars often attribute to them. As a rule they are proud, not ashamed of their cult, and they make phalloi which need no esoteric eye to interpret them. But if we

17. Wang, *I Shu*, I.1.5a.
18. Loc. cit.
19. This is usually absent in the forms on the oracle bones, but does perhaps occur; cf. *T'ieh Yün Ts'ang Kuei* 48.4, where it is so interpreted by Sun (*Chia Pien* 1.5a), but seems dubious. Cf. also *Chin Pien* 1.3a.
20. *BMFEA*, 1930, 2.1–54.

are going to find phalloi everywhere, and on the slightest provocation, it happens that the world is so well furnished with long and pointed objects that we shall never be able to finish cataloguing them. Of course, we should be alert to appreciate any real evidence of such practices wherever they may occur, but we should also avoid the tendency to turn everything which may be forced or twisted into such evidence, as is done all too frequently. There is good reason to suppose that the ancient Chinese may well have had phallic practices. But my own research has not yielded one scrap of real evidence that they did.

Menzies considers the character *tsu* to have been a pictograph of the Chinese grave mound, bound around with wattles[21]. This is a possible interpretation of the form 且, found on the oracle bones[22], although we do not know how old the use of such grave mounds is. Karlgren[23], myself, and others have supposed this to be the ancestral tablet. Some evidence for this is furnished by the form 且[24], occurring in a middle Chou bronze inscription, which shows it standing upon a table.

The one conclusion toward which all of these theories and this evidence point is that *tsu* was a term used to denote a dead ancestor. Yet we find it here used to introduce direct quotation of the words of a living man. Wang Kuo-wei thinks that this merely proves that it was written much later than the events, but even so this is very strange.

We have seen that there are many difficulties which stand in the way of interpreting the *Kao Tsung Yung Jih* as a genuine product of Shang times. Must we do so? By no means. For this book too, though supposed to date from the middle of the Shang period, is saturated with the religion of *T'ien*, who was unknown to the Shang cult, while it does not even mention the genuinely Shang god, *Ti*[25]. Its style is in general that of the Western Chou period.

21. Verbal communication.
22. *Yi Ch'ien Pien* 1.11.5.
23. Op. cit. 19. He considers it the tablet and a phallic symbol.
24. *Li Tai T'ieh* 75a, 78a.
25. Menzies believes that this text originally had *Ti* in the places where *T'ien* now occurs, and that *T'ien* was substituted in early Chou

If we understand the *Kao Tsung Yung Jih* as a forgery of Chou times it is easy to explain its difficulties. What apparently happened is that the name of Tsu Chi, handed down in Shang genealogies as that of an ancestor, was not understood by the men of Chou times because they knew that there had been no Shang king of that name. The scribe who wrote this document wished to put his moralizings into the mouth of some one whose fame would carry authority and therefore ascribed them to Tsu Chi, supposing that he was a famous minister of the Shang kings. The last words of this brief document are: "... follow the regular procedure in sacrifices, and do not be excessive in those made to your father *alone*"⁽²⁶⁾. It may be, therefore, that this book was written, in Chou times, by some scribe who wished to correct his ruler's irregularities in sacrificial procedure. We know that Duke Wên of Lu moved the tablet of his father, Duke Hsi, out of its proper order so as to come before that of Duke Min, the elder brother and predecessor of his father. And the *Tso Chuan* devotes a passage which is nearly twice as long

---

times (personal letter of Feb. 11, 1935. Cf. *Shang Tai Wên Hua*, in *Ch'i Ta Chi K'an*, 1932, No. 1, pp. 5–6). But I know of no textual basis for such an interpretation of the facts. And since the Chou people themselves called this deity *Ti* as well as *T'ien* from the very beginning of the Chou period (see *Shu* 385, 425, 428, 454, 455, 456, 457, 458, 475, 478, 480, 482, 495, 496; *Shih* 427, 433, 436; *K'ê Lu* 2.17b; *Li Tai T'ieh* 153a), there is no reason why they should have made such a substitution.

26. The last clause is given, not as in the usual text, but as 毋禮於棄道 by Ch'ên Ch'iao-ts'ung in the *Chin Wên Shang Shu Ching Shuo K'ao*, 7.5b, and also in the *Han Shih Ching Pei T'u* 11a. But both of the readings are based on the *Yin Pên Chi* of the *Shih Chi*.

It is a great weakness of the reconstructions of the text of the *Shu* by Chinese scholars that they have too much tendency to quote the *Shih Chi* as the original text. This especially mars the otherwise very valuable *Chin Wên Shang Shu Ching Shuo K'ao*. We know very well that Ssŭ-Ma Ch'ien made frequent, deliberate alterations in the texts which he used, to make them more clear for his readers. It is quite impossible, then, to take the *Shih Chi* as the standard for the *Chin Wên Shang Shu*.

In the particular passage in question, this reading which they take to be original is almost certainly a late alteration. For the style of the

as the whole *Kao Tsung Yung Jih* to condemning this act[27]. It is possible that this book was written on a similar occasion. At all events it is not a Shang document.

Hsi Po K'an Li

There remain two books of the *Chin Wên Shu,* attributed to Shang times, to be considered, namely the *Hsi Po K'an Li*[1] and *Wei Tzŭ.* These pose a problem for criticism different from that of the foregoing books, because both are supposed to have been written at the very end of the Shang period, while the Chou conquest was in progress. There is no anachronism, then, in the fact that their style is like that of Chou prose, the less so since the Chous appear to have learned writing from the Shang people. Our criticism must be based, therefore, solely on matters of content and on historical criteria, rather than on style as such.

There is one matter of vocabulary which must be taken up at this point. In the *Hsi Po K'an Li* we encounter, for the last time in the *Shu Ching,* the character 台 *t'ai.* The *Êr Ya* defines it as 我 *wo*[2], and it seems to function in the *Shu* as a first personal pronoun, sometimes possessive. It occurs only eleven times in the whole of the *Shu Ching* as we have it today, including *ku wên* as well as *chin wên* text. This character does not occur in any book attributed to Chou date, and with the exception of one occurrence in the *Yü Kung*[3] is found only in books ascribed to the Shang period. From this we ought to

---

Kao Tsung Yung Jih is, in general, that of early Chou prose, while the character *tao* was not used in the sense in which we find it employed in this substituted passage until about the time of Confucius.

27. *Tso Chuan* 232.

1. Since nearly every critic has his own version of the last two characters it does not seem worth while to do anything but follow the common reading; for others cf. *Chin Wên Shu K'ao* 8.1–2 and *Han Shih Ching Pei T'u* 12a.

2. SSC *Êr Ya* 2.1a. This does not agree with the definition of the *Shuo Wên.*

3. *Shu* 142.

suppose that this was a genuine property of Shang prose, and a mark of authenticity in these documents, except for the fact that completely overwhelming evidence of other sorts proving that they are not authentic rules out this possibility. In the *chin wên* text of the *Shu* we find this character only in the *Yü Kung* which is traditionally held to be pre-Shang, and in four supposedly Shang books, i.e. the *T'ang Shih* (twice), *Pan Kêng, Kao Tsung Yung Jih*, and *Hsi Po K'an Li*[4]. Even more remarkable, four of these five occurrences are in the phrase 其如台, which occurs once in each of these books. This construction, of a type which seems essentially late in origin, is found in the *T'ang Shih*, supposed to date from the very beginning of Shang times, appears in two books attributed to the middle of the Shang period, and is still present in the same identical form in the *Hsi Po K'an Li* which relates events of the Chou conquest.

It may be that the character *t'ai* was an actual property of Shang prose, which was copied by those who forged these books in the Chou period. Or it may be that it was used in the first of them to be perpetrated and thereafter was copied in making the others. However that may be, it is interesting to note that the person or persons who forged the *ku wên* text of the *Shu Ching*, probably after the beginning of the Christian era, were clever enough to use this character only in books which they ascribed to Shang date[5].

In the *Hsi Po K'an Li* the *T'ien* cult occupies the center of the stage, while *Ti* is not mentioned. The character *T'ien* occurs seven times, the philosophy of the Decree of Heaven is present in its completeness, the Shang king is called the Son of Heaven, and the Shang state is referred to as Yin. All of these things are contrary to what we should expect in Shang literature from our

4. *Shu* 173, 175, 222, 266, 271.
5. Cf. *Shu* 177, 187, 250, 252, 259.
The perpetrators of the *ku wên* text used twice the phrase 台小子, which they probably copied from the *T'ang Shih* of the *chin wên* text; cf. *Shu* 187 and 259 with *Shu* 173. The phrase 台德 may have been lifted from the *chin wên Yü Kung* cf. *Shu* 252 with *Shu* 142.

knowledge of the bone inscriptions, but yet they can not be considered quite conclusive evidence against its authenticity. For this book is supposed to be from the very end of the Shang period, and it could therefore be argued that at that time the coalescence between Shang and Chou culture had already taken place, so that these ideas and this phraseology are not necessarily out of place. This seems improbable, however, because the Shangs were definitely a more cultured people than the Chous, and so considered by the latter. And while it is quite certain that the Chous took on Shang ideas and characteristics before the conquest, it is doubtful that the Shangs would have copied their more barbarous neighbors until defeat forced them to.

The weakest point in this book is its historical improbability. It purports to record a speech made to the last Shang king by one of his retainers, Tsu I[6]. The Chou leader, Wên Wang, had carried his conquests to a point dangerously near to the Shang capital, and the news of the fall of Li frightened Tsu I so that he went to the king to remonstrate with him on his course. We should expect, in such a case, that the retainer would plead with the king, saying that this calamity was due to the king's unwisdom or even perhaps his wickedness, and that *if he did not change his course* the end of the dynasty was certain. But Tsu I does not speak so. He leaves no loophole for amendment, or for averting the catastrophe. He says:

"Son of Heaven[7], T'ien has already brought to an end[8] the Decree of our Yin dynasty. The wisest of men and the

6. General opinion of commentators makes this Tsu I a minister. Wang Kuo-wei, from the parallelism of the name to what we find on the oracle bones, supposes him to be a member of the royal family; see *I Shu*, I.1.5b.

7. The characters 天子 *T'ien tzŭ* are commonly omitted from this book by those who undertake to reconstruct the *chin wên* text; cf. *Chin Wên Shu K'ao* 8.1, *Han Shih Ching Pei T'u* 12a, and Wang Hsien-ch'ien, *Shang Shu K'ung Chuan Ts'an Chêng* 13.2b. But all base this solely on the fact that these characters are not quoted in the *Yin Pên Chi* (cf. *Shih Chi* 3.10a); neither the *Chou Pên Chi* nor the *Sung Shih Chia*, to which Wang Hsien-ch'ien refers, make a direct quotation at this point (cf. *Shih Chi* 4.5a and 38.1a).

But it is quite unwarrantable, as has been pointed out before, to

great tortoise alike do not venture to know anything fortunate for it. It is not that the former kings do not aid us, *their* descendants, but by your excesses and cruelty[9], O king, you are cutting off yourself. Therefore Heaven has rejected us.... Now among our people there is none who does not wish *the dynasty* to perish, saying, 'Why does not Heaven send down its terrors? Why does not *some one with* its great Decree make *his* appearance? What has the present king to do with us?'

"The King said, 'Oh! Is not my life secured by the Decree in Heaven?'

"Tsu I replied, saying, 'Oh! Your many crimes are heaped up above—can you charge your fate to a Decree from Heaven? Yin is going to destruction, and as for your deeds, they will certainly bring ruin to your state'[10]"

As a bona fide speech by a Shang minister or a member of the royal house to the Shang king, this is nonsense. It does not in any way attempt to change the course of events. It is simply and solely a torrent of abuse for the sake of abuse, with its only probable result the putting to death of Tsu I. And how, we

---

take the quotations of the *Shih Chi* as being ipso facto the original text of the *Shang Shu*. At least, if they are going to do so, these scholars should be consistent and render the whole passage as it appears in the *Shih Chi*, writing 告紂 instead of 告于王—which none of them does. Since the whole T'ien philosophy is present in this book anyway, there is no reason why 天子 should not occur.

8. Legge says, "is bringing to an end" (*Shu* 268). But the text makes the above reading imperative.

9. 虐 *nüeh*, instead of the 戲 *hsi* of the *ku wên* text, which Legge translates "sport" (*Shu* 271). This has not only the authority of the *Yin Pên Chi* (*Shih Chi* 3.10b) but also that of Chêng Hsüan (loc. cit., commentary) behind it. Moreover and more important, it is more fitting in the context and more in conformity with what we should expect from Chou prose and bronze inscriptions generally (cf. *Chün Ku Lu Chin Wên*, 1895, referred to hereafter as *Chün Chin Wên*, 3(2).56b, etc.). The latter character is a very easy textual corruption because of the complex form and lack of standardization in characters including *hu* (cf. *Chin Pien* 5.7–8).

10. *Shu* 268–72.

may ask, did such a book happen to come down to us? Apparently these admonitions were not in writing, but in speech. Who wrote them down, and why? It is hard to conceive.

This book takes for granted the certain success of the Chou conquest with an assurance which the Chous themselves were far from feeling, even years after they had nominally succeeded[11]. This complete certainty of the success of the Chou expedition is in itself enough to cause us to suspect that this book was written after that success had been consummated.

With the 祖伊 Tsu I of this book there is the same difficulty as with the Tsu Chi of the *Kao Tsung Yung Jih*; a living man is called by a name which we should expect, from the oracle bones, to be applied only to an ancestral spirit. The author of the *K'ung Chuan* links these two together as ancestor and descendant, supposing Tsu to be a surname[12], but we know from the bone inscriptions that it must mean "ancestor". Wang Kuo-wei, recognizing this, seeks to save the credit of the book by attributing its writing to an author who lived after the events in the State of Sung[13]. But why should a man of Sung have desired thus to calumniate his ancestors or their king?

There are, as we have seen, numerous discrepancies in the *Hsi Po K'an Li* if we regard it as a genuine production of the Shang state at the end of the Shang period. And as such it lacks motivation. But this is by no means the case if we consider it to be a fabrication of the Chou period for use as propaganda to consolidate the Chou position. The unmitigated condemnation of the Shang sovereign and the prophecy of the certain fall of the Shang state are just what would be most useful in this connection. And who but a Chou adherent could have written:

"Now among our people there is none who does not wish *the dynasty* to perish, saying, 'Why does not Heaven send

---

11. Cf. for instance the *Ta Kao, Shu* 362ff., and the *Chün Shih, Shu* 474ff.
12. *SSC Shang Shu*, 10.11b.
13. Cf. *I Shu*, I.1.5b.

down its terrors? Why does not *some one with* its great Decree make *his* appearance?'"(14)

There is no mystery about the identity of the "*some one with its great Decree*" intended here—it was obviously the Chou king, and no one else. The accusations made here against the last Shang king, supposedly by one of his own retainers, are word for word the same accusations which were made against him and the last Hsia ruler by Chou spokesmen, not once but repeatedly, in pronouncements of which some were undisguised efforts to persuade the Shang people to accept the Chou rule(15).

It is no accident that there are so many discrepancies in this book when we view it as a Shang production, and so many correspondences when we consider it to be a Chou forgery. There is, in my opinion, no doubt that it was written by a Chou adherent as a piece of political propaganda.

Wei Tzŭ

The *Wei Tzŭ* is a companion document to the last. Like it, it is supposed to date from the very days when the Chou conquest was in progress. Its style is that of Western Chou prose, showing great similarity to that of early Chou bronze inscriptions. In it the Shang state is called Yin, and the deity *T'ien* is fully established.

This book is supposed to be a colloquy between three high officials of the Shang government, *Wei Tzŭ* (supposed to be the

14. *Shu* 271.
15. There are only three definite charges made against King Chou in the *Hsi Po K'an Li*, namely that he is 淫 *yin*, that he is 虐 *nüeh* (according to the amended text), and that he refuses to correct his conduct depending instead on the Decree of Heaven. In Chou books, the first of these charges will be found in the *Chiu Kao*, the *To Shih* (twice), and the *To Fang* (*Shu* 408, 456, 457, 499). The second is made, against the last Hsia king, in the *To Fang* (*Shu* 498). The last occurs twice in the *To Fang* (*Shu* 496, 499).

elder brother of King Chou)[1], the Grand Tutor[2], and the Junior Tutor. It differs from the preceding book in one important respect. In the *Hsi Po K'an Li* the Shang king is damned in general and in particular, but the rest of the Shang people are left unsmirched. In the *Wei Tzŭ*, however, nobody in the Shang state, from the king down to the veriest commoner, is left with a shred of virtue. It says:

> "Wei Tzŭ spoke to the following effect[3]: 'Grand Tutor and Junior Tutor, *the House of* Yin can no longer govern the four quarters. Although there is the great array of our ancestors above, we, through being sunk in and maddened with liquor[4], have disordered and destroyed the effects of their virtue here below[5]. Among the Yin people there

1. According to the *Shih Chi*, 38.1a. It is a little difficult to reconcile this with his brother's having come to the throne while he was still alive. The *Lü Shih Ch'un Ch'iu* explains it by saying that when Wei Tzŭ was born his mother was still a concubine, so that his less noble birth kept him from succeeding (loc. cit., commentary). We do not yet know enough of the Shang rules of succession to say whether this explanation can stand or not; further study of the oracle inscriptions may clear up this point.
2. The *chin wên* text is given as Ta Shih instead of the usual Fu Shih. Although this is only on the authority of the *Yin Pên Chi* (*Shih Chi* 3.11a), it seems more reasonable, especially as set against Shao Shih.
3. This is Legge's translation of *jo yüeh*, which is reproduced here without comment. It will be discussed later.
4. There is some difference of opinion about the characters here (cf. *Shih Chi* 38.1a, *Chin Wên Shu K'ao*, 9.2a) but it does not seem to make much difference since their exact meaning is uncertain anyway.
    Merely because the *Sung Shih Chia* has them, those who reconstruct the *chin wên* text add 婦人是 at this point (*Chin Wên Shu K'ao* 9.2a and *Han Shih Ching Pei T'u* 12a). But this is not sufficient warrant, and gives us an essentially senseless passage. This may have been picked up from the similar passage in the *Mu Shih* (*Shu* 303); at any rate it seems out of place here, and is omitted.
5. This translation, as regards the interpretation of the terms *shang* and *hsia*, "above" and "below", is my own, for which I can quote no authority. Legge's interpretation which takes them as chronological is not only orthodox, but also apparently the way in which they were understood by the author of the *Shih Chi* (38.1). But in the light of Chou religious ideas and literary usage I believe that it is clearly mistaken.

are none, small or great, who are not given to highway robberies, villainies, and treachery. The nobles and officers imitate one another in violating the laws; all are guilty, and there is no certainty that offenders will be apprehended. The lesser people rise up and treat one another as enemies. Yin is now sinking[6] in ruin....'

"The Grand Tutor spoke to the following effect:... 'Now the people of Yin will even steal away the pure and perfect victims devoted to the spirits of heaven and earth[7], and their conduct is connived at, so that though they proceed to eat *the victims* they suffer no punishment. When I look down and survey the people of Yin, the methods of government to them are hateful exactions, which call forth enmity and hatred without ceasing. The guilt is shared by all[8]. Multitudes are starving with none to whom they may appeal. Now is the time of Shang's calamity....' "[9]

This compares favorably with the wildest of the propaganda levelled against each other by the belligerents in the World War[10]. It has an astonishing similarity to the stories which the Chous circulated about the Shang people and their last king

6. Legge's argument against reading *tien* here, as we find it in the *Shih Chi* (38.1b; cf. *Chin Wên Shu K'ao* 9.3a) is very apt; see *Shu* 275 footnote.

7. This rendering of *shên ch'i* is in accord with tradition, but the tradition has little basis that we can ascertain today. The commentators may have had some real information, now lost to us, as to the meaning of *ch'i*, or they may have done what they did so often—guessed.

8. Legge's addition of *in authority* here has no warrant from the text, and is in direct contradiction to the *K'ung Chuan*. More important, the reading I have given is directly warranted by the text itself, cf. *Shu* 273-5.

9. *Shu* 273-7.

10. To be sure, this does not include the fellow of the story of cutting off the hands of little children, but such stories were circulated about King Chou in later times. For instance cf. *Shu* 285, "He has ripped up pregnant women", and Legge's historical note (*Shu* 269-70) detailing the pastimes of this fiend in human form as described by the conscientious Chou historians.

in the early days after the completion of the conquest. It may be said that this is because it is true, but at least it is interesting to note the similarities. In the inscription on the bronze vessel known as the *Ta Yü Ting*, probably cast within the first seventy-five years of the Chou dynasty[11], we find the statement that Yin lost the Decree and went to ruin because its vassals and officials were addicted to liquor[12]. In the *Ta Ya*, one of the older sections of the *Shih Ching*, in a poem which is definitely Chou in origin, we read, "King Wên said, 'Alas! Alas! you *sovereign of* Yin Shang, It is not Heaven that flushes your face with spirits'"[13]. The following three passages are from the *Wei Tzŭ*, the *Chiu Kao* of the *Shu*, and the poem just quoted. All are describing the last Shang king or the Shang people:

沈湎於酒 [14]

湎于酒 [15]

湎爾以酒 [16]

It is interesting to see that an utterance credited to a high Shang official is couched in terms so very similar[17] to those used by Chou writers, avowed enemies of the Shangs, in denouncing them. And this similarity, among other things, justifies us in

11. This inscription ends with the date "In the twenty-third year of the king" (see *K'ê Lu* 4.13b). Wu Ch'i-ch'ang, in his *Chin Wên I Nien Piao* (1933; reprinted from *National Library of Peiping Kuan K'an*, vol. 6, nos. 5–6; referred to hereafter as *Chin Nien Piao*) no. 23, places it in the reign of Ch'êng Wang. Kuo Mo-jo (*Liang Chou Hsi* 33) attributes it to that of K'ang Wang. According to the traditional chronology this would place it, then, in 1093 or 1056 B.C.

12. *K'ê Lu* 4.12ab.

13. *Shih* 508.

14. This phrase occurs twice in the *Wei Tzŭ*, *Shu* 273 and 276, but is considered to appear only once in the *chin wên*. Instead of the second character the current, *ku wên* text has 酗 *hsü*. The present reading is based on the *Shih Chi* and the *Han Shu* (cf. *Chin Wên Shu K'ao*).

15. *Shu* 412.

16. *Shih* 508.

17. It is to be remembered that we can not be sure of complete identity here, because of the difference in *ku wên* and *chin wên* versions of the text noted above.

suspecting that this may have been a catch-phrase in a campaign of propaganda designed to break down the Shang prestige after the Chou conquest, like the catch-phrases used by the various countries in propaganda during the World War, and in economic propaganda at the present time.

With this book as with the *Hsi Po K'an Li* there is the problem of motivation. If such conversations had taken place, why would anybody have taken the trouble to write them down and preserve them? If it be held that they were letters exchanged between the three men, the content is rather strange for letters. This was highly treasonable material, and according to tradition King Chou did not hesitate to punish most cruelly those who offended him, even though they were his relatives[18]. All three of the men mentioned in the *Wei Tzŭ* are said to have had to flee for their lives[19]. We should expect, then, that if they were so indiscreet as to have written down such damning matter, they would have kept it strictly private. Furthermore, when a man writes a statement like that of the Grand Tutor at the end of this book, announcing his resolution to "present himself to the former kings"[20] and perish with the dynasty, one might suppose that he would have enough personal interest in the matter to write it himself. Yet the language of this book is such that, if it is genuine, Wei Tzŭ and the Grand Tutor merely gave their secretaries an outline of what they wished to say and left it to them to draw up the documents!

This book consists of only two speeches, although three men are mentioned. These speeches begin with the words 微子若曰 *Wei Tzŭ jo yüeh* and 大師若曰 *Ta Shih jo yüeh*[21]. Legge says of the *jo yüeh* construction that it "intimates that what follows is not all in the exact words of [in the case of which he is speaking] the king, but the substance of what he said"[22]. But this does

18. Cf. *Shih Chi* 3.10b-11a and 38.2b.
19. Cf. loc. cit. That at least Wei Tzŭ is to flee is suggested in the book itself, *Shu* 278.
20. *Shu* 278. What he says here is 自獻 *tzŭ hsien*, "sacrifice oneself". As will be shown later, *hsien* was a term used for human sacrifice.
21. *Shu* 273 and 276.
22. *Shu*, p. 225, footnote on par. 6.

not completely explain it. The *To Fang* begins:[23] 周公曰 王若曰[24], and the *Chiu Kao* (which is plausibly ascribed to the Duke of Chou) begins 成王若曰[25]. The Duke of Chou, who speaks in the king's name here, was the king's uncle, who acted as Regent during the youth of King Ch'êng. It is probably to his policies and ability, more than to any other single factor, that the firm establishment of the Chou dynasty was due. We can not suppose that the Duke was merely reporting the gist of what the king had told him in advance to say, acting as the mere mouthpiece of his young nephew. Rather, the Duke, as Regent or as one of the principal advisers of the king, was stating his own ideas in the king's name, with the consent or at least the acquiescence of the king himself. In such a case, then, we should not translate 王若曰 *wang jo yüeh* as "The king speaks to this effect:—"[26], but rather as "The king agrees in saying:" or even "It is as if the king said:" (i.e., "It is said in the name of the king"). This construction is frequent in the text of the *Shu Ching*[27]. It is also a prevalent feature of long bronze inscriptions, which give us further insight into the meaning which this phrase

23. I.e., after the date and place, which seem regularly to have been prefixed to documents entered in the archives, just as they were to documents embodied in bronze inscriptions.

24. *Shu* 492.

25. The current text, as found for instance in Legge (*Shu* 399) lacks the name of the king. But Lu Tê-ming, in the *Shang Shu Shih Wên*, states explicitly that the character *Ch'êng* was cut out of the text because it was considered to be the king's posthumous name which was wrongly added to the text by "vulgar scholars" (*SSC Shang Shu* 14.14b.). But the error here was made by him who "corrected" the text. For apparently all of the old texts, *ku wên* and *chin wên* alike, had this character. And we know now, on the basis of very recent research, that the use of posthumous names was by no means uniform if indeed it had arisen at all in this period; more will be said of this in a later paper.

26. This is Legge's translation, *Shu* 399.

27. In the *chin wên* text it occurs in the *Wei Tzŭ, Ta Kao, K'ang Kao, Chiu Kao, Lo Kao, To Shih, Chün Shih, To Fang, Li Chêng, Ku Ming*, and *Wên Hou Chih Ming*. Not all of these books are genuine.

sometimes had[28]. We read, for instance, as on the *Shih Hu Tun*[29], that on a certain day, after everyone was assembled and in his proper place in the court, "the King ordered the Nei Shih[30] Wu, saying, 'Command Hu with the document!'[31]" Immediately after the name Hu there ensue the characters *wang jo yüeh*[32], which introduce a long statement making known the royal commands. We can easily see what happened. When the king wished to confer a fief, bestow an office, order a military expedition, or grant rewards for services, the thing was done by means of a court ceremony. The terms of the command, reward, enfeoffment, etc., were drawn up beforehand, and merely read out in the formal ceremony by a secretary. Ordinarily the king himself did not even bother to dictate the exact words of the document used; he had officials to write them for him, just as modern rulers do. But unlike the modern custom it was not pretended that these were the ruler's words, but only his will, so that documents commonly began "The king agrees in saying", or "It is as if the king said".

28. Cf. *K'ê Lu* 4.2a, 4.12a, 4.17b, 5.3a, 5.10a, 9.15a, 9.18a (the inscription in the cover of this vessel, otherwise similar, lacks the character *jo*; cf. 9.17b), 11.2a, 11.7a, 11.16b, 11.22b; *Li Tai T'ieh* 14.148b, 14.153a, 14.155b.

29. The matter of the names of Chinese bronze vessels is a most vexing and chaotic one. There is sometimes disagreement among authorities even as to the type of a given vessel, and the proper names of types; as regards the names of the individual vessels there is little agreement. It would seem better to agree upon some conventional names, even though they might be unscientific, than to continue the present confusion which artificially multiplies the difficulties, intrinsically great enough, of the student of these materials. Conditions being as they are, all I am able to do is to use the name by which the particular vessel is known in the work to which I am referring.

30. 內史. This title, which appears frequently in bronze inscriptions, should perhaps be translated as something like "Interior Recorder". Those who held it seem to have been royal secretaries.

31. 册命虎 *t'sê ming Hu*. This is an awkward translation, but it seems the only feasible one. *T'sê* is the common word for a book or document on the bronzes as well as on the oracle bones, and *t'sê ming*, meaning "command by reading a document containing orders" is frequent.

32. For this whole inscription see *K'ê Lu* 11.7a.

Since so many of the documents produced in the early Chou period came into being under these circumstances, not only in the royal court but also in the courts of lesser rulers, this doubtless came in time to be thought of as a regular opening for documents. But when we find such highly important, dangerous, treasonable matter as that contained in the *Wei Tzŭ*, affecting the very lives of the authors of the statements, introduced by "Wei Tzŭ *jo yüeh*" and "Ta Shih *jo yüeh*," implying that these documents were drawn up by secretaries on the basis of outlines furnished by the principals, we are justified in suspecting that this is nothing more nor less than a slip on the part of the Chou scribe who forged the document.

It was not his only slip. He made the condemnation of the Shang people too complete and too wholesale to be convincing. It might be said that Wei Tzŭ could have produced such a document because he did, after all, desert the Shangs and become, a few years after the conquest, a Chou vassal, ruling the Shang people in the State of Sung[33]. But according to this same account he was almost uninterruptedly in authority of one sort or another over a part of the Shang people, as well as being a member of their own royal family, and we can hardly conceive him saying that "Among the Yin people there are none, small or great, who are not given to highway robberies, villainies, and treachery"[34]. The author of the *Wei Tzŭ* is even less plausible when he tells us that "Now the people of Yin will even steal away the pure and perfect victims devoted to the spirits ... [35]" It is impossible to believe that this occurred during what was, as the book itself tells us, a time of general calamity. The Shang oracle inscriptions make it abundantly evident that the Shangs were, if anything, even more profoundly religious, more completely assured of their dependence on the gods, than the Chous. And even in the sophisticated days of the present people who are normally indifferent frequently turn to religion in time of trouble.

33. Cf. *Shih Chi* 38.2b, 38.7b.
34. *Shu* 273–5.
35. *Shu* 277.

It is completely out of line with everything we know of early China to suppose that the Shangs would have tempted fate by insulting the gods when they were already in difficulties. On the other hand this is exactly the sort of story which their enemies would circulate about them.

Final evidence of the spuriousness of *Hsi Po K'an Li* and the *Wei Tzŭ* is found in the lack of any reference to the books or even to the events of which they treat in the *To Shih* and *To Fang* sections of the *Shu Ching*[36]. In these books, as has been said, the Duke of Chou is alternately pleading and threatening to persuade the conquered Shang people to cease all thought of resistance to the Chou rule and to acquiesce in their subject condition. He tells them repeatedly that the Chous were forced to dethrone the last Shang king because of his wickedness. But he states that wickedness only in the most vague and general terms[37]. One would think that a clever man like the Duke of Chou could not possibly have failed to see the value of, and to use, the argument that the king's guilt was proved beyond all doubt by the fact that his high officials and even his own brother turned against him, as is detailed in the *Wei Tzŭ*[38]. Yet he says not a word of these things. Nor does he, eager though he is for evidence, quote or even refer to the existence of such documents as the *Hsi Po K'an Li* or the *Wei Tzŭ*.

The evidence against the *Wei Tzŭ* is overwhelming. It must, like the four other books we have examined, be a fabrication of Chou date.

This brings us to a rather remarkable conclusion, namely, that in the whole of the transmitted Chinese literature there is not a single document which was produced in the Shang state. Not only this—there is not a single document earlier than the

36. *Shu* 453-63, 492-507.
37. See *Shu* 456, 499, 500-501.
38. It is impossible to argue that the Duke may not have known of these events, if one accepts the traditions. For the *Shih Chi* tells us that Wei Tzŭ went out and submitted, in the most public and spectacular manner, to the Chou king (*Shih Chi* 38.2b-3a).

beginning of the Chou dynasty, unless perhaps a part of the *I Ching* which was apparently a Chou book[39]. Chinese literature, as it has been preserved to us, takes its rise, therefore, with the Chou dynasty. And it takes it with a flourish. From the opening years of the Chous we have, as has been shown, eight documents in the *Shu*, beside the original portions of the *I Ching* and parts of the *Shih*. All these have been transmitted to the present; from an earlier time, nothing. Yet the Chous were, beyond question, a comparatively parvenu, unliterate people. These facts seem incompatible; they make us wonder if some of the supposedly early books may be early after all. But they are not; they simply will not do for the periods to which they are assigned. What is the answer?

I do not know, but I have one hypothesis to put forward. In connection with it it is interesting to compare an episode in the history of the Ch'ing dynasty. In a recent work, *The Literary Inquisition of Ch'ien-lung*[40], L. C. Goodrich has pointed out that that monarch carried on a highly successful campaign of suppression directed against books hostile or distasteful to the Manchu conquerors of China. Not only were "anti-dynastic or rebellious"[41] works, and those which gave "a biased, or, in Manchu eyes, unfavorable account of any incident or series of events in the Chinese-Manchu period of conflict of the seventeenth century"[42], consigned to the flames. The ban was also pronounced against books written as early as Sung or Yüan times which were considered to "insult previous dynasties which were, in a sense, ancestral to the Ch'ing ... Any unflattering reference to the Liao, Kin, and Yüan houses or to the Mongol and Ju-chen people" was considered cause for partial or total suppression of the work in which it appeared[43].

39. That the sections of the *Shu* which are supposed to date from pre-Shang times are actually no earlier than the Chou period will be shown at the beginning of the following paper.
40. Baltimore, 1935.
41. *The Literary Inquisition of Ch'ien-lung* 44.
42. Ibid. 51.
43. Ibid. 45–46.

The position of the Manchus, as a conquering dynasty, had some features in common with that of the Chous. Both were peoples whom the conquered undoubtedly considered "barbarian"[44], and both assimilated themselves to Chinese culture very rapidly. There is a curious likeness in the fact that in Chinese literature we find comparatively little abuse levelled against these two peoples, quite in contrast to what is the case with some of the other "barbarian" invaders. In fact, I know of only one protest against the Chou domination in all of the early Chou literature. In the *Shih* we read:

"In the States of the east, large and small,
  The looms are empty . . .
Slight and elegant gentlemen
Walk along that road to Chou.
Their going and coming
Makes my heart ache . . .
Alas for us the toiled people!
Would that we could have rest!
The sons of the east
Are only summoned [to service], without encouragement;
While the sons of the west
Shine in splendid dresses.
The sons of boatmen
Have furs of the bear and the great bear.
The sons of the poorest families
Form the officers in public employment.
If we present them with spirits,
They do not look upon them as liquor.
If we give them long girdle-pendants with their stones,
They do not think them long enough . . . [45]"

This poem probably dates from a late period, when the power of the Chous was already on the wane, and suppression of such

---

44. But it is doubtful that there was as much racial diversity between the Chous and the Shang people as between the Manchus and the Chinese; we have no accurate data on this point as yet, however.
45. *Shih* 353–355.

protests was no longer easy[46]. It is extremely significant that we have virtually no echoes of discontent from the time when the lands of the east were being parcelled out, as fiefs, among the leaders of the conquering hordes from the west, and the more cultured people of the east were having to learn to bear the unaccustomed yoke. That the Shang people did grumble we know, from the speeches of the Duke of Chou who threatens to transport them further or annihilate them if they do not stop it[47]. If we had not these we might suppose, from the transmitted literature, that the conquered people spent their spare time in singing paeans in praise of their conquerors, as rescuers from oppression.

Ch'ien-lung carried on his literary inquisition at a time when, it has been estimated, as many books had been published in Chinese as in all other languages combined[48]. Printing had been in use for many centuries, and books were widely diffused. Yet in these difficult circumstances he is estimated to have *completely wiped out* from 1500 to 2000 or more works[49].

If the Chous had chosen to undertake the suppression of literature which they considered to obstruct their program of consolidation, their task would have been far easier, for books were much rarer in their day. We know that they had a well developed system of propaganda, backed by a philosophy of history which must have been contradicted by many of the earlier records. We know that they were aware of the educational value of history[50], and that they were intelligent, bold, and when necessary ruthless.

Ch'ien-lung did his work so well that within less than two centuries it was all but forgotten that there had been a campaign of suppression, or that there had been such works as those suppressed[51]. If the Chous had prosecuted a similar campaign,

46. Cf. *SSC Mao Shih* 13(1).6; Legge's note, *Shih* 353.
47. *Shu* 460–463, 504, 507.
48. Cf. *Bulletin* No. 10, American Council of Learned Societies (Washington, 1929) 3.
49. *The Literary Inquisition of Ch'ien-lung* 61.
50. See pages 32–33 above.
51. *The Literary Inquisition of Ch'ien-lung* 6–9.

surely there would be nothing remarkable in the fact that we find no positive record of it after three thousand years.

I am very far from asserting that the Chous did systematically wipe out books from a period earlier than their own. We have no objective proof of it, and in the nature of the case probably never will have. But the hypothesis that they did fits the situation as we know it very well indeed, and is one of the most plausible of the explanations which can be advanced to account for the very mysterious disappearance of earlier records.

Summary

The materials available for the study of the history and the culture of the Shang period may be divided into two sorts, contemporary and non-contemporary. Non-contemporary materials are those traditions concerning and traces of the Shang period which we find in later documents. Contemporary materials include all objects, documents, and data of any sort which come to us directly from the Shang period.

Throughout these papers the principal emphasis will be placed upon contemporary evidence, for the reason that through accident or design, sometimes through mistakes of understanding and sometimes for purposes of deliberate political propaganda, a very large proportion of the facts concerning pre-Confucian China have been greatly distorted in traditional history—distorted so completely, in fact, that it is quite impossible for even the most gifted and inspired historian to discern the truth if he has access to nothing but the orthodox history.

For the Shang period the case was worse than for any ensuing time. Until the dawn of the present century we had virtually no contemporary materials whatever for Shang history. Even that which passed as contemporary material now shows itself, in the light of the new discoveries, to be of later origin. We are obliged, therefore, to start almost with tabula rasa and to attempt to reconstruct, as best we can, a picture of the history, the institutions, the culture of the Shang state, in so far as that picture can be pieced together, on the basis of a rigidly scientific examination of the contemporary materials now available to us. The first step in such an attempt must be a thorough examination of everything which has any serious ground for consideration, with the object of discriminating that which is from that which is not contemporary, and establishing a group of basic materials for research. This has been the purpose of the present paper.

Contemporary materials may be divided into objects, documents, and other data. The datable objects from the Shang period which are now in the possession of the National Research Institute and of Chinese and foreign museums and individuals run into the hundreds of thousands, though most of the things which make up this vast number are of minor interest and importance. The oracle bones must be mentioned first among objects as well as among documents. Next in interest come bronze vessels and objects of various sorts. Only a small proportion of the Shang bronzes known to us have been excavated under scientific conditions, but a very large number of those which have not, as well as other objects of various sorts, can be identified beyond question by comparison with objects which have been so excavated.

Among Shang documents the preëminent place is held by the oracle bone inscriptions. When it is considered that more than one and perhaps as many as two hundred thousand pieces of this inscribed bone are in the hands of collectors, and that these pieces contain an average of several characters each, it is plain that the sheer amount of written matter here is not small. On the other hand, the number of complete inscriptions is less than this, the inscriptions themselves are not often more than some twenty characters in length, and the range of their subject-matter is somewhat narrow. Yet exhaustive, painstaking study covering all of this material, using the method of legitimate controlled inference to derive from these inscriptions information concerning matters with which they do not directly deal, is capable of obtaining from them a picture, astonishingly adequate in some respects, of the life and times of the people who wrote them. Aside from the oracle inscriptions there is a small amount of other writing on bone, a single piece of inscribed jade, an inscription on a stone vessel, some characters scratched on pottery, and inscriptions on bronze. Shang bronze inscriptions consist for the most part of not more than three characters; the subject of longer bronze inscriptions in Shang times is fraught with problems which will probably be cleared up by future research.

While a section of the *Shih Ching* and five books of the *chin wên* text of the *Shu Ching* have been considered to be Shang productions, they are actually documents written in Chou times and wrongly attributed to the earlier date. Nevertheless, the *Shang Sung* of the *Shih* has a little more to recommend it as historical material than have the other documents. For it was written by the descendants of the Shang people at a time when they had not yet fully accepted the Chou version of history, and therefore retains something of the true Shang tradition. It is not contemporary material, but it does possess a certain validity.

Under the heading of other data which come to us directly from Shang times the chief and perhaps the only entries which can now be made are the various items of information resulting from the excavation of the Shang capital at Anyang by the National Research Institute.

This completes, for the present time, the list of the contemporary, and the only completely reliable materials, upon which the study of the history and culture of the Shang state may be based. It may be added that there are no contemporary materials, except the numerous objects and data found by excavators of a number of as yet undated sites of pre-Bronze Age men, upon which to base Chinese history for any period earlier than the Shang. In other words, at the present time we have no contemporary evidence whatsoever which has been proved to be related to any of the events or figures of Chinese history, orthodox or unorthodox, prior to about the fourteenth century B. C. Earlier records certainly existed, and they have as certainly disappeared. It is among the possibilities that they were deliberately obliterated at about the time of the Chou conquest, but this is a proposition which it is impossible to prove on the basis of our present data.

II. WAS THERE A HSIA DYNASTY?

1. TRADITIONS OF PRE-HSIA CHINA

The latter portion of the Shang period is the earliest time in China which we can call historical. For the Shang state previous to the time when the capital was moved to Anyang we do have, at least, the genealogy of the Shang kings which is certified by very early records, i.e., the bone inscriptions. But for any period earlier than Shang times we have scarcely a shred of thoroughly reliable material.

We do, of course, find a great deal of tradition concerning an earlier time in books of Chou and of Han date. And there are four books in the *chin wên* text of the *Shu Ching* which have been supposed to come down to us from pre-Shang times [1]. But the less conservative among Chinese scholars now agree that these books were written at a time not earlier than the Chou period, and it is not difficult to determine that they are undoubtedly correct in this view [2].

Chinese scholars have recently pointed out a curious circumstance in the manner in which we find traditions concerning pre-

---

1. I.e., the *Yao Tien, Kao Yao Mo, Yü Kung,* and *Kan Shih*. In the current *ku wên* text the last part of the *Yao Tien*, with twenty-eight added prefatory characters, is made a separate book, the *Shun Tien*. The last part of the *Kao Yao Mo* is likewise separated and called the *I Chi*.

2. In the *Yao Tien* we find a great many ideas which show that it can hardly be even as early as the Western Chou period. Most striking of these are the many sets of "fives", which are so conspicuous in the late Chou period, and totally lacking in early Chou literature. Here we find the "five punishments", "five ceremonies", "five utensils", "five teachings", etc., etc.; cf. *Shu* 31, 34, 36, 38, 44, 45. We also find the four directions coupled with the four seasons, according to the philosophical scheme which is of late origin; see *Shu* 35-37. The deity *T'ien*, which seems to have originated with the Chous, appears here; see *Shu* 50. We even find more advanced uses of the character *T'ien* (this character first denoted numerous ancestral spirits, then a single

Shang China cropping up in Chou literature. That is that these traditions, as they are found in late books, tell us of earlier periods and give us more details than do the traditions found in earlier books. There is a general tendency for this tradition to reach further backward and to add more of circumstances and particulars, in proportion as the literature recording the traditions is farther removed from the period with which the traditions

deity, and then developed into the sense of "sky", etc.; see my paper (in Chinese) in *Yenching Journal of Chinese Studies*, No. 18 (Dec. 1935), 59–71) as "sky" (*Shu* 24, twice) and in the expressions "*hao t'ien*" (*Shu* 18) and "*t'ien hsia*" (*Shu* 40). That we should have *T'ien* used in exactly the same ways, and in the same expressions, that we find in Chou literature, in a book really dating from the remote time ascribed to Yao and Shun, and yet find these ideas and the very character *T'ien* entirely lacking from the Shang inscriptions, is too much to believe.

In the *Kao Yao Mo* the presence of *T'ien* is even more striking. The deity of this name is mentioned nine times; see *Shu* 73 (three times), 74 (four times), 79, 89. The character appears twice in the sense of "sky", *Shu* 77, 83. There are even two references to the Decree of Heaven, *Shu* 79 and 89. The late philosophical pattern of regimenting things as "the three this", "the nine that", etc., is in full swing here. For the sets of "fives" alone see *Shu* 72, 73 (three times), 74 (four times), 80, 81 (three times), 85 (twice).

Quite apart from any particular anachronisms in their content, both the *Yao Tien* and the *Kao Yao Mo* differ from all the really early (i.e., early Chou) documents which we have in that they have no immediate practical purpose. Some of the early Chou books of the *Shu* contain a certain amount of moralizing and philosophizing, but it is for the purpose of persuading the people to whom it is addressed. But there is no immediate motivation to these two books. The actors move hazily across the stage, reciting their stilted speeches with the detachment of octogenarian philosophers emitting aphorisms, not so much for the benefit of their hearers as of the reader. Yet these books probably did have a definite, immediate purpose, though not the one which they were pretended to have. They were probably written by more or less philosophical members of the official class, in middle or late Chou times, for the purpose of showing the kings and feudal lords that the celebrated rulers of ancient times had honored their ministers, listened to their words with great respect, and even on occasion chosen their successors from among them. It is possible that in their composition fragments of really old documents were included.

The *Yü Kung*, or "Tribute of Yü" is a book concerning which there

deal[3]. This is so much the case that it justifies us in positing the tentative conclusion that certain traditional figures, such for instance as those of Yao and Shun, had no ascertainable basis in fact, and in leaving them out of account (at least until new material shall present itself) in seeking to trace the course of early Chinese history.

---

has been a tremendous amount of discussion and writing in Chinese scholarly circles in recent years (cf. for instance *Ku Shih Pien*, I.106–134, 165–86, 207–210). Professor Ku Chieh-kang has placed it in the late years of Duke Chuang of Lu, who reigned 693–662 B.C. (verbal communication of October 1933). It is impossible to go here into all of the complex questions which this document raises. It may be pointed out, however, that the China visualized in this book is much too large, stable and peaceful, too much subjected to the control of a central authority, even to have been conceived in pre-Chou times. The completely schematized geography of the last section of the document (*Shu* 142–150) is a conception worked out by philosophers thoroughly imbued with the natural philosophy of middle Chou times. We read, for instance, that a certain distance out from the center there was a territory, presumably three hundred *li* wide making a hollow rectangle, in which the barbarians called *I* lived, while in a still more remote similar territory were the *Man*. Thus we would have both *Man* and *I* in every direction. But actually these names were generally used to designate the tribes of the south and the east respectively, while other names were applied to those of the north and the west. We can not imagine such abstract geography being concocted, on this scheme which fits so perfectly with the thought of middle (but not early) Chou times, in the pre-Shang period.

The *Kan Shih* contains no real internal evidence of its date, so that we are wholly dependent upon tradition in this respect. The *Shih Chi* (2.19b–20a) tells us that it is a speech delivered by Ch'i, the son of Yü, to his army just before a battle designed to punish an insubordinate ruler of a small territory. This would make it a Hsia book. But here we find even the *wu hsing*, the so-called "five elements" mentioned, although they are unknown in Chinese literature generally until well into the Chou period. The book reads, in part: "The ruler of Hu has treated the five elements with violence and disrespect... Heaven therefore is cutting short his Decree. Now I am reverently carrying out Heaven's punishment" (*Shu* 153). This passage is so obviously a production of Chou date that the fact needs no enlarging upon.

3. Cf. Ku Chieh-kang's discussion of the development of the Yü traditions, *Ku Shih Pien*, I.106–134.

2. Hsia Traditions

But we can not do this with the so-called Hsia dynasty. It appears so early and so frequently in the preserved literature that it becomes an inescapable duty to investigate the substratum of this tradition. Its most developed form, in so far as it concerns the Hsia state or people as a whole, is that which maintains that there was a Hsia dynasty, ruling all of the China of its day, wielding the imperial[1] sway over feudal vassals who included the rulers of the Shang people. The end of the Hsia dynasty, according to this tradition, came when the Shang ruler, T'ang, renounced his allegiance, rebelled, and took the Chinese throne away from the last Hsia king. We find this story told in detail twice[2] and referred to more or less briefly five times[3] in the earliest books of the *Shu*, written during the opening decades of the Chou period. This same tradition is referred to once, but only once, in rather definite terms in the *Shih Ching*[4]. These are the only references to a Hsia dynasty in any of Chinese literature which can possibly be ascribed to a time as early as the Western Chou period. There is one additional reference in the *Shang Sung* of the *Shih Ching*[5], but there Hsia is obviously conceived as having been merely a state or even a tribe, not a dynasty ruling all China.

There are, of course, a number of references to a Hsia state or dynasty in the *Tso Chuan* and *Kuo Yü*, but both of these works were written so late that we have no way of being sure that their

---

1. It is sometimes held that the term "empire" should not be applied to China before the Ch'in dynasty. In my opinion this is a mistake. I do not, of course, believe in a Hsia empire. But if we accept the definition of "a state including broad territories and various peoples united under one rule", then there was certainly a Chou empire during a part at least of the Western Chou period. This is not, of course, any reason to abandon the convenient convention of translating *wang* as "king", especially since the term *wang* seems at first to have stood for a ruler of comparatively small territory and little power.
2. *Shu* 455–6 and 495–8.
3. *Shu* 427, 429–30, 432, 460, 499–500.
4. *Shih* 510.
5. *Shih* 642.

statements, even those which are supposed to come from an early period, do not reflect late influence. On the other hand, in the current inscriptions on Chou bronzes the very character *hsia* does not appear, even with its common meaning of "summer", until the seventh or sixth century B.C.[6]. In its two occurrences at this time it still does not stand for the dynasty. In the inscription on the *Shu I Chung*[7], which is attributed to the reign of Duke Ling of Ch'i (581–554 B.C.), we have what is probably another occurrence, in the form 𤓯[8]. To get this form we need only make a change in the "foot" element and put it on the side instead of at the bottom. This inscription is made by a reputed descendant of T'ang the Successful, founder of the Shang state, and says that "Ch'êng T'ang 唐[9] . . . received Heaven's Decree . . . to attack Hsia". It is somewhat remarkable, however, that we do not find mention of a Hsia dynasty in earlier bronze inscriptions, since it is the custom in these documents to make a good deal of general rhetorical reference to historical events.

6. I.e., it is not listed by the *Chin Wên Pien*, the *Shuo Wên Ku Chou Pu* (1898), or other works which analyze these inscriptions, except for the two occurrences on the *Ch'in Kung Tui* and the *Ch'in Kung Chung*; cf. *Chên I Wên* 6.14a, and *Li Tai T'ieh* 73a.

The inscriptions on these bronzes say that before their maker there had already been twelve dukes, presumably of Ch'in. This would bring us down to the seventh or sixth century B.C., depending on the method of reckoning, and the form of the characters in the inscriptions makes this seem reasonable. Cf. also *Liang Chou Hsi* 272.

Lin I-kuang in his *Wên Yüan* (1920) 4.3b, and following him Tung Tso-pin (*Anyang Pao Kao*, 512), identify the character *hsia* on the *Yu Hsi Li*; cf. *Chên I Wên* 4.11a. But this identification is extremely doubtful, and Lo Chên-yü wisely does not attempt to interpret this character in his transcription. The character appears in a proper name, so that we have no contextual clue to its identity. And it has very little resemblance to and differs considerably from the very few early forms of *hsia* which we know. In my opinion the reading of this character as *hsia* is definitely a mistake. I do not know what is the date of the *Yu Hsi Li*, but from the form of the characters it must be later than the opening years of the Chou period.

7. *Li Tai T'ieh* 78a. Cf. also *Liang Chou Hsi* 245.
8. Kuo Mo-jo identifies this character as *Hsia, Liang Chou Hsi* 245.
9. This is the form in which the name of T'ang is found on the oracle bones, rather than the usual 湯; cf. *Yin Ch'ien Pien* 1.47.1, etc.

If we attack the question of whether there was a Hsia dynasty from the point of view of historical probabilities, it is very difficult to bring irrefragable proof on the one side or the other. Yet it is very difficult to suppose that there could have been such a general dominion over anything approaching all of north China at a date prior to Shang times. The evidence from the oracle bones, while not definite, seems to indicate that the Shang state was hardly so large. The Chous were able to weld together broad territories only after a most spectacular coalition of tribes for a career of conquest, which was followed by the work of able statesmen conducting a very unusual political and religious propaganda. It is reasonable to suppose that roads and communications generally were more developed in Chou times than in the much earlier period of the supposed Hsia dynasty, and we know that media of exchange, vital to the administration of wide territories, improved considerably during early Chou times. Yet with all this the Chous were not able to exercise really effective sway, even over that part of north China which they claimed, for a very long time.

The Chous governed through a feudal system. In the conditions existing in very early China, with communications and finance comparatively undeveloped, some system of delegation of authority was inevitable. In each locality there had to be local rulers empowered to act as they thought fit, without the delay which would be involved in consulting the central authority. This meant that there would have to be either a feudal system or a system of rule by hereditary local rulers who merely acknowledged the overlordship of the king, but were really sovereign lords of their own territories. It appears that the latter system was that of the Shang kingdom. But such a state expands and contracts with the varying power and military prowess of its kings. It is not a satisfactory basis on which to build a stable rule, for the individual components of the larger kingdom are constantly on the alert to seize their independence when they can. And it could hardly have made possible an empire so large, stable, and powerful as tradition represents that of the Hsia dynasty to have been.

Tradition represents the Hsia system of government to have been feudalism. It also represents the Shang system as feudal; the Chous are supposed to have stepped directly into the place of the Shang rulers and kept the system going with little or no alteration. But the *Shang Sung*, which apparently reflects Shang traditions kept alive in the State of Sung, speaks of the Shang government in these terms:
> "Heaven appointed the many rulers,
> And established their capitals within the sphere of the labors of Yü,
> But for the business of every year they appeared before our king,
> Saying, 'Do not punish nor reprove us;
> We have not been remiss in our husbandry'"[10].

What is described here is not feudalism at all. It is rather the condition in which a ruling state, through conquest, forces the rulers of numerous adjacent states to acknowledge its overlordship, and to repair to its court from time to time to pay homage and, undoubtedly, tribute.

Furthermore, we have indirect but very good evidence from early Chou times indicating that feudalism on any extensive scale was a new development at that time. We know very well that the Chous were great admirers of Shang culture and that they took over a great number of institutions from the Shangs[11]. They took over the Shang method of writing, and a great deal of terminology. They pretended that they, the Chous themselves, had been docile feudatories of the Shang state. But it is evident, when we examine early Chou bronze inscriptions, that not even the titles for feudal lords of various ranks had been arranged into a graded hierarchy in the early Chou period. In the beginning these titles were used rather indiscriminately[12]. The system

10. *Shih* 645.
11. Cf. for instance the admonitions to a Chou official to follow the Shang legal code, in the *K'ang Kao*, *Shu* 390–391. Cf. also *Shu* 386, 395.
12. Thus we find a man succeeding to his father's fief called 侯 *hou*, while his father is called 公 *kung* (*K'ê Lu* 5.6b). This shows either that titles and fiefs were not yet wholly hereditary or that titles were used

of five orders of rank emerged and became clarified only gradually. This is exactly what we should expect if a feudal system had been created de novo out of the situation resulting from the Chou conquest, which made it imperative for the Chous to divide up the territorial spoils between the various chieftains who had assisted them in the expedition to the east. But if a feudal system had not been worked out in Shang times it probably did not exist in the still more remote Hsia period—at the least, we cannot accept the story of its unbroken continuance from remote antiquity. And without the aid of feudalism it is difficult to conceive that a state so large and so enduring as that of the traditional Hsia dynasty could have existed under the circumstances prevailing in China at that time.

Shang tradition, as reflected in the *Shang Sung*, does not consider Hsia to have been a dynasty, but only a state. According to the Chou version of Shang history the Shang rulers were vassals of the Hsia kings down to the time of T'ang the Successful, who rebelled and wrested the throne from the last Hsia sovereign[13]. But the *Shang Sung* tells us that "Hsiang T'u, the ardent, spread his dominion even beyond the seas"[14]. According to the accepted genealogy of the Shang kings, which is corroborated in most of its details by the oracle bones[15], Hsiang T'u was the twelfth Shang ruler *before* T'ang the Successful. He must, therefore, have lived at a time which Chou history represents to be about the middle of the period at which the

---

without any fixed rule. The latter is indicated even more strongly when we find the same individuals called, alternately in the same inscription, 公 *kung* and 伯 *po*; see *Liang Chou Hsi* 18, and *Chün Chin Wên* 3(3).8. *Po* is, of course, a term used to denote the head of a family as well as a feudal rank, and Kuo Mo-jo says that it is in this sense that it occurs in the latter of the two inscriptions just cited (*Liang Chou Hsi* 92). But the usage in such cases is that where it refers to the family the surname is used, while with the feudal title the name of the fief is used. When, as in these inscriptions, we find *po* and *kung* used with the same name, it seems definitely to reflect looseness of usage.
13. Cf. the *To Shih* and *To Fang*, *Shu* 456, 499–500.
14. *Shih* 640.
15. Cf. *Ts'ai Anniv. Vol.* chart 2 opp. 331; *Pu Tz'ŭ T'ung Tsuan*, *K'ao Shih* 73b–74a.

Hsia dynasty ruled all of China[16]. According to the *Shang Sung*, Hsia was merely one of several states, not a dynasty exercising general dominion, even at the time when it was attacked and conquered by T'ang the Successful. It says that "Having smitten *the princes of* Wei and Ku, he dealt with *the prince of* K'un Wu, and with Chieh of Hsia"[17].

It is worthy of note that there is little mention of Hsia as a dynasty in very early Chou times, and that the most detailed references to its traditional history come precisely in the *To Shih* and the *To Fang*, two harangues addressed to the Shang people to persuade them to submit to the Chou yoke. The whole tradition of Hsia as a dynasty is closely linked with the idea of the Decree of Heaven[18]. But the deity Heaven does not appear in the oracle inscriptions at all, and it is difficult if not impossible to suppose that the peculiar complex of religious, political, and philosophical ideas which make up the theory of the Decree of Heaven could have been in existence very long before the Chou conquest.

All of these circumstances make it not implausible to suppose that the existence of a Hsia dynasty, as such, was a fiction circulated as a part of the campaign of propaganda which legitimized and, as it were, sanctified the Chou conquest. It is probable that the Chous themselves believed it thoroughly. Certainly there were some traditions concerning a Hsia state, and if these took a form which was convenient for the purposes of the Chou conquerors at the moment, we need not be surprised if they took them up eagerly and elaborated them. A Hsia dynasty, which had ruled all of China, was a perfect precedent for the far-flung military expeditions launched by the Chou rulers. And a Hsia dynasty whose last ruler had become wicked, necessitating a holy rebellion on the part of the Shang chieftain, was a similarly apt

16. As was mentioned previously, Legge (*Shih* 640) and various Chinese scholars have interpreted this passage in the *Shih Ching* so as to obviate the conflict between the Chou and Shang versions of history. But their interpretations are distinctly forced; the conflict is real, not easily to be explained away.
17. *Shih* 642.
18. Cf. *Shu* 427, 429-30, 456, 460, 497, 499-500.

model from which to justify the Chou adventure. Nothing is more important, in seeking to influence a large number of people, than precedent. Whether it is genuine or false makes no immediate difference, so long as it is widely believed. One may doubt the scientific accuracy of the practice of the enemies of the Germans in the World War in calling them "Huns", but no one can doubt its practical efficacy. The memory of the Roman Empire and the name of Caesar have been worth many regiments to his numerous emulators. Japan has recently found it most convenient to hold that the course of the United States with regard to the Panama Canal Zone provides a precedent and justification for her own actions in Manchuria. In the same way the story of a Hsia dynasty, and its defeat by the Shangs, was used by the Chous as a precedent and justification for continuing their conquests "until", in the words of the Duke of Chou, "our reign is universal, and from the corners of the sea and the sunrising there shall not be one who is disobedient to our rule".[19]

In the present state of our knowledge we are justified in drawing at least the tentative conclusion that there was never, in Chinese history, a Hsia dynasty in the traditional sense. But this is not to say that the whole Hsia tradition was a fabrication. Indeed, we find so many early traces of a tradition concerning a Hsia state or people that we may be quite sure that it had some foundation. But what was that foundation?

The character 夏 *hsia* is something of a mystery. Its three most common meanings are "summer", the Hsia state or dynasty, and China as a territorial or cultural unit. The *Shuo Wên Chieh Tzŭ* gives it in the form 夒 and defines it as "Men of 中國 China. Composed of 夊, ᄀ two feet, 臼, two hands, and 頁 [a head]". This is rather obvious guess-work, an exercise in

19. *Shu* 485.
This reference is from the *Chün Shih*, a book which Ku Chieh-kang formerly stated to be an Eastern Chou forgery (cf. *Ku Shih Pien*, I.201). But after careful comparison of the style of this book with Western Chou bronze inscriptions I believe it to be genuine, and Professor Ku is now of the same opinion (verbal communication of October 1933).
The problem raised by the opening phrase of this book, 周公若曰, will be discussed when we come to criticise the book in detail.

which the author of the *Shuo Wên* was adept. The character was generally used to mean "China" long before his time, and it certainly contains a foot (*not* two feet)[20] and a head and possibly two hands; to conclude that it meant "men of China" required no great cleverness, nor did it help us any to understand the origin of the character. As Chinese scholars have pointed out, foreigners as well as Chinese are commonly possessed of head, hands, and feet. Lin I-kuang presents what he considers a more reasonable explanation. He says that this character "represents a man making himself comfortable during the summer heat, with his hands and feet exposed"[21]. But since the hands and feet of persons represented in ancient characters are never shown covered, this hardly sheds any further light.

In the opinion of many, perhaps of most Chinese scholars working in the oracle bone material, the character *hsia* has not been identified with any certainty in the Shang bone inscriptions. There is nothing which has even been held to be a reference to the Hsia state or dynasty on the oracle bones, but this is no evidence whatever against its existence. The bone inscriptions deal almost exclusively with questions of immediate practical action, whether to make war, whether to offer certain sacrifices and when, whether the gods will smile or frown on certain undertakings, etc. Unless there had been, at the time when the inscriptions were made, a contemporary state called Hsia, it is extremely unlikely that the name would have appeared on the oracle bones. Evidently there was not. But this can not be used as any kind of evidence against the previous existence of a Hsia state or even dynasty.

There are two kinds of characters on the oracle bones which have been supposed by some Chinese scholars to be ancestral forms of the character *hsia*, which they claim are used in the bone inscriptions with the meaning of "summer". The following

20. The *Shuo Wên* constantly misinterprets the element 夊, "seal" form 卩. As is shown by the characters in which it appears, it is nothing more than the conventionalized drawing of a single foot, thus 𠂆, which is common on the oracle bones and in bronze inscriptions.

21. *Wên Yüan* 4.3b.

chart, made up after one by Tung Tso-pin[22], illustrates these theories[23].

This chart was not copied after Tung's, but made by photographing squeezes of the original inscriptions to which he refers. It has been proved time after time that when one tries to draw these characters in facsimile it is virtually impossible to prevent his mental preconceptions from influencing the copy, try as he will to make nothing more nor less than a simple reproduction. This is why drawings of these inscriptions are considered to be of very little value as compared with photographic reproductions of the bone itself or of squeezes.

The theories on which this whole chart is based were originated by Yeh Yü-shên[24] and elaborated by Tung Tso-pin[25]. Characters (1) to (4) are forms, occurring on the oracle bones[26], which according to the theory represent the cicada. In four places where characters resembling these occur they are preceded by the character 今 chin, which is held with some plausibility to indicate that it refers to time. The phrases 今日 chin jih, "today", and 今夕 chin hsi, "tonight"[27], are common in the bone inscriptions. Yeh says that the Shang people named the four seasons after their most striking characteristics, and he is not without some reason when he says that the terrific humming of the cicada which is heard, in north China at any rate, during a large part of the summer, is one of the most unmistakable phenomena attending the season. Therefore, he says, chin followed by the pictograph of a cicada means "now in the summer season". Yeh considers form (5), which is the so-called "seal" form of hsia, to be a form mistakenly evolved and conventionalized from this. In my opinion, however, if one accepts

22. See *Anyang Pao Kao* 513.
23. See plate facing this page. This chart faithfully reproduces the order of Tung's chart except that the lower horizontal row has been moved to the upper position, and vice versa, to facilitate explanation.
24. Cf. *Yin Ch'i Kou Ch'ên* 2a; *Yen Ch'i Chih T'an* 9b.
25. *Anyang Pao Kao* 511–14.
26. They occur as follows: (1) *Yin Ch'ien Pien* 5.25.1. (2) *Yin Ch'ien Pien* 2.5.3. (3) *Kuei Tzŭ* 2.26.13. (4) Ibid. 2.18.3.
27. Cf. *Yin Ch'ien Pien* 1.39.5, 2.13.2. *Hsi*, which now commonly means "evening", seems to have meant "night" in Shang times.

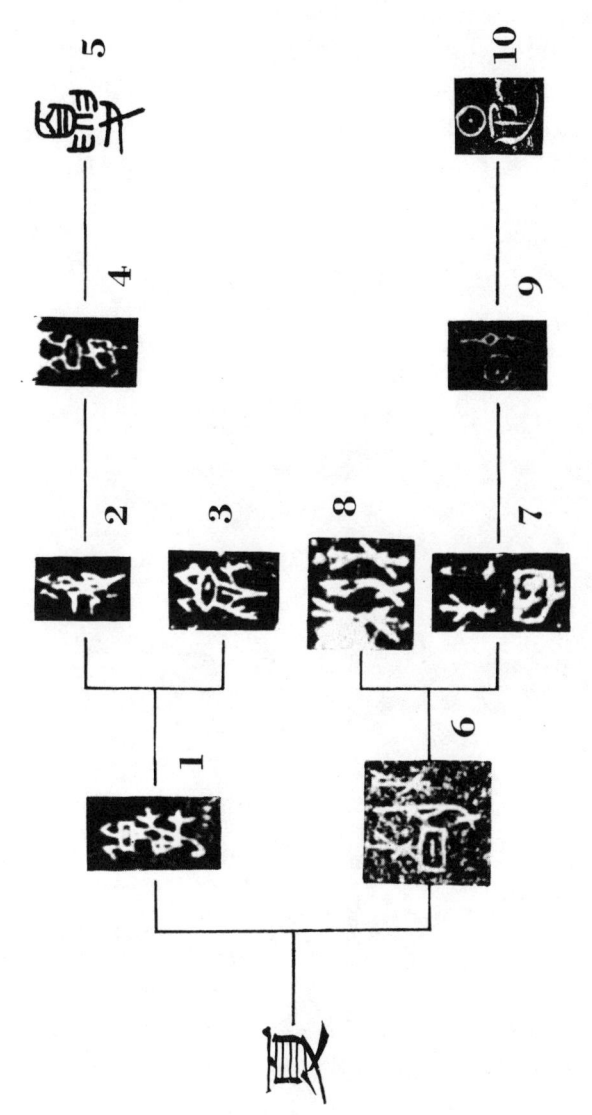

Ancestral Forms of the Character *HSIA*

Hsia Traditions 109

this theory there is far more likeness to be found between form (4) and form (10); (10) is the form given as *ku wên* "ancient script" on both the Han and the Wei "Stone Classics in Three Forms of Characters"[28].

Forms (6) to (9) are considered by Yeh to represent an entirely different form of *hsia* on the bones[29]. He points out that forms (7), (8), and (9) are found preceded by the character *chin*. Form (8) he identifies as the character 棥 *mou*[30], which the *Shuo Wên* defines as "trees flourishing". Form (8) is considered to be an abbreviation of (6), which has all of its elements plus a pictograph of the sun, standing for "day" or "time". Yeh therefore analyzes (6) as meaning "the days when trees are flourishing", i.e., "summer", and therefore an alternative form of the character *hsia*. He considers (7) to be yet another abbreviation of the same character, with one less tree, while (9) is a still further abbreviation of the same character with no trees at all. Yeh leaves it at this, as an alternative writing, without trying to link it up with the known ancient forms of the character *hsia* itself. But Tung Tso-pin seeks to link it with an unusual form of *hsia* which occurs in the stone classics, i.e. (10). He points out that both (9) and (10) contain a pictograph of the sun, and believes that the right half of (9) and the lower element in (10) are sufficiently alike to be accounted for by mere distortion in transmission. He, then, holds that both of these forms found in the bone inscriptions may be identified as the familiar character *hsia*.

28. In the above chart, (10) is photographed directly from a squeeze of one of the four fragments of the Han inscriptions which are now in the Lo Hê Library in Loyang. I saw the original stones and purchased the squeezes in Loyang in May 1935. For the Wei form, see *Shuo Wên Chieh Tzŭ Ku Lin* (referred to hereafter as *Shuo Wên Lin*) 2325.

29. These forms are quoted from the following squeezes: (6) *T'ieh-yün Ts'ang Kuei* (referred to hereafter as *T'ieh Kuei*) 227.3. (7) *Yin Ch'ien Pien* 6.39.3. (8) *Yin Ch'ien Pien* 7.28.4. (9) *Chien Shou T'ang So Ts'ang Yin Hsŭ Wên Tzŭ* (referred to hereafter as *Chien Yin Tzŭ*) 22.2.

30. For the identification of the middle element of this character, as it appears in the bone inscription, as the character *mao*, cf. Tung Tso-pin's discussion in *Anyang Pao Kao* 652–3. I personally consider this rather doubtful.

No one can deny that these theories are ingenious. They are not unrepresentative of the processes by which these and other scholars have unfolded the secrets of the bone inscriptions. But in the particular case of the character *hsia* they seem to be founded on too little real evidence. Even the primary point of whether these pictures do or do not represent the cicada is, in my opinion, open to question. They are characterized in every case by prominent, long "feelers", which bend down into an inverted v-shape; cf. the chart, forms (1) to (4)[31]. These feelers are the most striking and the most unvarying feature of the pictograph. But in so far as I am able to learn the feelers of the cicada do not turn back in this manner, but are straight. We have hundreds or thousands of representations of the cicada by the Shang people, on pottery and especially on bronze where it was a favorite motif, but none of these which I have ever seen shows anything resembling such feelers. Even the reproductions of these published by Tung to illustrate his theory have nothing of the sort[32]. In other respects also these bone characters are not strikingly like the cicada.

Even if they were it would not be certain that this character meant "summer", much less that it were an ancestral form of *hsia*. In the appendix to his *Chia Ku Wên Pien*, Sun lists thirteen occurrences of what appears to be this character[33]; there is at least one other[34]. Of these fourteen characters, only four are preceded by the character *chin*[35]. In the remaining cases the context, where it is present, does not give any indication that this character has to do with time. The quoted occurrences

31. In Tung Tso-pin's chart, his (9) which corresponds to my (4) does not have the feelers bending down into an inverted "v". He says that this form is quoted from *Kuei Tzŭ* 2.18, but unfortunately does not state which squeeze on this page. However, there are three forms of this character on the page referred to, and in every one of them the feelers do turn down in this manner very definitely.

32. Cf. *Anyang Pao Kao* 512–13.

33. *Fu Lu*, 23b. It is to be understood that Sun does not consider this character to be *hsia*, which is why he places it in the appendix.

34. *Kuei Tzŭ* 2.18.4.

35. *Yin Ch'ien Pien* 2.5.3; *Yin Hou Pien* 2.12.14; ibid. 2.42.3; *Kuei Tzŭ* 2.26.13.

of the other form are still fewer, and the case for it is even more ambiguous. It is possible that these characters are forms of *hsia*, but it is very far from certain.

For the early Chou period we have much more definite data on the use of this character. *Hsia* does not occur at all in the original text of the *I Ching*[36], nor in any early Chou bronze inscription now current. It occurs nineteen times, however, in the thirteen books of the *chin wên* text of the *Shu Ching* which we can be sure are both early and genuine[37]. In seventeen of these nineteen cases it is used as the name of the suppositious

36. This statement is based on my own examination of the text. By the original text is meant the text without the "Ten Wings" or appendices. References to names and events, and the general social and political situation reflected in this material, show that at least a good deal of it must come from about the end of the Shang and the beginning of the Chou period. This text will be discussed in some detail in a later paper.

37. These books are: *Ta Kao, K'ang Kao, Chiu Kao, Tzŭ Ts'ai, Shao Kao, Lo Kao, To Shih, Chün Shih, To Fang, Ku Ming* (with which is included, in the *chin wên* text, *K'ang Wang Chih Kao*), *Pi Shih* (this is the name of the book in the current text, and is preserved for the sake of simplicity; at least four names have been attached to this one book), *Wên Hou Chih Ming,* and *Ch'in Shih*. These books will be discussed in detail at the appropriate place in these papers.

The terms "early" and "genuine" require definition. By early books I mean books which were written, as judged by their style, in the same general period at which the events they relate took place. There are books, like the *Ku Ming*, which were undoubtedly put together into their present form some time after the events which they relate, but the style of which is still in general that of the period of the events. There are others, like the *Chin T'êng*, which may be genuine enough in the sense that no fraud was intended by their writers, but which quite evidently were produced in a period much later than the events they deal with. And there are still other books, such as the *Wei Tzŭ* and *Hsi Po K'an Li*, which seem to be quite early as Chinese literature goes, and to have been produced not very long after the events they relate are supposed to have happened, but which are not genuine because they are evident forgeries written with the attempt to deceive. I prefer as a rule not to use materials of this last class when dealing with questions like the present one because there is always an element of uncertainty concerning the date of deliberate forgeries.

Hsia dynasty[38]. There is one occurrence of the character in the *Shih Ching* which refers to the dynasty[39]. It should be noted, however, that all seventeen references to the Hsia dynasty in the *Shu* are found in three books, and every one of them occurs in a passage concerned either with the Chou conquest or with the establishment of the Chou power. Thirteen of them are found in the *To Shih* and *To Fang*, two books consisting entirely of exhortations addressed to the conquered Shang people. The one reference to the Hsia dynasty in the *Shih Ching* occurs in the course of an abusive tirade, supposed to have been uttered by Wên Wang, against the last Shang king and his government[40]. All of this supports the theory previously advanced, that Hsia as a dynasty was a fiction of Chou propaganda.

The character *hsia* is found fourteen times in the *Shih Ching*. Twice it is explained to mean "large"[41], and twice it occurs as a proper name[42]. In six cases it means "summer"[43]. It should not be supposed that "summer" as a meaning for *hsia* was necessarily late in origin merely because it is not found (unless one accept Yeh's theory) on early Chou bronzes and the Shang bone inscriptions. The names of the seasons were not commonly used in dating by the scribes of Shang and early Chou times. Instead they stated the day of the cycle of days and sometimes the phase of the moon, the month, even the year of the king's reign. But Kuo Mo-jo holds that the name of any one of the four seasons has not been proved to appear once either on the Shang bones or on early Chou bronzes[44].

38. *Shu* 427, 429 (twice), 432, 455 (twice), 456, 495 (twice), 496, 497 (four times), 498, 499 (twice).
39. *Shih* 510.
40. *Shih* 505–510.
41. *Shih* 203, 454. In the latter case there is a difference of opinion, Mao explaining it as 大 *ta*, Chêng Hsüan as 諸夏 *chu Hsia*; see *SSC Mao Shih* 16(4).13b.
42. *Shih* 213 (twice).
43. *Shih* 187 (twice), 205, 206, 357, 624.
44. *Chin Wên Ts'ung K'ao* (Tokyo, 1932) 30b. Cf. however a summary of the evidence for their appearance on the oracle bones by Tung Tso-pin in *Anyang Pao Kao* 507–18.

As has already been said *Hsia* occurs once as the name of the dynasty, in the *Shih Ching*⁽⁴⁵⁾, and once as the name, not of a dynasty at all, but merely of a state or tribe which was conquered by the Shang king T'ang⁽⁴⁶⁾. In the two remaining cases it means "China"⁽⁴⁷⁾. It has this meaning in two passages in the early and genuine books of the *Shu Ching*⁽⁴⁸⁾. We find 夏 *Hsia* or 諸夏 *chu Hsia*, in this sense, very frequently in Chou literature. The last phrase should perhaps be translated "all the Chinese states" or "the various Chinese states". But we must investigate just what was meant by the term "Chinese".

By investigating the occurrences of these terms in the *Tso Chuan* and the *Kuo Yü* it is possible to get a certain amount of specific data as to just what territory and what people were meant by the designations *Hsia* and *chu Hsia* during the *Ch'un Ch'iu* period (722–481 B.C.), and what states and peoples were not included. In the first place the barbarian peoples known as Jung, as Man, and as I were definitely outside the pale⁽⁴⁹⁾. We are told, in fact, that "Jung and Hsia are mutually opposed"⁽⁵⁰⁾. While only these three varieties of barbarians are specifically mentioned (in the material covered by my notes), yet the fact is that Jung, Man, and I were only general names applied to barbarians of the west, south, and east, and we know very well that the barbarians of the north were considered equally outside the Hsia circle.

The great and powerful State of 楚 Ch'u was not considered to be among the Hsia states. Ch'u, which took in both banks of the Yangtze and extended northward something more than halfway to the Yellow River, played a rôle in *Ch'un Ch'iu* times somewhat like that of Ch'in at a later period. Ch'u was constantly trying to gain control of the states to the north, and they

45. *Shih* 510.
46. *Shih* 642.
47. *Shih* 578, 580. Chêng Hsüan would add another reference here, *Shih* 454, but Mao does not agree.
48. *Shu* 383, 481.
49. See *Kuo Yü* 7.1b, *Tso Chuan* (all references are to the Chinese text unless otherwise stated) 179.16, 774.8.
50. *Kuo Yü* 7.1b.

on their part tried to maintain solidarity against the common menace of Ch'u's size and power. During this time Ch'u was gradually coming into the sphere of Chinese culture, and Chuang Wang (613–591 B.C.) of Ch'u is even considered for a time to have been Pa, leader of the Chinese states. Yet Ch'u was not considered, and did not even consider itself, to be a part of Hsia[51]. The small states of 沈 Shên and 蔡 Ts'ai were called "Eastern Hsia" even in Ch'u, although in relation to Ch'u itself they lay, not to the east, but directly north[52]. We find repeated indications that Hsia as a territory was considered to lie to the north of Ch'u[53] and to be "remote" from Ch'u[54].

One passage indicates that the State of 邾 Chu did not have an incontestable title to inclusion among the Hsia states, even though its territory, not far from the coast, was at one time almost completely surrounded by that of the thoroughly Hsia State of Lu[55]. Wu and Yüeh, on the coast south of the mouth of the Yangtze, were not considered among the Hsias[56].

We have specific references to the states of 晉 Chin, 齊 Ch'i, 魯 Lu, Shên and Ts'ai as belonging to the Hsia group[57]. One passage would give the impression that Chin was in Eastern Hsia[58], whereas it is really just about in the north of the center of the Chinese states of the *Ch'un Ch'iu* period. There are probably two reasons for this. In the first place, the episode in which this passage occurs is laid in the opening years of the Chou dynasty, when the Chou capital was in the Wei valley, far to the west. As compared with the seat of Chou power, Chin was eastern. In the second place, at that early time it is probable

51. See *Kuo Yü* 5.4a, 17.2b, 17.4b, 17.7b, 18.9a; *Tso Chuan* 456.7, 521.15, 673.17.
52. See *Kuo Yü* 17.4b.
53. *Kuo Yü* 17.2b; *Tso Chuan* 456.7.
54. *Kuo Yü* 17.7b; *Tso Chuan* 673.17.
55. *Tso Chuan* 179.14.
56. See *Kuo Yü* 19.2b; *Tso Chuan* 852.11.
57. Cf.: Chin: *Kuo Yü* 7.1b, 17.7b; *Tso Chuan* 505.2, 658.6, 673.8, 852.11. Ch'i: *Kuo Yü* 19.2b; *Tso Chuan* 774.8. Lu: *Tso Chuan* 179.14–16. Shên and Ts'ai: *Kuo Yü* 17.4b.
58. *Tso Chuan* 658.6.

that the Chou rule and even Chinese culture itself, as such, had not penetrated nearly so far to the east as they did later. We really know very little at present about the extent of the original Chou conquests, but it is probable that there is much of the apocryphal in the received accounts which carry them so far to the east. And it is probable that the signification of the term Hsia was extended with the extension of Chou rule and Chinese culture to a widening area. Hsia seems sometimes to have been used even as a political term, to designate the group of states adhering to the Chous or to those who ruled, as Pa, more or less in the name of the Chous [59].

But more than political or territorial, Hsia was a cultural term. We find it used twice in the *Shu Ching* to refer to the territories of Wên Wang, before the Chou conquest, presumably in the Wei valley, as belonging to the Hsia area [60]. Yet for various reasons it is very doubtful that the Chou people had been within the circle of Hsia culture for any very long time in the days of King Wên [61]. Even the Chou people themselves said that their original home was "among the Jung and Ti barbarians" [62]. But they had been "converted", as it were, or had converted themselves, to Chinese culture at a fairly recent time, and considered themselves to be a part of that culture. They therefore called their western territories a part of the Hsia region.

We have gleaned several items of information concerning the meaning of Hsia as designating a people or a territory. They may be divided into two classes, i.e., those which refer to an ancient, pre-Shang state and those which refer to a specific part of the territory of eastern Asia during Chou times. As to the early Hsia, orthodox Chinese history counts nothing more

59. Cf. for instance *Tso Chuan* 505.2.
60. *Shu* 383, 481.
61. Some of the evidence for this was discussed in the previous paper, and the whole problem will be gone into thoroughly in a later one.
62. *Kuo Yü* 1.2b. This speech, attributed to a minister who is said to be a descendant of the original Duke of Chou, says that the ancestors of the Chou kings, falling on evil times during the Hsia dynasty, "hid themselves among the Jung and Ti", though still keeping their Chinese culture.

certain than that there was a dynasty by that name, ruling broad territories including all, or virtually all, of the China of its day for more than four centuries (2205-1766 B.C.). The accepted chronology lists by name seventeen or eighteen rulers for the Hsia period [63]. But we have seen that there are no references to a Hsia dynasty in any known Chinese documents earlier than the Chou period. References even in early Chou times are surprisingly few, and all of them occur in literature of a highly propagandistic nature, designed to facilitate the firm establishment of Chou rule and to bring the people of the conquered territories to submission. This fact, coupled with the historical improbability of a Hsia dynasty and the fact that Shang traditions, as found in the *Shang Sung*, definitely contradict the dynastic theory, indicates that the story of Hsia as a Chinese dynasty was no more nor less than an item of Chou propaganda. Yet it was not a totally baseless fiction. Shang tradition tells us that there was a state, called Hsia, which was conquered by T'ang the Successful. And the wide use of the term "Hsia", in later times, as in some sense designating Chinese people or territory as opposed to non-Chinese, shows that there must have been some substratum of fact to the Hsia tradition.

The sense attaching to the term Hsia in Chou times was at once geographical and cultural. We can mark off its geographical limits roughly by bounding it with Shên and Ts'ai on the south, Lu and Ch'i to the east and northeast [64], Chin on the north, and Ch'in on the west (if we accept the statements in the *Shu* which include the original Chou territory of King Wên in Hsia) [65]. This gives us a territory roughly oval in shape, with its long axis running east and west and tilted slightly toward the northeast. And it includes virtually all of the territory over which the Chou kings ever had any real power for any great length of time.

63. Depending upon whether or not the first part of the reign of Shao K'ang is attributed to the supposed usurper Han Cho.
64. The state here referred to is 齊 Ch'i. The status of the small state of 杞 Ch'i, which was located to the east of the larger Ch'i in *Ch'un Ch'iu* times, is ambiguous; sometimes it was considered Hsia, and sometimes barbarian. See further discussion.
65. *Shu* 383, 481.

The essential significance of the term Hsia as it was used in Chou times was not, however, political or geographic, but cultural. The barbarians were not Hsia, but people who had been barbarians became amalgamated into the Hsia group by taking up Chinese culture. The reverse was also true—it was possible for a group or a state to cease to be Hsia on dropping Chinese culture and taking up that of the barbarians.

It is not possible at this point to go into the details of what constituted Chinese or Hsia culture. The essence of it seems to have been summed up in the term 禮 *li*. The character *li* originally meant "sacrifice"; from this it developed to mean the ritual used in sacrifice and finally to stand for ceremonies generally, the proper mode of conduct in general, and even for common politeness[66]. *Li*, or at least Chinese *li*, has been considered *the* distinguishing characteristic above all others of the Chinese individual. One even finds Chinese today who think that non-Chinese peoples have no *li*, that is, no fixed rituals or ceremonies or even any definite forms of courtesy.

This *li* included matters of religion, of course, but it also extended even to details of dress and personal appearance. It is related in the *Shih Chi* that the grandfather of Wên Wang wished his youngest son to succeed him. His two elder sons, realizing this, ran away and went to live among the Ching Man, i.e., the tribes of the south. And they "cut short their hair and tattooed their bodies", thus transgressing Chinese *li* and removing themselves from the possibility of succession[67]. The *Tso Chuan* has this same story in slightly different form[68]. Confucius, in praising Kuan Chung for keeping the Chinese states united in resisting the barbarian invasions, said, "But for Kuan Chung we should now be wearing our hair unbound and the lappets of our coats buttoning on the left side"[69].

66. Cf. *Lun Yü* 251: "... when you go abroad, behave as if you were receiving a great guest; employ the people as if you were assisting at a great sacrifice..."
67. *Shih Chi* 4.3b.
68. *Tso Chuan* 812.8. Here it is said that the elder brother kept to the Chou *li*, while the younger departed from it.
69. *Lun Yü* 282.

A part (but only a part) of this difference in culture between Hsia and non-Hsia people was the difference which still persists between the culture of the northern and southern Chinese, which is to a considerable extent the result of geography. The cutting of the hair and even the tattooing mentioned above are ascribed by commentators to the fact that the people of the south, being "constantly in the water", do this to make themselves look like "young dragons" so that they may avoid being harmed by the various creatures of the dragon variety who live in the waters [70]. A statesman of the southeastern state of Wu, in pointing out to his king the futility of an expedition against the northern states, said: "I have heard it said that landsmen must live on land, and men of the waters in the water. As for the Chinese states, if we attack them and conquer yet we cannot live in their territory nor can we ride in their chariots. But as for Yüeh, if we attack it and conquer we shall be able to live in its territory and to ride in its boats" [71]. The difference between north and south was stated in still more extreme terms by a messenger of Ch'u, protesting against an invasion in 656 B.C. He said that the borders of Ch'i [72] and Ch'u were so far apart, and the two had so little in common, that the very horses and cattle of the two states could not interbreed [73].

It is probable that there was a certain degree of linguistic significance to the term Hsia, that is, that there existed among the people designated by that term a somewhat greater similarity of speech and writing than existed between them and non-Hsia peoples. We know that the Shang oracle inscriptions and early Chou bronze inscriptions show a remarkable degree of similarity, and that the bronze inscriptions which have come down to us from the various Hsia states show a considerable amount of

70. *Shih Chi* 4.3b; *SSC Tso Chuan* 18.8a.
71. *Kuo Yü* 20.2a.
72. 齊.
73. *Tso Chuan* 139.2. For further discussion of the differences between the cultures of the north and south, see Bishop, "The Beginnings of North and South in China," in *Pacific Affairs*, 1934, 7.297–325, and Laufer, "Some Fundamental Ideas of Chinese Culture," in *The Journal of Race Development*, 1914, 5.162–164.

uniformity. Those inscriptions which appear to emanate from states outside the Hsia circle[74] have certain peculiarities in style and sometimes in the form of the characters. This is particularly true of those from Ch'u. A few Ch'u inscriptions have been known since the Sung dynasty, but a large number of new ones have been unearthed in very recent years. The inscriptions are in Chinese, but the characters are so different in form from those of the northern states as to be quite striking and in some cases undecipherable. And there are differences of content as well[75]. From the transmitted literature we know that Ch'u had special names for certain of its officials, different from those commonly used by the northern states[76].

Hsia was not a racial designation, applied indiscriminately to all of those who were supposed to come from a common ancestral stock and to no others. This is made plain by the references to the State of 杞 Ch'i which we find in the *Tso Chuan*. The rulers of this state claimed to be descended from the Hsia kings, and were generally considered to be so[77]. Yet they are repeatedly referred to as I, "eastern barbarians"[78]. Why? Because in spite of their supposed Hsia ancestry they have taken up and practised the *li* of the I[79]. In 544 B.C. an official who was defending the action of Lu in appropriating some of the territory of the State of Ch'i did not seek to deny (as he might well have done) the descent of its rulers from the Hsia kings—in fact, he affirms it. But he considers it sufficient, in order to show that Ch'i has no claim for help or sympathy on the Chinese states, to point out that it has "turned toward (Legge translates "assimilated to") the eastern barbarians"[80].

74. Cf. *Liang Chou Hsi* 177–200.
75. Cf. Liu Chieh, *Ch'u Ch'i T'u Shih* (Peiping, 1935).
76. For instance, their chief minister was called 令尹 *ling yin* (*Kuo Yü* 18.5a, *Tso Chuan* (76.11, etc.), and their minister of crime 司敗 *ssŭ pai* (*Kuo Yü* 18.7a, *Tso Chuan* 255.6). Such variations occurred in other states, but apparently were especially frequent in Ch'u.
77. Cf. *Tso Chuan* 545.9.
78. *Tso Chuan* 184.10 (Legge, in translating, omits this sentence), 200.1, 545.9–10.
79. See *Tso Chuan* 545.9–10; *SSC Tso Chuan* 15.8a, commentary.
80. *Tso Chuan* 545.9–10.

Fundamentally, then, the term "Hsia" stood for two things—a pre-Shang state (not dynasty) and the group of states, in Chou times, which adhered to Chinese culture. From this we may deduce that the substratum of the Hsia tradition was an ancient state which probably was the focal point and the leader of the Chinese culture of its day. That there was a culture which could properly be called Chinese, even on a linguistic basis, at the early date assigned to Hsia, is altogether probable. For the Chinese writing system as we find it on the Shang bones of the fourteenth century B.C. was amazingly complex; embodying almost every principle of the formation of characters which is in use today; it must have been preceded by many centuries of development.

3. THE LOCATION OF THE HSIA STATE

Tradition links numerous places with the Hsia dynasty. Its founder, Yü, is said to have been enfeoffed at the place now called Yü Hsien, almost in the middle of Honan Province[1]. The same authority says that upon becoming emperor he established his capital at 平陽 P'ing Yang[2]; this must have been near the modern city still known by that name though officially called Lin Fên, on the Fên River in southwestern Shansi[3]. But it may also, he says, have been at 晉陽 Chin Yang, which was probably near the present Taiyuan in central Shansi, or at 安邑 An I, a district which in his day comprised both the modern An I Hsien and 夏 Hsia Hsien, in the southwestern tip of Shansi[4]. According to quotations from the genuine Bamboo Books[5] Yü lived at 陽城 Yang Ch'êng, which is said to be located in

1. See *Shih Chi* 2.1a.1–2, and *Chung Kuo Ku Chin Ti Ming Ta Tz'ŭ Tien* (Shanghai, 1930; referred to hereafter as *Ti Ming Tien*) 961.
2. Huang-Fu Mi, quoted in *Shih Chi* 2.19a.6.
3. This district is also supposed to be that in which Yao made his capital. Just south of the city there is a temple to Yao, called Ku Ti Yao Miao. The images are rather interesting, but the temple is given over entirely to soldiers and I could find no one about the place who knows so much as when the temple was built, to say nothing of having any ancient traditions to relate.
4. *Shih Chi* 2.19a.6.
5. *Ku Chu Shu* 1b.

Honan only a few miles northwest of Yü Hsien⁽⁶⁾, but whether this was supposed to be his original fief or his capital is not clear. The current Bamboo Books⁽⁷⁾ says that he lived at 冀 Chi; whether this is intended to indicate the location of the ancient state of that name, in southwestern Shansi⁽⁸⁾, or, as Hsü Wên-ching says, merely to state that it was located in the ancient Chi 州 Chou which included Shansi, Hopei, and all of Honan north of the Yellow River⁽⁹⁾, is uncertain.

Yü's son, Ch'i, is said to have established his capital a few miles to the northwest of his father's original seat at Yü Hsien, in modern Honan⁽¹⁰⁾. The current Bamboo Books locates Ch'i at a place called 夏邑 Hsia I, which Hsü places at Yü Hsien⁽¹¹⁾. Both the genuine and the current Bamboo Books say that his son, T'ai K'ang, ruled from 斟鄩 Chên Hsün⁽¹²⁾. One opinion locates this place near the modern 鞏 Kung Hsien in Honan, close to the junction of the Lo with the Yellow River⁽¹³⁾; according to another it was far to the east, in the region of the modern 平度 P'ing Tu Hsien in the Shantung peninsula⁽¹⁴⁾. According to tradition T'ai K'ang was a degenerate ruler and was displaced by a rebel, 羿 I⁽¹⁵⁾. Accounts vary as to when this I usurped the throne, but the two texts of the Bamboo Books agree in locating him, too, at Chên Hsün⁽¹⁶⁾. The younger brother of T'ai K'ang, Chung K'ang, also had his capital there according to the current Bamboo Books⁽¹⁷⁾. With the varying accounts of the rebellions involving this sovereign and his successor it is not necessary to concern ourselves here save to note the locations of

6. *Ti Ming Tien* 959.
7. *Chu Shu* 3.3a.
8. Cf. *Ti Ming Tien* 1212; *Chu Shu* loc. cit.
9. *Chu Shu* loc. cit.
10. *Shih Chi* 2.19b.6–7.
11. *Chu Shu* 3.6a.
12. *Ku Chu Shu* 2a; *Chu Shu* 3.8a.
13. *Chu Shu* 3.8a.
14. *SSC Tso Chuan* 29.24a.
15. *Tso Chuan* 422.4–8.
16. *Ku Chu Shu* 2a; *Chu Shu* 3.8b.
17. *Chu Shu* 3.8b.

capitals. Hsiang is said to have had his capital at 商 Shang, also called Shang 邱 Ch'iu[18]. This place may be considered either to have been near the modern Shang Ch'iu Hsien in eastern Honan[19], or near the modern Shang Hsien in southeastern Shensi. He is also said to have later lived at 斟灌 Chên Kuan, supposedly located east of the present 壽光 Shou Kuang Hsien in Shantung[20]; whether he ruled from there, or merely sought refuge from his enemies, is uncertain.

The current Bamboo Books says that his son, Shao K'ang, returned to Hsia I[21], but later in his reign moved to 原 Yüan; Yüan was apparently near the present 濟源 Chi Yüan Hsien in north central Honan[22]. His son Chu[23] also made his capital in a place called Yüan, which, whether or not it was the same, was in the same general region[24]. From here he moved to 老邱 Lao Ch'iu[25], which is supposed to be a short distance east of the modern Kaifêng in Honan[26]. The locations of the capitals of the next rulers, Fên[27], Mang[28], Hsieh[29], Pu Chiang[30], and

18. *Ku Chu Shu* 2a; *Chu Shu* 3.10a (cf. ibid. 3.9b).
19. Cf. *Chu Shu* 3.10a.
20. *Ku Chu Shu* 2a; *Chu Shu* 3.10b; *Tso Chuan* 29.24a.
21. *Chu Shu* 3.13a, 14b.
22. *Chu Shu* 3.15b.
23. This is the name given by the current Bamboo Books, *Chu Shu* 3.15b, and apparently considered standard by Wang Kuo-wei, cf. *Ku Chu Shu* 2b. But the same ruler is called Yü in the *Shih Chi*, 2.21b, and by various names elsewhere.
24. *Chu Shu* 3.15b; *Ku Chu Shu* 2b.
25. The second character as it occurs in *Chu Shu* 3.15b is of course merely an old alternative form. Whether or not the *i* determinative is added to the right-hand side of this character makes no difference in either its meaning or its pronunciation.
26. *Ku Chu Shu* 2b; *Chu Shu* 3.15b–16a. Cf. *SSC Tso Chuan* 56.20b.
27. *Ku Chu Shu* 2b; *Chu Shu* 3.16b. The *Shih Chi* 2.21b, calls this ruler Huai.
28. *Ku Chu Shu* 2b; *Chu Shu* 3.17b; *Shih Chi* 2.21b. In one quotation from the genuine Bamboo Books this ruler is named Huang; *Ku Chu Shu* 2b.
29. *Ku Chu Shu* 2b; *Chu Shu* 4a; *Shih Chi* 2.21b.
30. *Ku Chu Shu* 3a; *Chu Shu* 4.2a; *Shih Chi* 2.21b. He was called Chiang in the *Shih Pên*, cf. *Shih Chi* loc. cit.

Chiung[31] are not specified in either version of the Bamboo Books, in the *Shih Chi*, nor by the commentators on these works. Chin[32] lived at 西河 Hsi Hê, according to both texts of the Bamboo Books[33], but it is only vaguely located as "in the west of Chi Chou"[34], which presumably means somewhere in modern Shansi. K'ung Chia is said to have lived in the same place[35]. The location of the capital of the next ruler, Hao[36], is not specified, but the *Tso Chuan* says that his tomb was located at 殽 Yao, in northwestern Honan[37]. Nor are we told the seat of his son Fa[38]. The last Hsia ruler, most commonly referred to as Chieh[39], is said to have ruled again from Chên Hsün[40]. As has been stated, one tradition locates this place in the region of the present P'ing Tu Hsien in eastern Shantung[41], another near the modern Kung Hsien in northern Honan[42]; the Honan region seems to be favored as the residence of Chieh. The current Bamboo Books says that in the thirteenth year of his reign he moved to 河南 Hê nan, "south of the Hê", but what Hê is indicated and exactly where this place was is not clear[43].

31. *Chu Shu* 4.2b; *Shih Chi* 2.21b.
32. Also called Yin Chia in both versions of the Bamboo Books.
33. *Ku Chu Shu* 3a; *Chu Shu* 4.3a.
34. *Chu Shu* 4.3a.
35. By the current Bamboo Books only, *Chu Shu* 4.4a.
36. So called in *Ku Chu Shu* 3a and *Chu Shu* 4.5b. But the *Shih Chi* 2.22a, calls him Kao, and the commentary on the current Bamboo Books gives this as an alternative; see *Chu Shu* 4.5b.
37. *SSC Tso Chuan* 17.12a; quoted in *Shih Chi* 2.22a and *Chu Shu* 4.6a.
The exact location of this place is difficult to determine, cf. *Ti Ming Tien* 1222 under Mien Ch'ih Hsien.
38. Thus called in *Shih Chi* 2.22a, *Ku Chu Shu* 3a, and *Chu Shu* 4.6a. Also called Ching (*Ku Chu Shu* 3a), Hui (loc. cit.) and Fa Hui (*Chu Shu* 4.6a).
39. *Ku Chu Shu* 3b. Also called Kuei (*Chu Shu* 4.6b) and Lü Kuei (*Shih Chi* 2.22a).
40. *Ku Chu Shu* 3b; *Chu Shu* 4.7a.
41. *SSC Tso Chuan* 29.24a.
42. Cf. *Chu Shu* 3.8a, 4.7a.
43. Cf. *Chu Shu* 4.8b and *I Chou Shu, Huang Ch'ing Ching Chieh Hsü Pien* 1032.5a.

From the traditions which have been cited it would appear that the Hsia capital was located some of the time in southern Shansi and some of the time in eastern Shantung, but chiefly in northern Honan. But it is very doubtful that any of these traditions is worthy of much credence. With little exception, the places mentioned have been located by scholars of Han or later date. In many cases they had very little reliable information to go on. They were frequently content to find, in their own day, a place bearing the name mentioned in an ancient document, and at once declare the two identical. Such a practice is indefensible when dealing with a period as remote as the Hsia.

The early Chou period was a time of expansion, of wide diffusion of Chinese culture and the establishment of new states and the building of new towns and cities. In this situation, we should expect that the names of persons and places important in Chinese tradition would be spread far and wide, and attach themselves to places far removed from their original homes. This is exactly what happened, in a similar situation, in North and South America, so that place-names there reproduce the names of places, saints, and heroes which originally belonged to every part of Europe. Similarly, in China, it does not follow that if a city is named Yü it was certainly the place of his birth or residence, nor does the name of Hsia attaching to a district prove, ipso facto, that it was a part of Hsia territory.

Nor does it agree with what we know of early China to suppose that the Hsia rulers could have moved their capitals about with the ease and frequency, and over the great distances, which these traditions take for granted. The Chou rulers, in the early days after the conquest, were very powerful, probably the most powerful rulers China had had up to that time. But while they controlled wide territories, they did not, and probably could not, move their capital about among them at will. They controlled their empire by virtue of the fact that the local rulers were made to value the king's assistance on the one hand and fear his punishments on the other. But if the king had tried to take direct charge of a remote piece of territory abruptly, and settle down on it with his capital, the end of the dynasty would probably have been close at hand. And if the Chous could not do it, it is even less likely that the Hsias could. It is interesting to note that the rapid changes of the capital, moving it over distances of scores of miles with the greatest frequency, which are a striking feature of the Hsia and early Shang traditions, cease abruptly as soon as we approach the historical period, after the middle of Shang times. In all of its more than eight centuries the first fully historic dynasty, the Chou, made only one such move [44]. And that was not, in reality, the moving of a capital but the end of a dynasty. From that time forward the Chou kings were under the "protection", and actually ruled by the sufferance, of the feudal lords who really controlled the district into which they had moved.

Concerning the location of the Hsia state, the most of solid information which can be gleaned from the traditions is the fact that it was generally supposed to have been located in the same general Yellow River valley region which has always been considered the ancestral home of Chinese civilization.

A great many sites showing cultures earlier than the Bronze Age (though not necessarily all earlier in time) have been excavated in various parts of North China during the last fifteen years [45]. But so far none of them has been shown to have any relation to the Hsia dynasty or to any of the figures or events of recorded Chinese history. Andersson wrote, in 1925, after his latest excavation: "Unfortunately nothing has so far been recognized among the furniture of the late Kansu sites which can be regarded as identical with objects of the San Tai. No painted pottery of the prehistoric type has been seen in any historical site, and the few and small metal objects found in my Kansu excavations are so simple and undecorated that they cannot help at present to link up the Kansu finds with early historical times. . . . The earliest dynasty of the Šan Tai, the Hsia, remains entirely legendary as, so far, no archaeological material has been found to support the scanty historical data" [46].

44. From the region of Hsian to Loyang, in 770 B.C.
45. See the following paper.
46. *Arch. Res. in Kansu* 28.

It would be almost impossible definitely to ascribe these sites to the Hsia or any other historical Chinese state or period unless writing of some sort should be found in the excavations. With all the richness of artifacts, remains of dwellings, etc., which have come from the Anyang site, it would still be impossible, in my opinion, to determine with assurance that this was a Shang city if we did not have the inscriptions to tell us so. With the inscriptions we are able to link up the artifacts, designs on carved bones and bronzes, etc., into a structure of proof which is unassailable, and working backward we can show that the culture thus reconstructed has a provable and necessary relation to early Chou history. But without the inscriptions we should lack the prerequisite key. Up to this time in so far as I am aware no writing of any sort has been found in any site in China earlier than the Bronze Age. A very few pictures painted on early pots have some resemblance to certain Chinese pictographs, but they occur singly, in isolation, and there is no indication that they were intended to be writing [47].

Andersson says, "In all our extensive excavations in the prehistoric sites of Kansu we never saw on any pottery vessel or other object the slightest indication of writing, in spite of the fact that our attention was constantly bent in that direction" [48].

Without writing, giving us contemporary records of Hsia times, it would be almost impossible to determine that any site were Hsia, no matter how much the cultural evidences found might agree with what tradition tells us of the Hsia period. For the actual, early traditions of Hsia which we have are almost nil—little more than the bare fact of the existence of a state by that name. This has left the Hsia period as a historical vacuum, a storehouse into which the politicians, philosophers, and pseudo-historians of a later day could pour all of their own ideas, at will, in order to point to them as precedents to justify themselves in doing whatever they wished to do. On the basis of such "traditions" one can prove nothing.

47. Cf. *Arch. Res. in Kansu* 17.
48. Ibid. 30.

Mr. Hsü Chung-shu has put forward the theory that the late Neolithic remains excavated at Yang Shao, in northwestern Honan Province, are those of the Hsia people. He cites various traditions which locate the tomb of a Hsia ruler and the Hsia capital in the general neighborhood of Yang Shao[49]. He points out that in the *Tso Chuan* we find 過 Kuo, 戈 Kê, and 有鬲 Yu Kê mentioned as place names of the ancient Hsia state or dynasty. 鬲 is also pronounced *li*, and is the name of a very ancient type of vessel, with three hollow legs, of which examples have been excavated at Yang Shao. Hsü says that the *li* excavated at Yang Shao all have a single handle, and therefore should properly be called 鬹. He mentions the well-known fact that the *li* form does not appear in Kansu until considerably later, as measured by cultural stages, than we find it in Yang Shao. He cites evidence both as to form and sound of the characters to show that 鬲, 戈, and 過 are closely related and concludes that they are three forms of the same name; from this and the fact that the one-handled *li* is found at Yang Shao he draws the further conclusion that Yang Shao is a Hsia site[50]. He also cites various books to show that tradition links the Hsia state with the making of pottery, and quotes the *Shuo Wên* as saying that the 壺 *hu* is "a round vessel of K'un Wu". Since K'un Wu is often mentioned together with Hsia, Hsü says that "their culture must not have been very different." And since pottery is the most abundant of the remains found at Yang Shao, and not a few vessels which may be called round *hu* are found among them, Hsü concludes that this is further evidence that Yang Shao was a Hsia site[51].

Mr. Hsü's article presents an interesting approach to an important problem, but his conclusions are not wholly convincing. Various sites have been connected by tradition with the Hsias. And there is a time as well as a place factor involved here. As for the identification of the three place names mentioned, which Hsü links with the *li*, this also could operate

49. *Anyang Pao Kao* 533-6.
50. Ibid. 536-9.
51. *Anyang Pao Kao* 539.

equally well for a large number of places, for the *li* was widely distributed over northeastern China in late Neolithic times. Nor is there anything in the evidence concerning the *hu* to force us to fix upon the particular spot at Yang Shao. Least of all is there anything in the fact of the Hsia people having made pottery which can help us to locate them. The making of pottery is a technique of unusually wide distribution.

Mr. Hsü has suggested that Hsia culture was not Chinese culture at all, but barbarian. In support of this he cites the fact that the states of 杞 Ch'i, 鄫 Tsêng, and 越 Yüeh, and the 匈奴 Hsiung Nu, were all said to be decended from scions of Hsia, and all are said to have adhered to barbarian rather than Chinese customs[52]. He recognizes, however, that the cultures of these various peoples, while not like the Chinese, were not mutually identical[53].

Chinese history is full of these genealogies which are traced back to an original Hsia ancestor. They may be compared to the Occidental theorizing which traces each nation back to some Biblical ancestor, or to the lost tribes of Israel. Such legends always grow up to fill the vacuum left by the lack of real knowledge. The Chinese conceived themselves as "the people", human beings in the truest sense of the word, the most intelligent and most cultured of beings. Since the people around them had something remotely resembling their culture, it was only natural to suppose that they had been the fortunate recipients of some Chinese influence at some time in the past. It is probable that some of these stories originated, not with the Chinese, but with the people concerned. In Chou times the circle of Chinese culture was constantly widening, and people who had been considered barbarians became respected members of the Hsia community. They merely followed a world-wide formula in acquiring genealogies—there is no quicker path to respectability. In early or middle Chou times it might have been a little difficult to trace back to a Shang ancestor. But the Hsia was so remote that there could be no embarrassing research into genealogies

52. *Anyang Pao Kao* 540-44.
53. Ibid. 542.

traced to it. Also, it had the lustre of high antiquity, and there must have been an additional halo about the name Hsia since it was still used to represent Chinese culture. Even the Chou conquerors were proud to trace their line to an official of the Hsia period—much as the Romans, coming under the influence of Greek culture, pointed to Aeneas the Trojan as their progenitor.

It is easy to see why the Chinese did not try to contradict these genealogies. They were very flattering to the Chinese. Time after time we read that some Chinese younger son, or official or hero in trouble, flees to live among the barbarian tribes, and is received with the greatest honor and set up as ruler. This immediately implies that the Chinese, as compared with the barbarians about them, were a sort of supermen. But it is easy to see, from the acts and achievements of barbarians which find their way into Chinese history, that this was not always the case. In character, in sagacity, even in learning we sometimes find the barbarian equalling if not surpassing the Chinese, even in accounts written by the Chinese themselves[54]. We do, it is true, find many cases of Chinese fleeing to live among the barbarians in historic times, and they are often treated with great courtesy and consideration. But they are not commonly set up as sovereigns to rule over their hosts[55].

In my opinion the fact of these many genealogies, even of barbarian peoples, being traced back to the Hsia does not at all show that Hsia culture was not Chinese. On the contrary, it goes far to prove the opposite. For such people as the Chous and the kings of Yüeh, anxious to secure a reception for themselves into the Chinese community, would hardly have bothered to advertise their descent from a barbarian state.

Summary

Orthodox Chinese history and Chinese tradition give us a great deal of information about a Hsia dynasty, which preceded the Shang. The *Shu Ching* contains several documents which have been supposed to have been written in Hsia times. Investigation

54. Cf. *Kuo Yü* 17.4a f.
55. Cf. *Tso Chuan* 155.1-8.

shows, however, that these documents could not have been written earlier than the Chou period. The traditions concerning a Hsia dynasty are mentioned very little in any literature as early as the early Chou period, and every reference to them occurs in literature of a highly propagandistic nature. This and other facts warrant the hypothesis that the story of a Hsia dynasty was a part of the political propaganda of the Chous, designed to give precedent and legitimacy to their displacement of the Shang house, and to secure acceptance of their rule by the subject population.

Yet the existence of a Hsia state of some sort was not pure fiction. Even Shang tradition, which denies the story of a Hsia dynasty, affirms that there was a Hsia state. The character *hsia* does not seem to appear on the oracle bones, although a few Chinese scholars have tried to prove that it does appear with the meaning of "summer". At any rate there is no reference in the bone inscriptions to a Hsia state or dynasty. Nor is the character found in the original text of the *I Ching*, nor in early Chou bronze inscriptions. It occurs several times, however, in the *Shu* and the *Shih*, and very frequently in the *Kuo Yü* and *Tso Chuan*. Aside from "summer" its principal meanings are "the Hsia dynasty" and "Chinese". In the *Ch'un Ch'iu* period it was used very commonly to refer to the group of states which possessed full Chinese culture, as distinguished from those which did not.

The evidence warrants us in concluding that while there was not a Hsia dynasty, in the traditional sense, there was a state by this name. And the fact that the term Hsia was later used so persistently to mean "Chinese" and "the Chinese states" in a cultural sense leads us to infer that this state was the leading exponent of Chinese culture in its day. As such it may have exercised political sway over a fairly large territory, and its cultural prestige may have given it a certain hegemony even beyond its proper borders. We have an example of this in the case of the Chou people, whom we know to have admired Shang culture and considered it superior to their own before and even after they conquered the Shangs. In a cultural sense, then, it is perhaps not completely erroneous to look upon Hsia as a Chinese dynasty. The term 三代 *san tai* has perhaps this much basis of truth, that the torch of Chinese culture was passed from Hsia to Shang to Chou.

But this is not at all to say that there is any proved basis to the Hsia dynasty of orthodox history. Thus far its dates, its kings, and its events appear to be wholly legendary. All attempts to link it up with the sites earlier than the Bronze Age which have been excavated in recent years have thus far failed. Even concerning the Hsia state which we know must have existed we have almost no specific facts. As to its location, we can only infer from traditions that it was somewhere in northeastern China, in the general region of the lower Yellow River valley. Various lines of interesting speculation suggest themselves in connection with this state—were its people, for instance, the first possessors, in China, of the technique of casting bronze, and did this give them military and cultural superiority? It may be so. But concerning this and a multitude of similar questions there is not, in the material now available, any evidence whatsoever.

III. WHO WERE THE SHANGS?

In a previous paper it was shown that all of the contemporary evidence concerning the Shang people which we now possess comes from Anyang. It is the purpose of the present paper to investigate the antecedents of the Shang people, to try to determine the background from which they emerge when they first come into our field of vision at the time of their move to Anyang. In order to do this we shall first have to try to determine the approximate date at which they took up their residence there. Some of the evidence on this point is connected with the amount and nature of the culture deposits at Anyang; therefore we must also try to fix the approximate time at which Anyang ceased to be the Shang capital.

1. The Period of Shang Residence at Anyang

We have a number of pieces of inscribed bone which must date from not earlier than the time of Ti I, the next to the last Shang king, who reigned from 1191 to 1155 (according to the conventional chronology used throughout these papers). Three inscriptions speak of 武祖乙 Wu Tsu I[1]. This Wu Tsu I must be the Wu I of history. *Yin Ch'ien Pien* 1.18.1 mentions both him and Wên Wu Ting, who is the T'ai Ting of history as has been shown[2]. And *Yin Ch'ien Pien* 1.10.3 was produced after the time of K'ang Ting (the Kêng Ting of history)[3] since it speaks

1. *Yin Ch'ien Pien* 1.10.3, 1.10.4, and 1.18.1.
2. Cf. p. 12, above, note 23.
3. Among the names of the Shang kings, and indeed in so far as I know in Chinese literature generally, the combination Kêng Ting is a complete anomaly. Both of these characters belong to the ten stems, whereas the practice in combining such characters is that the first shall belong to the ten stems and the second to the twelve branches. But in the names of Shang kings the usual practice is that the first character shall be a relationship term, like Tsu, or an adjective such as Ta, Wên, or K'ang, while the second is one of the ten stems.

Kêng Ting is obviously a misreading for K'ang Ting. This error was very easy to make, for there was never very much difference in

of him as K'ang Tsu Ting (i.e., Grandfather K'ang Ting) and the second generation after Wu I since he is spoken of as Wu Tsu I. We know that this inscription, and others of its sort, could not have been produced by the immediate successor to Wu I. For the *Shih Chi* says that he had a son who came to the throne as T'ai Ting[4], and this is confirmed by the fact that the same inscription which mentions Wu Tsu I mentions Wên Wu Ting (T'ai Ting)[5]. It is certain, then, that pieces of inscribed bone dating from not earlier than the reign of Ti I have been found at Anyang[6]. It has been held that we also have inscriptions from the time of the last Shang king, Ti Hsin, but this is generally considered uncertain[7].

From this, and from the fact that the king is mentioned frequently in such inscriptions, we may deduce that the capital of the Shang state was located at Anyang in the reign of Ti I. There is no reason why these bones should have been taken to the site of this city and buried there at a subsequent date if they had

---

form between the characters *kêng* and *k'ang* on the bones, and sometimes they were so written as to be identical, only the context serving to distinguish (cf. *Yin Ch'ien Pien* 3.2.4 and 1.12.7). The *Shuo Wên*, in its discussion of the character 穅, says that *k'ang* is made up with the character *kêng* as its phonetic.

That K'êng Ting is the Kêng Ting of history and no other is shown, for instance, by an inscription quoted by Lo Chên-yü which places him between Tsu Chia and Wu I (*Yin K'ao Shih*, shang 4a).

4. *Shih Chi* 3.8b.
5. *Yin Ch'ien Pien* 1.18.1. Tung Tso-pin considers this inscription to date from the time of Ti Hsin; see *T'sai Anniv. Vol.*, chart opp. 344. This is perhaps possible, but not proved, since it lacks the character *tsu*.
6. It may be objected that these particular pieces of inscribed bone were not excavated scientifically by the National Research Institute, and therefore that the above statement is false. None of the pieces under immediate discussion was so excavated. But their genuineness has not been called in question, and can be verified by comparison with the finds of the excavators. As for their having been found elsewhere than at Anyang, the possibility is negligible. Such inscriptions have never yet been found, to my knowledge, outside the Anyang area; if they should be they would possess a rarity value which even the peasants, and certainly the dealers, would not fail to capitalize.
7. See second note above.

not been produced there. The inscriptions tally, in various ways which will be mentioned later, with the rich cultural remains excavated on the Anyang site. And in the many thousands of pieces of bone found there we have inscriptions which can be proved to have been written during the reign, probably of every king, certainly of nearly every Shang king between Wu Ting (1324–1266 B.C.) and Ti I. Whether or not we have inscriptions from a time earlier than that of Wu Ting is still a question.

Both texts of the Bamboo Books, and the *Shih Chi*, agree that the Shang capital was moved in the time of Pan Kêng, although they disagree on the place to which it was moved[8]. All three agree that the capital was not again moved until after the time of Wu Ting[9]. If we may deduce, from the continuity of the deposits of bone inscriptions from the time of Wu Ting to the time of Ti I, that the capital was located at Anyang in Wu Ting's day, it then appears from the traditions just cited that when Pan Kêng changed his capital he removed to the site at Anyang. And there is much to support this view. The genuine Bamboo Books, as quoted in a commentary on the *Shih Chi*, said that after Pan Kêng's removal the Shang capital was not again moved until the state was conquered by the Chous[10]. The genuine Bamboo Books also says that Yin, the place to which Pan Kêng moved, is located "thirty *li* south of 鄴 Yeh"[11]. The ancient place of that name was located west or southwest of the present 臨漳 Lin Chang Hsien in the northern tip of Honan[12], which puts the site of Yin almost exactly at the place of the Anyang excavations.

8. *Ku Chu Shu* 5a; *Chu Shu* 5.18a; *Shih Chi* 3.7a.
9. The genuine Bamboo Books says that Pan Kêng, Hsiao Hsin, Hsiao I, and Tsu Kêng (Wu Ting's successor; Wang has not located any entry for Wu Ting himself) all had their capitals at Yin; *Ku Chu Shu* 5ab. The current text locates Pan Kêng, Hsiao Hsin, Hsiao I, Wu Ting, and Tsu Kêng, all at Yin; *Chu Shu* 5.18a, 5.19b, 6.1a, 6.4b. The *Shih Chi* records the move of the capital in the time of Pan Kêng, but mentions no further move through the time of Wu Ting; *Shih Chi* 3.7–8.
10. *Ku Chu Shu* 5a. In a note on this passage, Wang Kuo-wei questions that it was genuinely a part of the original text.
11. *Ku Chu Shu* 5a; *SSC Shang Shu* 9.1b.1.
12. See *Ti Ming Tien* 1247.

Contrary to this, the *Shih Chi* says that in the time of Pan Kêng the Shang capital was located north of the Hê, presumably the Yellow River, and that he returned the capital to the south of the Hê, to the ancient residence of T'ang the Successful[13]. The *Shih Chi* and the current Bamboo Books say that Wu I (1198–1195 B.C.) moved back to the north of the Hê[14]. The Yellow River is a migratory stream, and there is some uncertainty as to where it ran in late Shang times. But it has never, I believe, run north of Anyang, and general opinion agrees in placing it to the south at that time. Furthermore, we know from the deposits of oracle bones that the Shang people must have been at Anyang after the time of Wu I. Therefore, if we accept the account of the *Shih Chi*, the Anyang site could hardly have been the Shang capital, at the most, for more than some seventy-odd years, from 1198 down to the conquest in 1122 B.C.

Those who suppose this to be the case hold that the inscribed bones from previous periods, which have been excavated at Anyang, were carried to that spot when the capital was moved there[15]. On its surface this seems plausible enough, but there are several reasons for serious doubt of it. Least important is the literary evidence. The genuine Bamboo Books not only says that the Shang capital was not moved from the time of Pan Kêng to the end of Shang times, but also that "Pan Kêng... moved to ... Yin"[16]. As this passage is quoted in two separate places by two different commentaries on the *Shih Chi* it reads 殷虛 Yin Hsü instead of Yin[17]. The *Hsiang Yü Pên Chi* says explicitly that Yin Hsü was located on the Huan River, and one commentator places it in the Anyang district[18]. This evidence is definite enough if we can depend on it. But since the Bamboo Books is not, after all, a great deal more ancient than the *Shih*

13. *Shih Chi* 3.7a.
14. Ibid. 3.8b; *Chu Shu* 6.7b.
15. Cf. W. P. Yetts in the *Journal of the Royal Asiatic Society*, London (referred to hereafter as *JRAS*) 1933, p. 684.
16. *Ku Chu Shu* 5a.
17. *Shih Chi* 3.1a.3, 7.10b.5.
18. Ibid. 7.10b.2–3.

Chi, and since the name Yin is not found in the oracle bones, it can not be considered conclusive.

After Wu I there were three more Shang kings. Many believe, on the basis of a statement in the *Ti Wang Shih Chi*[19], that Ti I moved his capital to Ch'ao Kê; if he did, this means that only two kings died while the capital was at Anyang. But if, as the genuine Bamboo Books says, the capital was not moved, then four kings might have died there, supposing that Anyang was the capital only from the time of Wu I on. But we have already seen that four tombs of tremendous size have been excavated at Anyang, and another is known, which from their size and the objects found in them are almost certainly royal[20]. This means, beyond much doubt, that five Shang kings were buried within a few minutes walk of the capital at Anyang. All five of these tombs were found within a year's time, and there may be still more in the vicinity. This alone seems to make the theory that the capital was moved in the time of Wu I very dubious.

Even more important is the manner in which the inscribed bones from the earliest certain period, that of Wu Ting, have been found. They are surprisingly numerous, making up perhaps a third of the total number we have[21]. If they had been carried to Anyang, when the capital was moved there at a late date, we ought to find them more or less all together. But they are not so. Nor is this distribution to be attributed to confusion when the city was sacked and the archives scattered, or to dispersal by a flood as was first suggested. In many places at least these divination records were apparently stored, as is shown by the fact that those found together are more or less homogeneous in time, and sometimes even in orderly arrangement as they lie in the ground[22]. Seven large tortoise shells found in 1934 in an outlying dwelling site at Hou Chia Chuang, just north of the Huan River, had evidently been stored, for they lay together like

19. Quoted in *Chu Shu* 6.11b.7.
20. See page 18 above.
21. Cf. *Ts'ai Anniv. Vol.* 345.
22. See *Anyang Pao Kao* 424.

so many leaves of a book, and had been pressed so tightly that the characters on the front of one were found standing out in relief on the back of that against which it had lain.

The inscriptions from the time of Wu Ting had evidently been stored in numerous places, not in one [23]. Of the five areas in which the National Research Institute has excavated, four have yielded bones of this period. This distribution is rivalled only by that of the second period, and is twice as great as that of any other [24]. It is not plausible to suppose that if these inscriptions had been hoarded together, as royal archives, and moved in such large numbers to the site at Anyang, they would have subsequently been distributed so widely. The only solution to the problem is that the capital was at Anyang all the time, just as the genuine Bamboo Books tells us it was.

Speaking strictly, we have no proof that the capital was moved to Anyang in the time of Pan Kêng. The Bamboo Books and the *Pan Kêng* of the *Shu Ching* apparently agree in saying that it was. But the *Pan Kêng* is a relatively late book, as has been shown, and both of these documents probably rest on the same tradition. That tradition is none too reliable in such matters has just been shown, in the case of the conflict between the genuine Bamboo Books and the *Shih Chi* on the date of the move to Anyang. It might be argued, then, that the Shang capital may have been located at Anyang much earlier than the time of Pan Kêng. But the bone inscriptions give some support to tradition on this point. Whether we have any inscriptions earlier than those of the time of Wu Ting is a question; it has been held that we have a few going back as far as the time of Pan Kêng, but proof of this has not yet been presented. At all events, while the names of Shang kings and ancestors running many generations back of Pan Kêng have been identified on the bones, no inscription produced at a time earlier than that of Wu Ting has been generally accepted as such, and no one has even seriously claimed that we have inscriptions produced earlier than the time of Pan Kêng. With so many scholars working on this material

23. Cf. *Ts'ai Anniv. Vol.* 351-62.
24. *Ts'ai Anniv. Vol.* 362.

the claim would probably have been made if any basis for it existed.

It is highly improbable that the earliest divination bones which we possess are the earliest which the Shang people produced. The technique of divination, which represents a great advance over that of the uninscribed divination bones found in Neolithic remains in Shantung[25], changes little if at all from the time of Wu Ting on. There are a few changes in the phraseology of the inscriptions, but nothing basic, save such matters as the names of the diviners not being given in the later time. Furthermore, the technique of carving the characters on the bone had been well developed in the time of Wu Ting, for the inscriptions from this period are among the best. Carving characters on such bone is very difficult, even with good modern tools, as I know from having tried it. All these things indicate that the technique had a considerable history before our earliest bones were produced. But the beginning of the reign of Wu Ting[26] is only seventy-seven years after the accession of Pan Kêng[27]. Since our earliest bones are found sometime within this period, since these people must have been producing bones of this sort previous to this time[28], and since (as we have bones from every subsequent period) there is no reason why earlier bones should have disappeared if they had been produced at Anyang, we are justified in concluding that the Shang people had removed to Anyang at about this time. And this is just what tradition tells us they did do.

We may fairly say, then, that Chinese history begins with the

25. See pages 176–177 below.
26. In my opinion virtually the whole of the reign of Wu Ting must be represented in the bones we have, and not merely the latter part, because they are exceedingly numerous.
27. According to the traditional chronology Pan Kêng acceded in 1401, Wu Ting in 1324.
28. It would hardly do to explain away a gap by saying that the Shangs had merely ceased to use the divination technique for awhile and then happened to take it up again. It played a completely vital part in their lives, and could hardly have been laid down and taken up again like a garment.

Shang people living at Anyang in the fourteenth century B.C. From that time forward, while our record is very sketchy in some places and has gaps in others, we never completely lose sight of the history of the Chinese people and Chinese culture. But from that time back we know almost nothing which can be linked, with certainty, to Chinese history.

Who were these earliest Chinese we know? What was their origin? To answer this question in so far as it can be answered at this time let us divide it into three parts, having to do with the racial origin, the geographic origin, and the cultural origin of the Shang people.

2. Racial Origins

Until late in 1934 the scholars of the National Research Institute had not found a single skeleton at Anyang which they felt justified in assigning definitely to Shang times. Most of the skeletons found were plainly from later graves. As has been mentioned, most of their work had been limited to excavating dwelling sites, while the tombs were opened by those looking for bronzes to sell. The result is that the excavators frequently heard, through their workmen, of skeletons which were no doubt probably Shang being dug up and thrown away in pieces, while they themselves were unable to excavate even one of the large tombs rich in bronzes and other indubitable evidences of Shang date. They had, however, found five skeletons which, they agreed, must be placed not far from Shang times, if not in them [1]. Four of these, recorded in their reports as 18.2, 18.3, 18.4, and 18.5, were excavated in October 1929 [2]. One was excavated at a point stated to be three or four *li* due west of the main site, in April, 1931 [3]. Very little specific data are given concerning the finding of the latter individual, save that the locality in which it was found was characterized by artifacts, such as divination bone and tortoise shell (without characters), very

1. *Anyang Pao Kao* 447–80.
2. Ibid. 449–51, 461.
3. Ibid. 568, 627–8.

similar to those found in the Shang capital, and that it was buried facing downward[4].

Two of these skeletons, 18.3 and 18.4, I believe are indicated by the published reports to be very probably Shang. There is a distinct probability that 18.2 is also. My reasons for this belief are several.

In the first place these three burials, together with the one located to the west of the main site, mentioned above, have in common the fact that the dead were placed in a very peculiar position, that is, prone. When the excavators found the first such skeleton they were greatly surprised, they report, and immediately started inquiries as to the existence of parallels to this discovery. They wrote to Mr. Lodge, Curator of the Freer Gallery, who replied that within his knowledge and in so far as he could learn from archeologists and anthropologists in Washington the prone burial had not been previously found anywhere else in the world[5]. A Kansu grave found by Andersson, from his most recent culture, was reported to be a prone burial, but examination of the report showed that it was impossible to determine whether it really duplicated the Anyang find or not. The upshot of the inquiry seemed to be that this burial position had at least no clearly proved parallels anywhere[6]. And since this is a type of burial not found in such historic Chinese interments as are known, or in Neolithic or later prehistoric graves in China (with the one possible exception mentioned), it follows that this common factor indicates that the three skeletons probably belong to the same period.

Shang burials found late in 1934 and early in 1935 prove beyond question, according to Liang Ssŭ-yung, that prone burial was practiced by the Shangs, not only in the case of sacrificial victims but also of persons who appear to have been accorded honorable burial. Forty-one cases of the latter alone had been excavated

4. Loc. cit.
5. *Anyang Pao Kao* 448.
6. Loc. cit. But according to Mr. Bishop the sweeper caste in India uses prone burial at present, to keep the ghost from walking.

up to May 2, 1935. Prone burial was not, however, the universal practice in Shang times[7].

No trace of any coffin was found with these skeletons. Dr. Li Chi argues that there could not have been a coffin with 18.4, since the leg of a goat[8] (presumably placed there as food for the dead) was so close to the skull, and in such position, that it could not have been fitted inside a coffin nor could it have lain outside and still left room for a coffin between it and the skull[9]. But although no remains of coffin wood were found, the pattern of matting was found below the hand of 18.4[10]. From this it is argued that the bodies were wrapped in matting before interment, thus corresponding to the character 葬 *tsang*, "to inter", which shows the dead surrounded by grasses[11]. If so, this is a factor pointing toward Shang date. For Shang weapons dug up

7. Verbal communication from Liang Ssǔ-yung at Anyang, May 2, 1935.
8. For authority for this identification cf. *Anyang Pao Kao* 450, footnote.
9. It is a question, in fact, how early coffins were used in China at all. The excavators of the National Research Institute have found none, in all the great numbers of burials they have discovered up to this time. The early Chou tombs at Hsün Hsien show no trace of a coffin, but only a wooden tomb chamber about three meters long by two meters wide (verbal communication from Mr. Kuo Pao-chün at Kaifêng, May 6, 1935). And even of the much later Chou burial with which were associated the famous Hsin Chêng bronzes, Bishop says: "I noted particularly, while getting out the mandible, that there was no trace of anything suggesting a coffin" (*Chinese Social and Political Science Review*, 1924, 8.2.85). On the other hand, Mr. Tung Tso-pin told me, at Anyang on April 25, 1934, that word had come to him through his workmen that people of the countryside, in digging up large tombs, had on one or more occasions come upon nails spaced in orderly rows so that they must represent the remains of a coffin. If, as was supposed, Shang bronzes were found in connection with this, then it is possible that the coffin was sometimes used in the Shang period. But it is noteworthy that at least one undisturbed tomb of what must have been a person of some importance, since it contained a great number of bronzes, was excavated in 1934, but contained no coffin.
10. *Anyang Pao Kao* 450, 460–461. Note illustration on 460.
11. Ibid. 460–461.

at Anyang which come on the antique market very commonly have matting around them, and judging from the illustration of that found on the skeleton[12] the matting is virtually the same. From the designs found on them the weapons can often be determined to be Shang beyond doubt. I have recently seen a knife, identical in form with Shang pieces scientifically excavated, in the hands of a Peiping dealer, which had first been covered with matting and then with cloth laid over that; the pattern and apparently some of the original material of both cloth and matting were remarkably well preserved[13]. Since we know that the Shang people frequently wrapped matting around objects to be buried with the dead, it is not unreasonable to suppose that they may have prepared their dead for burial in a similar way.

One of the prone burials, 18.2, is said to have had "the whole body covered with red pigment"[14]. This does not, however, take it outside the sphere of Chinese culture. Such deposition of red pigment is, of course, found in many burials of Paleolithic and Neolithic age in Europe. In the numerous finds of remains dated from before and during the Bronze and Iron Ages in Kansu, made by Andersson, "from every major site in which human skeletal remains were recovered, one or more of the graves contained bones which were colored with a bright red pigment"[15]. Red pigment was found by Bishop next to human bones in the interment associated with the well known Hsin Chêng bronzes, dating from late Chou times[16].

The chief links connecting these three skeletons with Shang culture are five. The first, and least important, is what is described as "a small piece of fire-marked divination bone"[17].

12. Cf. ibid. 460.
13. See "On Shang Bronze", Plate VI.
14. *Anyang Pao Kao*, 449, 461.
15. Black, "A Note on the Physical Characters of the Prehistoric Kansu Race", *Arch. Res. in Kansu*, 55.
16. Carl W. Bishop, "The Bronzes of Hsin-Cheng Hsien", in the *Chinese Social and Political Science Review*, 1924, 8.2.84–86. This pigment was said to be oxide of iron.
17. *Anyang Pao Kao* 450.

Presumably this was similar to the divination bones found in the Shang culture stratum, and like ninety per cent of them lacked characters[18]. It is of only slight value for dating, however, since we know from the *Shih Chi* and other sources that the practice of divination in a manner similar, at least, to that used in Shang times, persisted until long after that period[19], and on the other hand we have no data by which to fix the time when this practice commenced.

The other four of these criteria are bronzes, two weapons of the type called 戈 *kê*[20] and two vessels, a 爵 *chüeh* and a 觚 *ku*[21].

18. Cf. ibid. 575.
19. Cf. *Shih Chi* 128.
20. There has been a great deal of discussion among Chinese scholars as to whether weapons of this type should be called *kê* or 瞿 *ch'ü*. The supposed distinction comes in connection with the 胡 *hu*, that projection made of bronze which runs down along the handle approximately at right angles to the blade, strengthening the connection of the blade with the handle. Only those weapons of this type which have *hu* may properly be called *kê*, according to certain scholars; all others must be called *ch'ü*. Cf. Li Chi's summary of this discussion, *Anyang Pao Kao* 466–8.

It has long been my opinion that the weapons without the *hu* are called *kê* with as good, and if anything better right, than are those with it, for the weapons first called by that name did not, I believe, have the *hu*. In recent years I have seen a very large number, probably running into the hundreds, of weapons of this type which were dug up at Anyang and which there is good reason to believe are Shang (see text below). It is typical of these weapons that they do not have the *hu* in the proper sense of the word, and it is agreed among dealers in antique bronzes that the *hu* is for the most part a feature of post-Shang weapons. In *Anyang Pao Kao* between pages 480 and 481, in plates 5, 6, 7, and 8 (in the last only no. 6), eleven weapons of the types under discussion are reproduced, all of which are believed to emanate from Anyang. Three of these were excavated by the National Research Institute (5.2, 3; 7), seven were bought at Anyang, and one is reproduced from another work as having been obtained from Anyang. Of the eleven weapons, only one has a *hu* (5.4). But the whole shape of this weapon is distinctly different from the others pictured, and to my eye it looks undoubtedly late. The two edges of the blade run almost parallel for some distance, in contrast to the almost triangular shape of the typical Anyang *kê*. Furthermore, the blade is set at an angle of one hundred

During the last several years I have had the opportunity of examining some hundreds of bronze vessels and weapons, in public and private collections and in the hands of dealers, which there is good reason to believe to date from the Shang period. I have made comparisons of their designs and inscriptions with the dated inscriptions of the Shang oracle bones, and discussed them in many informal conferences with Chinese experts and Occidental connoisseurs. As a result of this study I believe that I am able to distinguish bronzes which fall into certain well-defined Shang types. The coup de grâce has finally been dealt to the contention of some non-Chinese connoisseurs that there are no provably Shang bronzes. At the end of the autumn sea-

---

five degrees to the handle. In the typical Anyang kê, proved by its pattern, etc., to be Shang, I have rarely observed more than a ninety-five degree angle here, and I believe that the rule is ninety degrees or less. A large number of weapons of this type were excavated from Shang tombs in May, 1935. They have not yet been studied, but according to Mr. Liang Ssǔ-yung the hu, if present, was quite short (verbal communication of July 1, 1935).

But the ancestral form of the character kê is very common on the oracle bones; cf. *Chia Ku Wên Pien* 12.12a. Where it occurs as a separate character it is difficult to determine its identity with absolute certainty from the context, but in combination as in 伐 *fa* and other characters we have it unmistakably scores of times (cf. *Chia Ku Wên Pien* 8.4–6; *Yin Ch'ien Pien* 6.20.3, etc.). The forms in which it occurs on the oracle bones are very like, and in some cases virtually identical with, the forms found on bronzes, which in turn are unquestionably the character kê (cf. *Chin Wên Pien* 12.15a, appendix 15a). We have, therefore, a series of graphic forms which runs from the modern character kê directly back to a form of this character widely used in Shang times. But these written forms do not indicate that the weapon had a hu; we could hardly expect so much detail, however, in pictographs. Far more important is the fact that the considerable number of Shang weapons examined by me indicate the hu to have been very rare if not non-existent until late in Shang times, while the character kê was commonly used in the bone inscriptions to designate weapons of this type. Therefore I believe that it is correct to call weapons without the hu, kê.

21. These four bronzes are illustrated in *Anyang Pao Kao*, following page 480, plates 5.3, 7, 9, 11, and 15.1–2.

son of excavation in 1934 the National Research Institute opened several tombs at Hou Chia Chuang, north of the Huan River and some five *li* west and north of the main site. Here, together with highly decorated pottery and other artifacts typical and only typical of the Shang culture stratum at Anyang, were found a number of fine bronze vessels. None of this material has yet been published, and I am not at liberty to describe the finds in detail. But through the courtesy of Mr. Liang Ssǔ-yung, who had charge of this excavation, I had the privilege of examining the bronzes thoroughly in Peiping on February 18 and again on February 21, 1935. All of these bronzes were of the type which those of us who have been studying them in Peiping have been calling "Shang". Anyone of us would have classified any of the pieces as "Shang bronze from Anyang", no matter where or under what circumstances it had been shown to him. There is astonishing variety in the decoration and design, but a certain characteristic style runs through all of it which, once thoroughly apprehended, is not forgotten. The same style is found in additional bronzes excavated in the spring of 1935, which I had the privilege of examining on a visit to Anyang on May 2, 1935.

The *kê* associated with skeleton 18.2[22] is of the "Anyang type". Such weapons come on the market very frequently as having been dug up by grave robbers at Anyang, and some of them have decoration which it is possible to connect definitely with the Shang cultural complex. This *kê* appears from the illustration to be undecorated, however, which makes it more difficult to date with any certainty. But since the shape is like that of Shang weapons, and since burial 18.2 shares the prone position with 18.3 and 18.4 which have more definitely Shang artifacts, I believe that there is a very distinct possibility that 18.2 is a Shang burial. A very similar *kê*[23] was found associated with burial 18.5, which was found directly over burial 18.2. Of great interest is the fact that while the lower burial, 18.2,

22. See *Anyang Pao Kao* following 480, plate 5.3.
23. Cf. *Anyang Pao Kao* following p. 480, plate 5.2.

was prone, the upper one, 18.5, was supine[24]. This may indicate a time sequence in the two methods of burial.

With burial 18.4 there were found the traces of matting which have been mentioned and a *chüeh* and a *ku*. The *chüeh* is apparently without decoration[25]. Its shape, however, is similar to that of a large number of *chüeh* which come from Anyang and which are indicated by their designs and inscriptions (where these exist) to be Shang. The *ku* was broken in two pieces when found[26] but fortunately has a good deal of decoration in low relief[27]. Rubbings of this decoration have been published in the reports of excavation. For comparison a photograph of a clay bronze mold excavated in 1929 in the Shang culture stratum at Anyang is published with them[28]. The resemblance between the patterns is very considerable, although the mold illustrated was probably intended for the casting of a vessel of finer quality and a little more careful workmanship than the *ku* associated with burial 18.4. On one point there can be no question. The pattern on this *ku* is Shang, in spirit and in details of treatment. Whether it is Shang in date is a question to be discussed later. But certainly it belongs to a definite Shang type.

Together with burial 18.3 a piece of "fire-marked divination bone" and a bronze *kê* were found. As has been said, the mere finding of a piece of divination bone, if it lacks characters, can not be used to fix a date. But the *kê* in question is decorated with a dragon in low relief which is in typical Shang style[29]. The same sort of dragon is found on bone hairpins as well as weapons which come from Anyang. A number of *kê* of this same shape with the same decoration have come onto the market from Anyang; they range from small and very common ones to large handsome pieces, nearly two feet long, with this same design set with a mosaic of turquoise.

24. Cf. *Anyang Pao Kao* 462. The depth of these burials from the present surface was 2.6 meters and 2.95 meters respectively.
25. See ibid. following 480, plate 9.
26. *Anyang Pao Kao* 451.
27. Cf. ibid. after 480, plates 11 and 15.1–2.
28. Cf. *Anyang Pao Kao* following 480, plate 15.3.
29. Cf. *Anyang Pao Kao* following 480, plate 7.

In my opinion the *ku* associated with burial 18.4 and the *kê* associated with 18.3 are definitely of Shang type, and it is on this basis that I think that these two skeletons are probably those of Shang men. But this does not necessarily mean that they date from the Shang period. We have no reason to suppose that the Shang technique of bronze casting and decoration ceased abruptly with the Chou conquest, although it is probable that it underwent a decided decline in quantity and quality; the reduction of the Shang people to a state of subjection would normally entail this[30]. Nor do we know enough about the history of the Anyang site to be able to say definitely whether Shang people were or were not living in this area after the conquest.

Officials of the National Research Institute hesitated, with scholarly caution, to assign these burials to Shang times, chiefly because of the location of burial 18.4. This, they calculated would have been in the very city of the living in Shang times[31]. Also it is said that this grave was located in the very stratum of earth which is considered to be the Shang culture stratum, so that the burial must have been impossibly shallow if it was made in Shang times[32]. But the problems of stratification at Anyang are very complex. A single burial inside the city might possibly have occurred. Furthermore, the site at Anyang was occupied during something like two centuries, and it is by no means impossible that burial 18.4 occurred at a time when the inhabited district had not yet taken in its neighborhood. The location of burials 18.2 and 18.3 was felt by the excavators to be not unappropriate for graves made in Shang times[33].

These questions leave us with uncertainty. But on one point we may be sure. Bronze ceremonial vessels and their decoration, and the dragon (which appears in the decoration of the *kê* associated with burial 18.3) have definite religious asso-

30. My examination of bronzes excavated from 衛 tombs, at Kaifêng on May 4, 1935, causes me to believe that such a degeneration did take place very rapidly.
31. *Anyang Pao Kao* 451.
32. Ibid. 458.
33. Ibid. 451.

ciations. And when we find such things, of typical Shang style, carefully laid with men who were apparently given honorable burial, in graves at Anyang, it is highly probable that the people buried in those graves were Shang people, whether they were buried before or shortly after the Chou conquest. Therefore skeletons 18.3 and 18.4 are probably, and skeleton 18.2 is quite possibly, Shang skeletal material. These skeletons vary in their states of preservation; unfortunately no complete data on them has been published as yet. But the incisors of skeleton 18.4 are said to be definitely "shovel-shaped", indicating that the individual belonged to the Mongoloid division of mankind [34].

Further evidence that the Shangs were probably a Mongoloid people comes from the form in which they represent the eye. Whether in decorative carving on bone or stone, in the designs on bronzes, or in the various characters in which the pictograph of an eye occurs on the oracle bones [35], it is almost unvaryingly a "slanting" eye, with the inner corner drawn down by the manner of attachment of the eyelid peculiar to the Mongoloid peoples.

This agrees precisely with what we should expect a priori. The late Davidson Black summed up his study of a large number of skeletons from various Neolithic burials in China as follows: "I have already shown in the report on the Sha Kuo T'un and Yang Shao remains (loc. cit. supra) that the people there represented appear to conform to a physical type closely similar to that of the modern inhabitants of these regions and which I have termed North Chinese. If this be true it follows that the proto-Chinese Yang Shao and Sha Kuo T'un peoples are in general physical type similar to those of the Kansu prehistoric sites since both broadly conform to the modern type termed North Chinese or Homo Asiaticus proprius" [36].

34. Ibid. 451, 454.
35. Cf. *Chia Pien* 4.1–2, etc.
36. *Arch. Res. in Kansu* 54.

In a more recent publication based on further study (*A Study of Kansu and Honan Aeneolithic Skulls and Specimens from Later Kansu Prehistoric Sites in Comparison with North China and Other Recent Crania*, Part 1, *On Measurement and Identification, Palaeontologia*

The isolated burials which have been described are of interest, but they would hardly allow us to draw any very definite conclusions with regard to the physical type of the Shang people as a whole. Fortunately the government excavators located a veritable Shang cemetery in the fall of 1934, a short distance north of the Huan River, northeast of the village of Hou Chia Chuang. Up to May 2, 1935, more than three hundred tombs had been scientifically excavated. Many hundreds of skeletons, many of them excellently preserved, were first photographed in situ and then skilfully removed and treated so as to remain intact awaiting expert study.

That these burials date from Shang times is proved by a great variety of criteria. No inscribed oracle bones were found with

---

Sinica, Series D, Vol. 6, Fasc. 1; Peiping, 1928, 81) he concluded: "As a result of the foregoing investigation into the group measurements and form relations of the Honan and Kansu prehistoric crania in comparison with recent North China material, it would seem to be established beyond any reasonable doubt that the prehistoric populations were essentially Oriental in physical character. Further, the resemblances between these prehistoric and recent North China populations would appear to be such that the term 'proto-Chinese' may with some propriety be applied to the former." Cf. also Black, *The Human Skeletal Remains from the Sha Kuo T"un Cave Deposit in Comparison with those from Yang Shao Tsun and with Recent North China Skeletal Material* (*Palaeontologia Sinica*, Series D, Vol. 1, Fasc. 3; Peking, 1925), 98.

In *Arch. Res. in Kansu*, 54–55, Black mentioned three skulls from early Kansu sites which he designated as "Type X", possessing characteristics which might indicate that they were "due to a mixture of western and proto-Chinese strains". But in *A Study of Kansu and Honan Aenoelithic Skulls* . . . , 5, he said, "I am now convinced that the skulls tentatively referred to as 'Type X' do not constitute a distinct sub-type and should be included as normal variations within the Aeneolithic series. The skulls in question certainly differ from the majority of that series in respect to the degree of their facial flatness but the degree of this difference seems to fall well within the range of the normal variability of this character as seen among the specimens of my recent North China skull series of known age, sex, locality and race."

them—apparently they were not buried with the dead—and the writing found was limited to inscriptions of a single character on some three bronze vessels, and a longer inscription on the handle of a fragment of a vessel beautifully cut out of marble; the characters on the latter were like those found on the oracle bones. But it is not inscriptions but other artifacts which chiefly serve to date these finds. Bronze vessels found correspond, in their patterns, to the bronze molds found with the oracle bones in the dwelling site. Bronze knives and other utensils duplicate, in type, examples found in the dated city. Elaborately decorated white pottery vessels, most distinctive in their designs, are virtually identical with those which have been excavated in association with bones bearing datable inscriptions. The sculptures found in the great, probably royal tombs, show a close kinship of design with the Shang bronzes, and the patterns carved on a few pieces of inscribed bone.

Further evidence of Shang date is furnished by the occurrence of a great number of headless skeletons, evidently those of the victims of human sacrifice. We have long known, from the oracle bones, that the Shang people made a practice of sacrificing human beings by decapitation[37], and now, in 1934 and 1935, the skeletons of more than one thousand of such victims have been excavated[38].

This skeletal material has not yet been subjected to thorough examination, since it is only a matter of months since the first certainly Shang skeleton was discovered. When it has been studied exhaustively, we may expect to have a very adequate idea of the physical character of the Shang people. It must be remembered, however, that we can not be sure that all of these skeletons belonged to Shang men. We have good reason to believe, in fact, that the sacrificial victims were probably captives of war; this is indicated by the oracle bones[39]. But some of them undoubtedly did belong to Shang individuals of the domi-

37. See pages 214–217 below.
38. Verbal communication from Liang Ssŭ-yung, July 1, 1935.
39. This point will be dealt with further in a future paper on human sacrifice.

nant class, since they were buried with a profusion of bronzes and other costly objects.

Mr. Liang Ssŭ-yung has kindly acquainted me with the results of his preliminary examination of the teeth of a small number of representative skulls. They were selected to include each locality from which skeletal material was procured, and each type of individual, sacrificial victims, persons accorded honorable and even sumptuous burial, etc. He found that in every case the incisors were "shovel-shaped", indicating that the individuals were Mongoloid.

At the present moment, with so much pending, it would of course be unwise to attempt to draw more than tentative conclusions. Yet it is not without significance that all of the materials so far studied indicate that the inhabitants of north China, from the earliest Neolithic period we know down to the present time, have been essentially similar in racial characteristics. In so far as our present information goes the Shang people appear at least to have been Mongoloid, so that we may expect that further study will show them to fit into that sequence. There is nothing in the skeletal material so far studied to support the theory, sometimes advanced, that the bronze using aristocrats of the Chinese Bronze Age were an intrusive race from the west. On the contrary, the hypothesis which at present seems most plausible is that the Shang people, of the ruling class as well as their slaves and captives, were of the same general racial stock as the Neolithic inhabitants of north China.

3. Geographical Origins

So much for the racial origin of the Shang people. What of their geographical origin? No more than a decade or two ago it was thought that man might be a comparative newcomer in China, since little trace of human beings earlier than late Neolithic man had been found in China proper. But in 1926 two teeth of what was believed to be a type of human being were found in the deposits of the Chou K'ou Tien cave, some fifty kilometers southwest of Peiping, associated with a fauna said to be "not younger than the earliest part of the Pleistocene age"[1]. They attracted widespread attention in scientific circles, and when the discovery of another tooth made their human character certain the name of Peking Man was given to the find. The true nature and place of this type in relation to the human species were subjects of debate for several years. As a result of subsequent discoveries in the same cave a number of teeth, several jaws, several fragmentary and two complete skulls of this type of man are now known. Various characteristics, including the apelike form of the lower jaw, have caused this to be accepted by scientists as one of the very earliest of all known hominids, called *Sinanthropus pekinensis*. Associated with these skeletal remains there were charred wood and burnt bone, thought to show that *Sinanthropus* used fire, and pieces of stone which have been accepted by authorities as manufactured stone implements[2]. From the point of view of the antiquity of human remains, then, China has virtually as good a claim to be the oldest known home of the people now living there as any other place.

There has been much debate on the question of whether *Sinanthropus* is or is not an ancestor of modern man; many have held that he is not, but rather represents an early offshoot from the same family tree[3]. But Professor Franz Weidenreich, successor of the late Davidson Black at the Cenozoic Research Laboratory of the Geological Survey of China, has recently announced that his researches lead him to believe, not only that "Sinanthropus is the ancestor of recent man"[4], but also that the evidence "indicates direct genetic relations between Sinanthropus and the Mongolian group of recent mankind"[5]. This state-

1. *Children of the Yellow Earth*, by J. Gunnar Andersson (London, 1934), 102–103.
2. For a general, non-technical account of these discoveries see ibid. 94–126.
3. Cf. C. W. Bishop, *Man from the Farthest Past*, Smithsonian Scientific Series, vol. 7., Washington, 1930, p. 182, and Keith's chart reproduced in *Children of the Yellow Earth* 119.
4. Weidenreich, Franz, "The Sinanthropus Population of Choukoutien (Locality 1) with a Preliminary Report on New Discoveries", *Bull. of the Geol. Soc. of China*, 1935, 14.435.
5. Ibid. 438.

ment is based not only on the occurrence of shovel-shaped incisors in *Sinanthropus*, but also on certain "hyperstoses" or thickenings of the jaw, which are marked and striking. Professor Weidenreich was kind enough to show me the materials and explain his findings, in Peking; they seem quite convincing. Since he dates *Sinanthropus* as having lived about five hundred thousand years ago, this places the residence of the ancestors of the modern north Chinese in China at a date so remote that the question of whether they lived elsewhere previously becomes of little more than academic interest. A migration of ancestors of *Sinanthropus* to the Chinese area from outside can hardly be held to have brought in enough of alien culture to give a decidedly foreign tinge to Chinese civilization.

As against this, it is not yet certain that men have lived in China continuously from the time of *Sinanthropus* to the present. Until a short time ago, the very existence of Paleolithic man in the Chinese area was considered dubious. But Paleolithic implements resembling those of the Mousterian and Aurignacian period in Europe were found in Mongolia by the French Fathers Licent and Teilhard de Chardin. They were associated with animals, many of them belonging to species now extinct, typical of the Pleistocene age[6]. Still more recently, in 1929, Teilhard de Chardin and Young carried on investigations which allowed them to conclude that "As a result of these last archeologic finds, it is proved that, not only the N. Kansu and the Ordos border, but also the whole Huang Ho valley between Shansi and Shensi, were inhabited during Paleolithic times"[7]. But while a large number of utensils and even charcoal from campfires believed to have been made by Paleolithic man have been found, none of his skeletal remains have yet come to light in this area, with the

6. Cf. *Children of the Yellow Earth* 146–55.
7. P. Teilhard de Chardin and C. C. Young, *Preliminary Observations on the Pre-Loessic and Post-Pontian Formations in Western Shansi and Northern Shensi* (*Mem. Geol. Surv. of China*, Series A, No. 8, Peiping 1930), 34–5.

exception of a single tooth which may or may not have belonged to him[8].

A considerable number of skeletons, associated with remains of what has been described as a late Paleolithic industry, were found in excavating a cave adjoining that of *Sinanthropus*, in 1933 and 1934[9]. Weidenreich, who has examined them, says that they are not Mongoloid in type but rather resemble the Paleolithic Europeans; he suggests that they may represent the intrusion of a wandering tribe[10].

Because we have no remains of the early Neolithic period in China it has frequently been suggested that man did not live in China during this stage, but came in from elsewhere bearing a well-developed Neolithic culture with him. It is said that the Chinese climate was probably not favorable for human beings during the period which would have corresponded to this cultural epoch[11]. On the other hand Andersson has taken the position that the period immediately prior to that of the Neolithic sites which we know was a period when the Chinese climate was favorable for human occupancy, and that sites from this time will probably be found eventually[12]. As yet it is too early to say. Fifteen years ago the excavation of Stone Age sites in China had hardly begun, and there were those who doubted that Stone Age man had lived in China at all. Now we know some dozens of Neolithic sites, and several deposits even of Paleolithic utensils have been discovered. Archeology in China, in so far as scientific excavation is concerned, has barely begun. Almost all of the conditions which have made possible the rich

8. Cf. Licent, Teilhard de Chardin, and Black, "On a Presumably Pleistocene Tooth from the Sjara Osso Gol", *Bull. of the Geol. Soc. of China*, 1927, 5.285–290.
9. W. C. Pei, "A Preliminary Report on the Late-Paleolithic Cave of Choukoutien", *Bull. of the Geol. Soc. of China*, 1934, 13.327–350.
10. Verbal communication of November, 1935.
11. Cf. C. W. Bishop, "The Neolithic Age in Northern China," *Antiquity* 1933, 390; Bishop, "The Rise of Civilization in China with Reference to its Geographical Aspects," *The Geographical Review*, 1932, 22.617–618.
12. *Arch. Res. in Kansu* 49.

finds of the last century in Europe and America have been lacking in China. In the first place, digging for any purpose is frowned upon, because of certain beliefs connected with magic and because of the sanctity of graves. Therefore the accidental finds so numerous in Europe are less likely to happen here. And if such finds are made, there is still very little chance of their coming to the knowledge of trained scientists, for there is little general awareness of the importance of such things among the mass of the people. What the future may hold for Chinese archeology we can only conjecture.

During the last fifteen years cultural and skeletal remains of late Neolithic men have been found in Fengtien[13], Shantung[14], Honan,[15], and Kansu Provinces. Andersson wrote as early as 1925 that no less than thirty-eight sites of the late Neolithic and Copper Age periods were known at that time[16]. We have already seen that the people who inhabited north China at that time were essentially like the modern inhabitants of the same area. It seems not unreasonable to suppose, in view of the little we know, that the Shangs were descendants of certain of these Neolithic people—albeit it would be almost impossible to prove this in the present state of our knowledge. Theoretically they might represent a separate wave of the same people coming from some earlier homeland outside of China. This is doubtful, not only because of *Sinanthropus* but also because their culture seems to link them to eastern Asia. But that encroaches on the next question; our present problem is their geographical origin.

13. Cf. "An Early Chinese Culture," by J. G. Andersson, *Bull. of the Geol. Surv. of China*, 1923, 5.1.13–17; Andersson, *The Cave-deposit at Sha Kuo T'un in Fengtien, Palaeontologia Sinica*, Series D, Vol. 1, Fasc. 1 (Peking, 1923); Black, *The Human Skeletal Remains from the Sha Kuo T'un Cave Deposit in Comparison with those from Yang Shao Tsun and with Recent North China Skeletal Material.*

14. Cf. *Ch'eng-tzŭ-yai* 城子崖, edited by Li Chi, Liang Ssŭ-yung, and Tung Tso-pin. *Archeologia Sinica*, No. 1 (Nanking, 1935; dated 1934). This report, which has fifty-five plates, is published in two editions, one entirely in Chinese and one with an English summary.

15. Cf. "An Early Chinese Culture."

16. *Arch. Res. in Kansu* 40.

Fundamentally this goes back to the question of the place of origin of the Mongoloid stock. Bishop says that "Ethnologists seem agreed that the Mongoloid or Xanthoderm branch of the human family was specialized in Inner Asia. That region—after a last period of intense cold had given place to warmer conditions—became and long remained genial parkland and meadow, with lakes and streams fed by the melting glaciers of the neighboring mountains. Such an environment was favorable for human progress, and in Mongolia evidence has been found of development from a purely hunting and fishing and food-gathering economy into a cultural stage that practiced the rudiments of planting"[17]. On the other hand, Weidenreich's data on *Sinanthropus* would seem to place the ancestors of the Mongoloids in the very region of Peking, at a very early date indeed. But detailed inquiry into such remote origins is quite beyond the scope of this paper. Here we must limit ourselves to trying to determine the place from which the Shang people removed when they went to Anyang, or, at most, where they had lived during the few centuries immediately preceding their residence there.

For this investigation we shall have to depend almost wholly on tradition. In so far as I know there is no direct evidence on this question in any of the bone inscriptions or any of the results of excavation. The chief sources of the traditions on this point are the *Yin Pên Chi* of the *Shih Chi*, that Preface to the *Shu Ching* which is very questionably attributed to Confucius[18], and the genuine Bamboo Books.

The *Yin Pên Chi* goes back to the mythical period of the

17. "The Rise of Civilization in China with Reference to its Geographical Aspects," pp. 617–18.
18. *Shu* 1–14. It is to be noted, however, that with the exception of the passage introducing the *Pan Kêng* all of the sections of this Preface which refer to early locations of the Shang capital, and will be cited in this paper, were missing from the text of the Han stone classics, according to the reconstruction in the *Han Shih Ching Pei T'u* 10b. This reconstruction is probably essentially correct, although the fact that the lines do not come out even leaves it open to question in details. But most of the information on this point contained in this Preface is paralleled in the *Shih Chi* or the Bamboo Books, in any case.

founder of the Shang line, Hsieh. His mother is said to have come from P'u Chou, which is just east of the Yellow River in the extreme southwest tip of the present Shansi Province[19]. Hsieh himself is said to have been enfeoffed at Shang, from which the house took its name[20]. Where this Shang was the text of the *Shih Chi* does not tell us, but the *Chi Chieh* and *Chêng I* commentaries quote three authorities who agree in placing it on the eastern edge of Shensi Province, almost due south and some fifty miles from the great bend of the Yellow River[21].

But Wang Kuo-wei does not agree. He points out that the capital of the state of Sung, established after the fall of Shang, was called 商邱 Shang Ch'iu, which he says is similar to the name Yin Hsü which was given to the city at Anyang[22]. And he quotes a passage in the *Tso Chuan* which relates that anciently Kao Hsin had two sons who fought with each other, and the emperor therefore "moved Ê Po to Shang Ch'iu[23] to preside over Ch'ên[24]. The people of Shang followed him and Ch'ên is therefore the star of Shang"[25]. The *Tso Chuan* also specifically

19. Cf. *Shih Chi* 3.1a, col. 7, *Chêng I* comm. This is the modern Yung Chi.
20. Ibid. 3.1a.
21. Ibid. 3.1ab. The *Chi Chieh* quotes Chêng Hsüan as saying that Shang was located at 太華之陽 T'ai Hua chih yang, which presumably means to the south of the Hua mountain. This is in approximate agreement with the other locations. It also quotes Huang-Fu Mi as locating it at Shang Lo. Shang Lo is located in the present Shang Hsien; cf. *Ti Ming Tien*. The *Chêng I* quotes the *K'uo Ti Chih* (a now lost geographical work of T'ang date) as saying that this Shang is located "eighty *li* to the east of Shang Chou in 商洛縣 Shang Lo Hsien". This Shang Lo Hsien is the modern Shang Hsien; cf. *Ti Ming Tien*.
22. Wang, *I Shu*, I.12.1b.
Wang supports this by two quotations from the *Shuo Wên*, as follows: 虛大丘也昆侖丘謂之昆侖虛又云丘謂之虛从丘虍聲
23. Wang, in quoting this passage, gives 邱, while Legge's text of the *Tso Chuan* (573.2) and *SSC Tso Chuan* 41.20b have 丘; the two are interchangeable.
24. This is said to be another name for the star 大火 Ta Huo; cf. *SSC Tso Chuan* 41.20b col. 4.
25. *Tso Chuan* 573.2; *SSC Tso Chuan* 41.20b.

Geographical Origins

links the Shang ancestor Hsiang T'u with Shang Ch'iu[26], and elsewhere specifically locates this Shang Ch'iu in the territory of the State of 宋 Sung[27]. Wang quotes Tu Yü's *Ch'un Ch'iu Shih Ti* as saying that Shang Ch'iu is the same as Chü Yang of the State of Liang, and that Sung, Shang, and Shang Ch'iu are three names for the same place. Chü Yang is the modern Kuei Tê Fu or Shang Ch'iu, on the eastern border of the present Honan Province, some twenty miles south of the old course of the Yellow River[28]. Wang believes, therefore, that the Shangs started in the same location in which they ended, in the territory of the State of Sung[29].

The Preface to the *Shu* and the *Yin Pên Chi* both say that "From Hsieh down to T'ang the Successful there were eight moves" of the Shang capital[30]. K'ung Ying-ta[31] gives his opinion as to four of these locations. For the first he quotes the *Shang Sung* to prove that Hsieh lived at Shang, which he apparently puts in the modern Shang Hsien in eastern Shensi[32]. He quotes the *Shih Pên*[33] as saying that Hsieh's son, Chao Ming, had his seat at a place called 砥石 Chih Shih; of the location of this place there is, he says, no record[34]. The *Tso Chuan*, he says, locates Hsiang T'u at Shang Ch'iu[35], which he

26. *Tso Chuan* 437.1–2.
27. *Tso Chuan* 666.12. I.e., Sung is here linked with Ta Ch'ên, which in 573.2 is linked with Shang Ch'iu.
28. Cf. Wang, *I Shu* I.12.1b, and *Ti Ming Tien*.
29. Wang, *I Shu*, I.12.1b–2a.
30. *Shu* 3–4; *Shih Chi* 3.2a.
This passage in the Preface of the *Shu* is quoted by the *Chin Wên Shu K'ao* 32 shang, 14a. But the author of the *Han Shih Ching Pei T'u* (see 14.b7) omits it, evidently not considering it a part of the original text of the Preface. This is not very important, however, since the passage does occur in the *Shih Chi*.
31. The T'ang dynasty author of the *Shang Shu Chêng I*.
32. *SSC Shu* 7.14b–4–5. The quotation from the *Shang Sung* occurs in *Shih* 639.
33. A Han work compiled by Liu Hsiang, now lost, except for numerous quotations in various other books.
34. *SSC Shu* 7.14b.6.
35. This statement is apparently based on *Tso Chuan* 437.1–2; cf. *SSC Shu* 7.14b.5–6. In Wang's reconstruction of the genuine Bamboo

identifies with the capital of the State of Sung, on the eastern edge of modern Honan [36]. Lastly, the Preface to the *Shu* says that "T'ang first lived at Po". K'ung Ying-ta quotes Chêng Hsüan who apparently located Po in a district in the north of modern Honan, some fifteen miles east of Loyang [37]. He also quotes a commentary on the *Han Shu* which located it in what was called "the present 濟陰亳縣 Chi Yin Po Hsien" [38], and Tu Yü who located Po some forty *li* north of Shang Ch'iu in eastern Honan [39]. K'ung further cites the statement of Huang-Fu Mi, who said, "Mencius relates that when T'ang resided in Po, Kê was a neighboring state, and when the chief of the Kê family did not sacrifice T'ang sent the people of Po to till the ground for him [40]. Kê is the present Kê 鄉 Hsiang, in Ning Ling of the State of Liang [41]. If T'ang had lived at Yen Shih [just east of Loyang, as Chêng Hsüan says he did], more than eight hundred *li* distant from Ning Ling, how could he have sent people to till the

---

Books (*Ku Chu Shu* 2a) we read that "Hou Hsiang came to the throne and lived at Shang Ch'iu". This Hou Hsiang is supposed, of course, to be the Hsia ruler, Ti Hsiang (cf. *Shih Chi* 2.20b). I suspect, however, that one tradition concerning an ancient ruler named Hsiang, living at Shang Ch'iu, has bisected, giving us on the one hand a Hsia king and on the other a Shang ancestor.

36. *SSC Shu* 6.14b.6.
37. Ibid. 7.15a.4.
38. I have been unable to place this district. There was a Chi Yin Hsien in the district which is now Kê Tsê Hsien in the southwest corner of Shantung Province, but there seems little likelihood that this was the place intended here.
39. Ibid. 7.15a.5. He says, "In the State of Liang, to the north of Mêng Hsien there is the city of Po". Liang was in the region of modern Shang Ch'iu, twenty-two *li* to the north of which there was located, in the time of Tu Yü, a Mêng Hsien, since abolished. And forty *li* north of Shang Ch'iu was located a city called Po or Mêng Po (cf. *Ti Ming Tien*).
40. For this incident cf. Legge, *Chinese Classics*, Vol. II, *The Works of Mencius* (Oxford, 1895; referred to hereafter as *Mencius*) 271-2.
41. There is still a Ning Ling Hsien in about the same location, some twelve miles west and a little north of Shang Ch'iu.

ground there? Po was located in the present State of Liang, in Ku Shou Hsien"[42]. This Po is located forty *li* to the southeast of the present Shang Ch'iu[43]. K'ung Ying-ta concludes his discussion of the location of Po by saying that "the various explanations do not agree; we cannot tell which is correct". He also says that the four locations of the capital up to the time of T'ang which have been mentioned are all that are given in literature, while as to the rest of the eight there is no specific information[44].

But Wang Kuo-wei has sought to fill some of these gaps. In the first place, he says, since Hsieh was the son of Ti K'u[45] he must originally have lived at Po[46]. The *Chü P'ien* of the *Shih Pên* said that he lived at Fan, which Wang locates near the center of the southern border of the present Shantung Province[47]; this, then, must have been the first move. As we have already seen, the *Shih Pên* said that his son, Chao Ming, lived at Chih Shih, which is the second place moved to. The *Ch'êng Hsiang P'ien* of *Hsün Tzŭ* says that Chao Ming "lived at Chih Shih and moved to Shang"[48]. This is the third move. The *Tso Chuan* locates his son, Hsiang T'u, at Shang Ch'iu[49]. But elsewhere it says that K'ang Shu, when enfeoffed with Wei, was given "a portion of the lands belonging to the eastern capital of Hsiang T'u that he might be able to attend the king's inspec-

42. *SSC Shu* 7.15a.5–7.
43. Cf. *Ti Ming Tien*, 1187, under "Ku Shou Hsien".
44. *SSC Shu* 7.14b.5.
45. At least his mother is supposed to have been the concubine of this mythical ruler, but Hsieh himself is said to have been miraculously conceived, so that it has also been said that he was not the son of Ti K'u; cf. *Shih Chi* 3.1a.
46. Wang, *I Shu*, I.12.1a. The *Chi Chieh* commentary on the *Shih Chi* quotes Huang-Fu Mi to the effect that Ti K'u had his capital at Po, which he locates at Yen Shih, east of the present Loyang.
47. I.e., in the Fan Hsien of Han times, which is represented by the present T'êng Hsien.
48. *Hsün Tzŭ* 18.5a.
49. *Tso Chuan* 437.1–2.

tions in the east"⁽⁵⁰⁾. Since these meetings or inspections were supposed to take place near the "eastern peak", T'ai Shan, commentators place this capital near that mountain⁽⁵¹⁾, which is some one hundred fifty miles northeast of Shang Ch'iu. Wang suggests that Hsiang T'u first moved to the region of T'ai Shan and later returned to Shang Ch'iu, thus making the fourth and fifth moves of the Shang capital⁽⁵²⁾. The current Bamboo Books says that "In the thirty-third year of Ti Mang⁽⁵³⁾ the Marquis⁽⁵⁴⁾ of Shang moved to Yin"⁽⁵⁵⁾, and a quotation from the genuine Bamboo Books in a commentary on the *Shan Hai Ching* is supposed to confirm this⁽⁵⁶⁾. Yin is identified by Wang with the city at Anyang⁽⁵⁷⁾, and he considers the move to it to have been the sixth. Under the ninth year of Ti K'ung Chia the current Bamboo Books records that "The Marquis of Yin again returned to Shang Ch'iu"⁽⁵⁸⁾; this is the seventh move. Finally we have

50. Wang mistakenly attributes this passage to the ninth year of Ting Kung (*I Shu*, I.12.1a); it occurs under the fourth year, *Tso Chuan* 750.8.
51. Cf. *SSC Tso Chuan* 54.18.
52. This looks as if Wang were grasping at straws to fill out his quota of eight moves. For we have given a situation in which, according to tradition, Hsiang T'u originally lived at Shang Ch'iu and in which he is mentioned as having lived there and perhaps, though this is not even certainly intended in the tradition, to the northeast near T'ai Shan. The natural inference is that he moved from the one place to the other; to assume that he moved back again without any further authority is rather remarkable.
53. Wang (*I Shu* I.12.1a) says that this comes in the reign of Ti Fên, but this is evidently an error since not only other editions of the current Bamboo Books but even his own put it in the time of Ti Mang; cf. Wang, *I Shu*, III, *Chin Pên Chu Shu*, shang 9b, and *Chu Shu* 3.18a.
54. Of course there was not a graded feudal hierarchy in the late Chou sense in the early day to which this tradition is supposed to relate, so that *hou* ought perhaps merely to be translated "lord" or "ruler". But this whole tradition is probably mythological, and the mythology did read the later feudal system back into the earlier period.
55. *Chu Shu* 3.18a.
56. Cf. Wang, *I Shu*, I.12.1a.
57. Ibid. I.12.4b–5a.
58. *Chu Shu* 4.6a.

the statement of the *Shih Chi* and the Preface to the *Shu* that "T'ang first lived at Po"[59], which Wang locates just to the north of Shang Ch'iu approximately at the present border between Honan and Shantung[60]. This completes the eight moves, according to Wang's reconstruction[61].

The *K'ung Chuan* of the *Shu*[62] says that "From T'ang down to P'an Kêng there were in all five changes of the capital"[63]. Only three locations of the capital between the reigns of these two rulers are mentioned, however. Chung Ting is said to have moved to Hsiao, also called Ao;[64] this place has been variously located in an undetermined spot north of the Yellow River, near the modern city of Kaifeng, and near Jung Yang which is some eighty miles west of Kaifeng[65]. Hê Tan Chia is said to have lived at Hsiang, which commentators agree in placing north of the Yellow River and in the region, at least, of Anyang[66]. The Preface to the *Shu* says that 祖乙圮于耿 *Tsu I p'i yü Kêng*, which Legge translates "Tsu I met with calamity in Kǎng"[67]. The *Shih Chi* says that 祖乙遷于邢 *Tsu I ch'ien yü Hsing*[68], "Tsu I moved to Hsing". Most critics consider Kêng and Hsing two names for the same place[69]. The exact meaning of the

59. *Shih Chi* 3.2a; *Shu* 4.
60. Wang devotes a whole paper to proving this location; cf. *I Shu*, I.12.2a–4a. Most of the evidence he gives has already been cited. Wang locates this Po in Shantung Province, at Ts'ao Chou Fu, more than twenty *li* south of Ts'ao Hsien. The *Ti Ming Tien* says that it is in Honan, north of Shang Ch'iu, adjoining Ts'ao Hsien (see 1295, under "Pao Hsien").
61. Wang, *I Shu*, I.12.1b.
62. I.e., the commentary on the *Shu Ching* attributed to K'ung An-kuo. It is now generally considered to have been forged along with the *ku wên* text of the *Shu*.
63. *SSC Shu* 9.1a.4.
64. *Shu* 6; the *Shih Chi* calls what is apparently the same place Ao, cf. 3.6b.
65. Cf. *SSC Shu* 8.30a.6–7; *Shih Chi* 3.6b.1–2.
66. Cf. *SSC Shu* 8.30a.9–10; *Shih Chi* 3.6b.2–3.
67. *Shu* 6.
68. *Shih Chi* 3.6b.
69. Cf. *Shih Chi* 3.6b.4; Wang, *I Shu*, I.12.4a; *Chin Wên Shu K'ao* 32 shang, 38b.

passage in the *Shu* is a subject of debate, but no one questions that both passages indicate that the capital of Tsu I was at some time located on this spot. Two commentaries on the *Shih Chi* agree in placing it near the present Hê Ching Hsien, in modern southwest Shansi, a few miles northeast of the confluence of the Fên with the Yellow River[70]. But Wang Kuo-wei does not agree with this. He points out that the previous locations of the capital were grouped rather closely together, while this location in western Shansi is remote, too remote to be plausible. He interprets *Tsu I p'i yü Kêng* as meaning that Kêng was flooded during Tsu I's residence there[71]. But the Kêng in Shansi, Wang says, is rather distant from the Yellow River, and there is no tradition of disastrous floods there. He therefore identifies it with a place called Hsing Ch'iu, which was located on the north banks of the Yellow River some twenty *li* east of the present Wên Hsien in Honan[72]. Chêng Hsüan considers that Tsu I, having met with disaster in this location, moved yet again; he quotes the genuine Bamboo Books to the effect that Pan Kêng moved from 奄 Yen to Yin, concluding that Tsu I moved from Kêng to Yen[73]. The exact location of Yen seems to be uncertain[74], but it is said to have been in the region of the modern Ch'ü Fu, in southwestern Shantung[75]. But the fact is that the genuine Bamboo Books, as quoted by the *T'ai P'ing Yü Lan*, says that Tsu I, Ti K'ai Chia, Tsu Ting, and Nan Kêng all lived at a place called 庇 Pi[76]. Hsü Wên-ching identifies this with the Hsing of the *Shih Chi*, which he says is not the same as the Kêng of the Preface to the *Shu*, and locates it in the region of Hsing T'ai and P'ing Hsiang in southwestern Hopei Province[77]. Finally Pan Kêng is said by the *Shih Chi*

70. *Shih Chi* 3.6b.4-5.
71. Wang, *I Shu*, I.12.4a.
72. Wang, loc. cit.; cf. *Ti Ming Tien* 669 under "Hsing Ch'iu", and 213 under "P'ing Kao Hsien".
73. *SSC Shu* 8.30b.7-10.
74. Ibid. 17.4b.5-6.
75. Cf. *Ti Ming Tien* 441.
76. Cf. *Ku Chu Shu* 4-5.
77. *Chu Shu* 5.15a.

to have moved to Po[78], which Huang-Fu Mi locates at Yen Shih just east of Loyang. This is held by Wang Kuo-wei to be an error based on the Preface to the *Shu*, which says that Pan Kêng 將治亳殷 *chiang chih Po Yin*[79]. Shu Hsi of the Chin dynasty suggested that this passage originally read 將始宅殷 *chiang shih chai Yin*[80]. This is quite possible, because the ancient forms of *chih* and *shih*, *Po* and *chai*, were even more similar and more easily confused than are their modern equivalents[81]. At all events, whether or not this be the correct explanation, there can be no serious doubt that by the time of Wu Ting at any rate the Shang capital was located at Anyang, rather than staying south of the Yellow River until the time of Wu I as the *Shih Chi* says[82]. The evidence for this was given at the beginning of this paper.

These many traditions locating the places of residence of the Shang ancestors probably have little historical value. Their sources are, for the most part, late. The oracle bones make it possible for us to check on traditions concerning religion, political institutions, and other phases of Shang culture. This check reveals a high percentage of inaccuracy in the received traditions relating to the Shang period; this fact does not encourage us to suppose that traditions concerning geography are thoroughly reliable. Also the wide differences of opinion between various scholars who report traditions concerning what is supposed to be the same spot, but locate it with equal assurance in places separated by scores of miles, can not but decrease our confidence in such information.

The frequency with which the Shang capital is said to have been moved is inherently improbable. It has been argued from this that the Shang people were nomads, but this remains to be proved. There are scholars who still insist that the Shangs at Anyang were in a "pastoral stage" of culture, but this is untenable

78. *Shih Chi* 3.7a.
79. *Shu* 7.
80. Quoted in Wang, *I Shu*, I.12.4b.
81. Cf. *Shuo Wên Lin* 4915, 5564b, 2268a, 3213b.
82. *Shih Chi* 3.8b.

for various reasons[83]. As early as the time of Wu Ting the Shangs were erecting large buildings of complicated construction on essentially the same principles of design as those underlying the Chinese buildings of today[84]; these must reflect a long experience in building, and it is difficult to suppose that that could have been acquired by a nomadic people.

Nor is it easy to believe, for reasons which have already been pointed out[85], that the Shangs would have been allowed to move back and forth at will across north central China with the frequency with which tradition says they did. Whether they were nomads or not, we know that the late Neolithic dwellers in north China practiced agriculture and raised large numbers of pigs[86], both of which indicate settled habitations, and the depth of culture deposits proves that some sites were inhabited during long periods. Further, we know that the Shangs were troubled by a good deal of warfare while they lived at Anyang. In these circumstances it is not reasonable to suppose that they could have moved from Shantung to western Shansi and back again at will, without meeting opposition on the way, with the freedom which the traditional accounts imply.

Yet these traditions do possess a value for our investigation into the geographical origins of the Shang people. Among the traditional locations of the Shang capital discussed above there are fifteen which it is possible to place approximately on the modern map. The most widely separated of them are T'ai Shan on the northeast and Shang Hsien, in Shensi, on the southwest, well over four hundred miles apart. The most northern is in southern Hopei; Shang Hsien in Shensi is the most southern as well as the farthest west; T'ai Shan and T'êng Hsien, in Shantung, are farthest east.

The identification of some of these places rests on nothing

83. See p. 243, note 31.
84. See *Anyang Pao Kao* 711–715.
85. See pages 124–125 above.
86. Cf. Bishop, "The Neolithic Age in Northern China", 394–6; Black, *The Human Skeletal Remains from the Sha Kuo T'un Cave Deposit* . . . , 5 and 7.

more than the fact that a name, which occurs in history, happens to be found there—it is almost as if one should insist that the Trojan war took place in New York State, because it contains a city named Troy. Particularly dubious are the three locations claimed for the Shang capital in the far west, at Shang Hsien and to the east of Shang Hsien in Shensi and at Hê Ching Hsien in western Shansi. These appear to be based on nothing but names, and as Wang Kuo-wei has shown they are out of the general field of action in which tradition places the Shangs. If we eliminate these three sites, the remaining twelve are grouped in a relatively small area in northern Honan, southern Hopei, and western Shantung.

This is the area in which, in so far as tradition goes, the Shangs took their rise, and we know that it is here that they flourished during the latter part of the Shang period and during the existence of the State of Sung in Chou times. It is plain country, centering more or less about the bend which the Yellow River makes to run northeast after its long easterly crossing of northern Honan. The present bend in this direction has existed, of course, only since 1852. But apparently the course of the river in very ancient times was not wholly different from what it is now. Yetts says that "before 602 B.C. the Yellow River turned northward at a point some sixty-five miles to the west of the present bend which is twenty miles east of K'ai-fêng. Thence it ran north-east in the direction of Tientsin, and thus passed some fifteen miles east of An-yang".[87] He does not say on what evidence he bases the conclusion that this was its location in Shang times, but this agrees in general with the opinion of Chinese scholars with whom I have discussed the question. If this was the location of the river at that time, it approximately bisected the area of Shang residence indicated by these traditions, if we leave out of account the three sites in Shansi and Shensi. In general, then, these traditions indicate that the Shangs were a people who had for many centuries inhabited the plains region of what is now northern Honan, southern Hopei, and southwestern Shantung. And it is also worth noting that however we may

87. *JRAS*, 1933, p. 660.

calculate the position of the river in Shang times and even if we include the sites in Shansi and Shensi, the most remote of these sites is not much more than a hundred miles from the Yellow River, while most of them are a great deal closer.

4. Origins of Shang Culture

There is no absolutely necessary connection between the racial, geographical, and cultural origins of the Shang people. It might be within the bounds of possibility for such a group to be of North European stock, to have lived for many centuries on the coast of the Bering Sea before moving to Anyang, and to have taken over a culture developed in northern India. But however possible it might be, such a history is highly improbable. In all likelihood there is a very considerable amount of interrelation between these three aspects of their origins. We come, then, to the final and in many respects the most important of our questions, that of the origins of Shang culture. In dealing with it we are also dealing, to a very large extent, with the question of the origins of Chinese culture as a whole.

According to the general opinion of scholars many of the fundamental elements of the Chinese culture of the Bronze Age were imported into China from outside. Bishop says "It seems certain ... that the Bronze Age civilization, as an integrated complex, reached China by way of the Central Asiatic steppe belt"[1]. The late Dr. Berthold Laufer wrote that "ancient Chinese culture in its earliest stage cannot be the product of an isolated seclusion, but has its due share and its root in the same fundamental ideas as go to build up the general type of Asiatic-European civilization".[2]

That Shang culture evolved entirely on Chinese soil is a proposition which it would be impossible to prove. The potter's wheel, the horse-drawn chariot, and the casting of bronze, possibly by the *cire perdue* process[3], to mention only these, are complicated

1. *Pacific Affairs* 7.307.
2. "Some Fundamental Ideas of Chinese Culture" 166-7.
3. The technique of bronze casting in the Shang period is a subject which stands in need of thorough investigation, by technical experts

inventions which were very important in Shang culture and which were shared with ancient peoples inhabiting a large proportion of Europe and Asia. And there is some reason to believe, as has been frequently held, that the technique of casting bronze and perhaps some other things came into China, as Bishop says, "as an integrated complex", rather suddenly. But even if we could definitely determine this to be the case we should still have an even more important problem to solve, namely: did these several techniques and forms which entered, as items of material culture, enter as part of a new and alien cultural complex which in large measure swept away a previous, indigenous culture for which it was substituted; or was it rather the case that these techniques and forms were assimilated into an already existing cultural pattern so that it was altered, to be sure, but so that the result remained a culture distinctively eastern, and not merely a repetition with variations of the Bronze Age culture of Europe and the Near East?

---

in this field, on the basis of our new materials. It is generally supposed that the *cire perdue* process was employed, and indeed it seems that some of the amazing results achieved could hardly have been attained in any other way. But a great many bronze molds from Anyang have come to light in recent years, and some of them are composed of regular sections, with lugs and depressions on their edges so that they may be fitted together. I have published photographs of several of such pieces of molds in a paper entitled "On the Origins of the Manufacture and Decoration of Bronze in the Shang Period", *Monumenta Serica*, 1935, 1.1.39–69 (referred to hereafter as "On Shang Bronze"), Plates IX–X. Cf. also *Anyang Pao Kao*, following 480, Plate 15.3.

It has been suggested that these molds were used to cast wax models, which were then retouched. This is perhaps possible. We not infrequently find, on Shang bronzes of poor quality (cf. "On Shang Bronze", Plate IV A) and even occasionally on very fine ones, ridges which appear to show joinings between sections of a mold. It has been said, that these might result from a wax model which came from a mold. But this explanation is definitely inadequate to explain some cast ridges I have seen. The whole subject is a perplexing one on which I am able to draw no conclusions at present.

Neolithic Cultures in North China

We must first inquire what was the relation between the Shang culture and the late Neolithic and other prehistoric cultures of north China. In a paper published in 1923, reporting his work at Yang Shao in northwestern Honan, Andersson said:" the facies of this ancient culture is decidedly Chinese. The only fact I can mention against this statement is the custom of burying the dead with the head in most cases towards the SE. ... In all other features the Yang Shao culture seems to respond well to the denomination of Early Chinese"[4]. But after further study, and the excavation of a number of Neolithic, Copper Age, Bronze Age, and Iron Age sites in Kansu[5], he wrote two years later: "Unfortunately nothing has so far been recognized among the furniture of the late Kansu sites which can be regarded as idential [sic] with objects of the San Tai"[6]. He went so far as to reverse his earlier opinion, stating it to be a "fact, as best exhibited by Arne's comparative research on the painted pottery from Honan, that the early cultures studied by us offer comparatively little relationship to objects of early Chinese dynasties, but have very much in common with the Aeneolithic cultures of the Near East ... "[7]

The explanation of this change of opinion may lie in a fact what was not yet evident at the time Andersson wrote this. The Neolithic culture which he first excavated, in Honan, has proved to have considerably more in common with Chinese culture than does that of Kansu, in which he worked subsequently.

Hou Kang and Yang Shao. In 1931 the excavations of the

---

4. "An Early Chinese Culture" 32.
5. For the attribution of Andersson's Sha Ching stage to the early Iron Age, see *Kansu Mortuary Urns of the Pan Shan and Ma Chang Groups,* by Nils Palmgren (*Palaeontologia Sinica,* Series D, Vol. 3, Fasc. 1; Peiping, 1934), 4. According to Dr. Palmgren, iron has been found among the excavated materials from this culture, and Professor Andersson himself now assigns it to the Iron Age (verbal communication from Dr. Palmgren at Peiping, June 14, 1935).
6. *Arch. Res. in Kansu* 28.
7. Ibid. 10.

National Research Institute at Anyang brought to light material of the highest importance bearing on this problem. The discoveries were made under the direction of Liang Ssŭ-yung. At Hou Kang, a low hill about two miles east and south of the main site, which forms a promontory of the south bank of the Huan River, were found the remains of three successive cultures, in strata which left no doubt of their relative chronology. The earliest proved to be a Neolithic site, with painted pottery. This painted pottery is, of course, completely lacking in the Shang cultural remains. After the people represented by this culture left the site was apparently unoccupied for a time, and then came another Neolithic people with quite a different kind of culture, characterized by "black pottery", a polished, lustrous ware. It is thought that the makers of this black pottery may have been living at Anyang when the Shangs moved in, and conquered by them[8]. Finally there is a Shang culture stratum. Although these three are not at any point completely overlapping, the earliest is almost entirely covered by the middle stratum and all of the Shang stratum lies over the middle one[9].

Mr. Liang, who specializes on pottery, has written a very interesting paper on the significance of these finds in relation to the problem of the origin of Shang culture[10]. On the basis of his study of the painted pottery and other artifacts found in the lowest stratum he believes that they show a great many detailed correspondences to the objects excavated by Andersson at Yang Shao, and concludes that "the objects contained in this stratum are beyond doubt relics of the 'Yang Shao culture' "[11]. However, the decoration on the painted pottery found in the lowest Hou Kang stratum (which we shall call Hou Kang (I)) is very simple as compared with the designs found at Yang Shao. For this and other reasons Liang believes that Hou Kang (I) represents a stage of the Yang Shao culture which is somewhat earlier than that of the Yang Shao site itself; on the other hand, since

8. Verbal communication of Mr. Tung Tso-pin, April 25, 1934.
9. For the report of this excavation and illustrations of some of the objects found, cf. *Anyang Pao Kao* 609-626.
10. *Ts'ai Anniv. Vol.* 555-68.
11. Ibid. 558-559.

certain pottery types characteristic of Yang Shao itself are exactly paralleled in Hou Kang (I) he believes that the latter can be only slightly earlier than the former[12]. But Hou Kang (II), the "black pottery culture", has very little in common with Hou Kang (I)[13].

In 1930 and 1931 excavation at 城子崖 Ch'êng Tzŭ Yai in Shantung discovered remains of a Neolithic "black pottery culture" under another stratum of remains of uncertain date containing bronze[14]. The Neolithic culture, although it lacked the painted pottery of Yang Shao, shared with Yang Shao certain types of black and grey sherds and certain typical styles of decoration, and had certain pottery forms identical with those found at Yang Shao.

But Hou Kang (II), while having little in common with Yang Shao or with Hou Kang (I), has so much in common with the Ch'êng Tzŭ Yai culture that Liang says that "there is no question" that they are to be assigned to the same cultural stage[15].

The highest stratum at Hou Kang, Hou Kang (III), contains objects of pottery, stone, and bone identical with those of the Shang culture stratum, and even has the typical divination bone and tortoise shell and a single piece of inscribed bone, which Tung Tso-pin considers to come from a rather late period in the occupancy of the Anyang site by the Shang people[16]. Hou Kang (III) without doubt is a Shang cultural deposit[17].

Shang culture does not appear, even in its pottery, to have been merely a borrowing from any of the Neolithic cultures which have been mentioned. Nothing like the beautifully carved white pottery ceremonial vessels, numerous in the Shang deposits[18],

12. Ibid. 559.
13. Loc. cit.
14. See *Ch'êng-tzŭ-yai*, 1–25.
15. *Ts'ai Anniv. Vol.* 558.
16. *Anyang Pao Kao* 707.
17. Cf. *Ts'ai Anniv. Vol.* 557–8.
18. Some astonishingly fine pieces of this ware, with beautiful designs like those on bronzes carved in the wet clay, were excavated in the autumn of 1934, by the National Research Institute, in what is thought to have been a royal tomb at Anyang. They have not yet been published, but I have had the privilege of examining them.

is found in the Neolithic remains. The painted pottery typical of the Yang Shao stage in Honan and of later periods in Kansu is entirely lacking from the Shang ruins [19].

There are, on the other hand, certain aspects of Shang culture which show close relations between it and the preceding Neolithic cultures of north China. The "Yang Shao culture", named after the type site at Yang Shao in northwestern Honan, is considered to have strong western affiliations, especially in its painted pottery which is considered to be related to similar ware found even in the Near East [20]. But even in this culture we find types of artifacts which are also found in Shang culture and *which are not found in Europe or the Near East.* An example, according to Andersson, is the stone knife of semilunar and rectangular shape. He says: "...we must point out that the handleless crescent-shaped and rectangular knife blades which play such an immensely important rôle in prehistoric China are not known at all in the Near East or in Europe, where crescent-shaped flint saws are the only, and very uncertain, parallels to the stone knives of Eastern Asia. But just as these knife blades were unknown to the prehistoric peoples of the West, so also they seem to have been equally widespread among all the Mongolian races. In Baron Erland Nordenskiöld's rich collections from prehistoric South America I have seen stone knives which remind me very much of the rectangular knife-blades of Eastern Asia. It is thus possible that this stone knife was such an early possession of the Mongolian peoples that it accompanied them when, during the New Stone age, a section of this populous human tribe found its way across the Bering Strait and gave to America its first population" [21]. "Torii also called attention to the fact that similar stone-knives, mostly semi-lunar in shape, are found in the

19. It is true that a single potsherd, painted in two colors, was excavated in undisturbed strata together with a group of inscribed oracle bones, in the autumn of 1929 (cf. *Anyang Pao Kao* 337). But no others like it have been found, and its occurrence is obviously accidental.
20. Cf. *Arch. Res. in Kansu* 10.
21. *Children of the Yellow Earth* 208–9.

ancient sites of the Asiatic Chukchee, as well as of the American Eskimo"[22].

Knives of this type are not limited to prehistoric sites in China. They were among the most common tools used by the Shang people at Anyang, as the excavation of a very large number of them has proved[23]. As early as 1929 Li Chi wrote that "more than a thousand" of them had already been excavated[24]; they are so plentiful that I myself have been able to pick up a number of broken but nearly complete ones, from the rubbish heaps left by the excavators at Anyang. Some knives of these types, from Anyang and from the Yang Shao culture, are almost indistinguishable in form[25]. What appears to be a fragment of a knife of the typical semilunar form, made of mussel shell, was excavated by Liang in Hou Kang (II), i.e., the Ch'êng Tzŭ Yai cultural deposit at Anyang[26]. Semilunar knives of both mussel shell and stone, of the same forms as those used by the Shangs, were found in the Neolithic stratum at Ch'êng Tzŭ Yai, near the center of Shantung[27]. Andersson has made the interesting point that knives of this type, both rectangular and semilunar, are not only found in Neolithic remains in China and in the Shang culture, but even persist, made of iron, in China at the present day[28].

Andersson also mentions the fact that a stone spinning whorl which he bought from a Chinese whom he found using it in Hsi Ning "in no way differs from the stone whorls which we found

22. "An Early Chinese Culture" 3.
23. Cf. *Ts'ai Anniv. Vol.* 89-91.
24. *Anyang Pao Kao* 249.
25. Cf. illustrations in ibid. 248, *Ts'ai Anniv. Vol.* 89, and *Children of the Yellow Earth*, 203 (apparently, from his discussion in ibid. 202-203, Andersson found both the rectangular and the semilunar knives in the Yang Shao stage, but this is not completely clear).
26. *Ts'ai Anniv. Vol.* following 568, Plate 2, 2.34. Since Liang publishes a drawing of this among the typical artifacts of this stratum, more than one such piece was probably excavated.
27. Cf. *Ch'êng-tzŭ-yai* 75, 78, 84-5, and Plates XXXVII.6-12, XLI. 6-11.
28. "An Early Chinese Culture" 4-5.

in the Yang Shao dwelling-sites"[29]. Nor was this an isolated instance for he found many whorls in current use in Honan and Kansu which greatly resembled the Yang Shao whorls[30]. Traces of rice, a most important item in the modern Chinese diet, have been identified among the remains of the Yang Shao culture[31]. We can not yet be sure whether rice was raised by the Shang people, but there is evidence which makes it appear that it very possibly was. The very fact that it was apparently cultivated by the Yang Shao people on the one hand and has been an important staple of the historic Chinese on the other raises a certain presumption that it was known to the Shangs, although its culture might of course have been discontinued and reintroduced later from the moist south, where it probably originated. There are six occurrences on the oracle bones of a form which has been identified as the character 米[32]. But the contexts do not give much assurance that this is the correct meaning and even if it were we could not be sure that *mi* at that time meant rice[33]. There is some slight indication in the oracle inscriptions that irrigation was practised by the Shangs[34].

We can see, therefore, that even though the painted pottery of the Yang Shao stage disappeared completely, there does not appear to have been a complete break in continuity between this Neolithic culture and Chinese culture proper. Another sort of artifacts which constitute a striking link between the Yang Shao and Shang cultures is the *li* tripod and its related pottery forms. But it will be more suitable to discuss these at length in connection with the Ch'êng Tzŭ Yai Neolithic culture, which must next engage our attention.

29. *Children of the Yellow Earth* 217.
30. Loc. cit.
31. *Children of the Yellow Earth* 335–6.
32. *T'ieh Kuei* 72.3; *T'ieh* I 4.16; *Yin Ch'ien Pien* 4.41.2; *Yin Hou Pien* 1.25.7 (twice; Sun mistakenly gives 25.9), 2.23.5.
33. The *Shuo Wên* defines *mi* as "kernels of grain", but gives some presumption that it originally referred to rice.
34. *Yin Ch'ien Pien* 4.12.2 has a character made up of a pictograph of a field and streams of water.

Ch'êng Tzŭ Yai. The type site of this culture is in Lung Shan Hsien, about seventy-five *li* east of Tsinan, a little north and west of the center of Shantung Province. It is just north of T'ai Shan, and less than a hundred miles from the seacoast. Ch'êng Tzŭ Yai was excavated twice, by the National Research Institute, in 1930 and again in 1931. To say that the finds made at this spot were sensational is no more than the sober truth. They revealed the culture of a late Neolithic people, quite different from any previously discovered in China, who inhabited a rectangular walled city about 450 by 390 meters in size, who used the potter's wheel to make pottery of which some is no thicker than one millimeter, knew and perhaps raised horses and cattle, and practised scapulimancy in a manner strongly reminiscent of the Shang oracle bones. In various respects which we shall examine in detail, this culture resembles that of the Shangs more closely than does any other Neolithic culture we know.

It has already been referred to as "the black pottery culture". This name comes from a fine type of ware, black and commonly glossy, which is probably the most numerous of its distinctive artifacts. But it is perhaps necessary to emphasize that this is merely a conventional name, used by Chinese archeologists, to designate the peculiar and definite type of Neolithic culture, characterized by numerous definite criteria, which is found in the lower stratum at Ch'êng Tzŭ Yai, in Hou Kang (II), and elsewhere. Pottery somewhat resembling this is found in other cultures. And it is of course no more the case that every culture including black pottery is a "black pottery culture" in this sense, than it is true that we live in the Bronze Age because we make some use of bronze.

The most striking resemblance between the Neolithic culture found at Ch'êng Tzŭ Yai and Shang culture is in connection with the divination bones. Strictly speaking we can not be mathematically certain that the bones found at Ch'êng Tzŭ Yai were used for this purpose, for they do not contain writing explaining their use as the Shang bones do. But they were similar in material, in the first place. Of the six pieces found, four were pieces of ox scapulae, one of deer scapula, and one of the scapula of an unidentified animal[35]. The divination bones found at Anyang include many ox scapulae[36]. Three of these pieces were used in their rough, natural condition, but three of them were prepared as Shang divination bone at Anyang was frequently prepared. They were scraped and polished, and then bored with small round pits[37]. This boring with round pits was a crude method compared with the oval pit made by the Shangs, but it may be that the supplementary round boring sometimes made by the Shangs beside the oval pit was a survival of it[38]. Six somewhat similar pieces of bone were found in a later culture stratum, of undetermined Bronze Age date, on this same site. Three of them had the round borings in sets of three in a straight line overlapping[39]; this technique (which did not occur in the Neolithic culture) may represent a transitional stage to the oval pit of the Shangs. Finally, all six of the bones found in the Ch'êng Tzŭ Yai Neolithic culture had been touched with hot points or fire, presumably to produce cracks for divination, in the same way in which the Shang divination bones were treated[40]. Divination bone has also been been found in the Hou Kang (II) culture[41]. The detailed correspondences between the bones found at Ch'êng Tzŭ Yai and those found at Anyang are so many that they appear to preclude the possibility of independent development in the two cultures. In so far as I am aware no bone resembling this has been found in any Neolithic site except those of the "black pottery culture" represented at Ch'êng Tzŭ Yai. This constitutes, then, a link of considerable importance between the two cultures.

Another link of some importance is the technique of building

35. *Ch'êng-tzŭ-yai* 86.
36. Cf. *Yin Ching Hua*, in which the large plates are all of inscriptions on scapulae.
37. *Ch'êng-tzŭ-yai* 86. Compare the process of preparing bone and tortoise shell used by the Shangs, *Anyang Pao Kao* 80–95.
38. Cf. *Anyang Pao Kao* 95–6.
39. See *Ch'êng-tzŭ-yai* 86.
40. *Ch'êng-tzŭ-yai* 86.
41. Cf. *Ts'ai Anniv. Vol.* 558. This bone is not described, but it was apparently similar to that found at Ch'êng Tzŭ Yai.

with "pounded earth". This is still used in the village which stands on the very site of the ancient Shang capital; I have observed it in general use in modern Honan, Shensi, and Shansi. It consists of constructing a framework of boards, much like a mould for concrete, throwing in loose earth, and pounding it hard. When one layer is firm, the frame is moved higher, more earth is thrown in, the pounding is repeated, and the process is continued until the desired height is reached. I have seen walls in the Anyang region, built within the last decade by this method, which stand quite firmly twelve feet high although they are only two feet thick at the base. This pounded earth survives remarkably well; some of it which dates from Shang times is almost as hard as concrete when excavated.

The method is well described in ancient Chinese literature. We read in the *Shih*:

"He called his superintendent of works;
He called his minister of instruction;
And charged them with the building of the houses.
With the line they made everything straight;
They bound the frame-boards tight, so that they should rise regularly.
Up rose the ancestral temple in its solemn grandeur.
Crowds brought the earth in baskets;
They threw it with shouts into the frames;
They beat it with responsive blows;
They pared the walls repeatedly, and they sounded strong." [42]

It is frequently referred to in Chinese literature generally, and clearly was widely used [43].

Such pounded earth is one of the most characteristic features of Shang culture as it appears at Anyang. A large number of house foundations, one of them 28 by 8 meters and about one meter high, made by this technique, have been excavated [44].

42. *Shih* 439–40.
43. In addition to the above references see *Shih* 304; *Mencius* 254, 446; *Tso Chuan* 309.4; etc.
44. *Anyang Pao Kao* 711–15.

What appears to be the remains of a piece of wall within the city has been found[45], but as yet no traces of walls surrounding the city have been discovered. The circumstances make it very probable, however, that such walls will be found when the field of excavation has been widened sufficiently. In constructing their tombs especially the Shang people used this technique on a lavish scale. A hole of considerable size was dug in the ground, and after the interment was completed the entire opening was filled up with earth laboriously pounded, layer by layer. In the case of one tomb excavated in 1935 the cavity thus filled with pounded earth measured about twenty meters square and thirteen meters deep, while three others were only a little smaller[46]; the amount of labor required to fill them by this method must have been stupendous.

As to when and where this method of pounding earth originated, and whether or not it was independently discovered more than once, I have no information. It is said to have been used by the Scythians[47], but in so far as I am aware the earliest excavated Scythian materials are dated from about the seventh century B.C.[48]. Mr. Bishop says that this technique "is known from end to end of the North Temperate Zone, and is common in the Near East in antiquity. It occurs, for example, at Al 'Ubaid, in a very early prehistoric settlement."[49] But evidence of the use of this technique has not been found, according to my information, in any Chinese Neolithic sites except those of the Ch'êng Tzŭ Yai or "black pottery" culture. In reporting his Kansu excavations in a large number of sites of Neolithic and later periods, Andersson says that "Of housefoundations we have never found any trace, probably because the ancient people most likely built huts of the everywhere present,

45. *Anyang Pao Kao* 713.
46. Verbal communication from Liang Ssŭ-yung, May 2, 1935.
47. Verbal communication from Liang Ssŭ-yung, August 5, 1934.
48. Cf. M. Rostovtzeff, *The Animal Style in South Russia and China* (Princeton, 1929) 20, 24.
49. Quoted from a letter of August 15, 1934.

easily handled and easily eroded loess"[50]. But if foundations had been built of pounded earth, as they were at Anyang, they would have been found, for such earth is by no means easily eroded. It is so resistant, in fact, that the rectangular walls at Ch'êng Tzŭ Yai filled up with earth and formed an artificial terrace which still persists. Andersson also says, "Mud walls thrown up for defense have been noticed only in the case of the sites of the Sha Ching stage"[51]. But the Sha Ching stage is now dated as late as the Iron Age[52]. It is the most recent of the six cultural stages distinguished by Andersson in Kansu, and he has recently assigned to it a probable date of 600–100 B.C., thus placing it much later than Shang culture itself[53]. And the description of "mud walls thrown up" does not sound as if even these late walls had anything in common with the pounded earth walls which are erected with great care and labor.

In the spring of 1934 a pounded earth wall, which must originally have been of imposing width and height, was excavated at Hou Kang, at Anyang. The excavators assigned its construction to the people of Hou Kang (II), the Anyang black pottery culture, because it marked the limit of that culture deposit, because of the accumulation of rubbish heaps against it, and for other reasons. I saw this wall on a visit to the site, and discussed the reasons for its dating with the excavators. No description of it has yet been published. Much more is known about the walls surrounding the Neolithic town at Ch'êng Tzŭ Yai. The following description is quoted from the English summary of the report:

"The ancient builders probably built their walls in the following manner. A shallow round bottomed foundation trench about 13.8 m. wide and 1.5 m. deep was first dug in the ground.... It was then filled up with layers of hard stamped earth which served as the foundation. On this foundation was built the wall proper, also of layers of hard stamped earth which was

50. *Arch. Res. in Kansu* 5.
51. *Loc. cit.*
52. See page 170, note 5.
53. "Der Weg Über die Steppen", *BMFEA*, 1929, 1.152–153.

mixed with a quantity of stones that acted as a sort of concretion. The thickness of the layers, which vary between 0.12 and 0.14 m. are quite regular and each upper layer recedes about 3 cm. from the one below resulting in a slight batter. . . . When dug up, they show very distinctly the marks, round bosses and hollows of about 3-4 cm. in diameter, made by the stamps. The remaining height of the west and the south wall, where they are best preserved, stand about 2.5-3.0 meters. . . . Because of the destruction of the outside of these walls, their original thickness can no longer be determined. But calculating from their present thickness at one point . . . and the degree of battering, which is 3 cm. in 13 cm. or 0.7 m. in 3.0 m., the thickness at the base is approximately 10.6 m., at the height of 2.5 m. 10.0 m., and at the height of 6.5 m. 9.0 m. . . . "[54]

"The walls were built and in use, at least in their main parts, during the occupation of the site by the people who left the remains of the lower stratum [i.e., the Neolithic, 'black pottery' people]. That they were not built on unoccupied land is proved by the deposit of black pottery culture remains under them and the presence of similar remains in the wall earth. And that they were of the black pottery period is proved by the accumulation of rubbish heaps of that period against the foot of the walls . . . "[55]

This corresponds almost exactly to the examples of the use of this technique at Anyang, not only in the wall presumably belonging to Hou Kang (II) but also in the building of house foundations, etc., by the Shang people. As we might expect, the work in the latter case seems to have been done in a more careful manner; whereas the pounded layers in the wall at Ch'êng Tzŭ Yai are said to be 0.12 to 0.14 m. thick, those measured in certain Shang structures were only 0.05 to 0.07 m. thick[56], which means that a smaller quantity of loose earth was put into

54. *Ch'êng-tzŭ-yai*, English Summary 8-9.
55. Ibid. 9. For complete, convincing proof of this dating, with diagrams, see ibid. 28-30. There seems no possible doubt about the date of this wall.
56. *Anyang Pao Kao* 584.

the frame before each pounding and the result should have been a more closely amalgamated product. The round marks of the stamps were found in the Shang pounded earth just as in the wall at Ch'êng Tzŭ Yai [57].

What and where was the origin of this technique we do not know. But we do know that it was used by the Neolithic black pottery people before the Shangs moved to Anyang [58] in a manner almost identical with the Shang technique, and we know that the Shangs used it from the time of their move to Anyang and probably had been using it well before that time [59]. It is not found, on the other hand, in any Neolithic sites, even those to the west in Kansu, except those of the "black pottery" culture. While it may be possible to explain this otherwise, it is probably another indication of an important relationship between the black pottery culture and Shang culture.

Bishop, writing of the Neolithic cultures known before the discoveries at Ch'êng Tzŭ Yai, said, "On the basis of its possession of domestic animals, the Neolithic culture of China cannot be rated as a high one. That of Europe had the ox, goat, sheep, pig, and dog." In a footnote he added, "The horse as a domestic animal *may* have appeared in the Occident just before the close of the Neolithic there". "In China it is only the dog and the pig which certainly go back to Neolithic times. Their bones, and especially those of the latter, occur in enormous numbers,

57. *Anyang Pao Kao* 584.
58. Because the Shang remains overlie the black pottery remains at Hou Kang.
59. The Shang character 㐭, of which the meaning is not altogether certain, is unquestionably a ⌂ view of one of the typical large buildings of the period as seen from the end. It shows the pounded earth platform perfectly. This element appears in the character 㐭 in *Yin Hou Pien*, 1.6.7, which is dated by the name of the diviner 〣 as belonging to the period of Wu Ting. This shows that the complicated technique of house construction revealed by the excavations must have been developed before that early date. It follows that the technique of pounding earth to make platforms must have been known to the Shangs for some time before that date.

while those of other animals are almost wholly absent. Thus on the large site already mentioned, along with vast quantities of dog and pig bones and a very few of wild animals like the leopard and water-deer, there were found only a few vertebrae of a small bovid and the fragmentary mandible of a young sheep; and there is no assurance that even these did not belong to wild individuals."[61]

To the Neolithic culture here described, Shang culture stands in sharp contrast. Not only the bones of the pig and the dog but also those of horses, cattle, and sheep have been excavated at Anyang in large numbers[62]. Bones of the ox and the pig are the most numerous[63]. We know from inscriptions which contemplate sacrifices of as many as fifty sheep[64] or three hundred cattle[65] at one time that these animals must have been domesticated. Moreover, we find the character 牧 *mu*, "to herd cattle", on bone inscriptions even from the very early time of Wu Ting[66]. A variant form of the same character, found on the bones, is made up of "sheep" and a hand holding a crook[67].

Cattle grazing was, in fact, a very important activity with the

61. "The Neolithic Age in Northern China", p. 396.
62. *Anyang Pao Kao* 574.
63. Loc. cit.
64. *Yin Ch'ien Pien* 3.23.6.
65. *Ibid.* 4.8.4.
66. Cf. *Yin Ching Hua* 2, 6; the name of the diviner dates 2. The form of the character *mu* which occurs here is not the usual one showing a hand holding a stick or a crook, but instead the hand holds what appears to be a brush, and on one form of the character in 2 there are several short dashes about the pictograph of the ox. Lo Chên-yü interprets these dashes as water, and therefore says that the pictograph represents the washing of cattle with a brush (*Yin K'ao Shih*, chung 70b). I commented to Mr. Bishop that this seemed excessively close care for a herdsman to take of his charges, and he responded with the suggestion that the character might depict "simply a fly-flapper such as modern mafoos use to brush away flies". This is quite possible, in which case the dashes might represent the flies. On the whole this theory seems more plausible than Lo's.
67. Cf. *Yin Ch'ien Pien* 5.45.7–8.

Shang people, as early as the time of Wu Ting. Quarrels over the use of grazing lands apparently led to wars. In the oracle inscriptions from his time we read that a certain person "informs saying, 'The *people of the* 丨 [hereafter referred to as X][68] country have come forth and grazed cattle on our ... lands, seven men.'"[69] "The X country also grazed cattle on the lands of our western border settlements"[70]. "If the order is given to attack the X country will we receive *aid*?"[71] "Shall three thousand *men* be ordered to attack the X country?"[72] Again it is said that someone "informs saying, 'The 土 T'u country grazed cattle on our lands, ten men'."[73] "The T'u country attacks our eastern border ... two towns"[74]. "... shall the king attack the T'u country?"[75]

68. This character has not been certainly deciphered, in spite of many attempts to read it; cf. *Pu Tz'ŭ T'ung Tsuan*, K'ao Shih 112.
69. *Yin Ching Hua* 2; dated by diviner's name in time of Wu Ting.
70. Loc. cit.
71. *Yin Ch'ien Pien* 7.35.1; dated by diviner's name in time of Wu Ting. The last character in this section of the inscription is 受 *shou*, which is partially missing but clearly identifiable. The word "aid" is added by analogy with other inscriptions of this kind; cf. ibid. 7.2.4, 7.38.1. This is probably the aid of the gods, since in other inscriptions of this type we find such statements as "Ti sends down compliance" (ibid. 7.38.1, etc.).
72. *Yin Hou Pien* 1.17.1; dated by name of diviner in time of Wu Ting. The word *jên* is broken off at the top of this inscription, but is present in another inscription on this same bone and is made quite certain by its presence above the number in a great many inscriptions which are virtually identical with this; cf. *Yin Ch'ien Pien* 6.34.2, 7.2.3, etc.
73. *Yin Ching Hua* 6. The "ten men" are presumably men in charge of the cattle. Unfortunately this bone does not contain the name of a diviner. But there are many detailed correspondences between its inscription as to size and form of characters, grammar, phrases, etc., and inscriptions on bones which are indubitably from the time of Wu Ting (cf. ibid. 1, 2, 3, 7). Moreover, it refers to events which seem to be peculiar to that period, so that I have no doubt that it is from the time of Wu Ting.
74. Ibid. 2. This inscription is dated in the time of Wu Ting, by the diviner's name.
75. *Kuei Tzŭ* 2.9.1; this inscription is dated in the time of Wu Ting by the diviner's name.

We can not, of course, be absolutely certain that the wars of the time of Wu Ting were caused by disputes over grazing lands. But when we find repeated complaints against encroachments on pasture lands by certain peoples, and find that wars were waged with these peoples in the same period—especially when we find these things mentioned on the same piece of divination bone—[76] this is rather good evidence that there was some connection between the two. And if cattle grazing was carried on by the Shangs and their neighbors, in the early time of Wu Ting, on a scale large enough to cause repeated clashes and even wars in various localities, then it was probably a well established part of Shang culture when the Shang people moved to Anyang, probably a few decades earlier than this date.

Horses were well known, domesticated, and driven to chariots even as early as the time of Wu Ting. The pictographs both for "horse" and for "chariot" occur in at least one inscription which we can date certainly, by the diviner's name, from his time[77]; they also occur in several other inscriptions which probably come from this time but which are too fragmentary to be dated with precision. Not only did the Shang people have the horse and the chariot in the time of Wu Ting; they hitched the horse to the chariot.[78] In the inscription just referred to this is not only

76. As in *Yin Ching Hua* 2.
77. *Yin Ching Hua* 1.
78. How many horses were hitched to one chariot at this time it is not possible to say with certainty. Some of the "chariot" pictographs on the bones clearly indicate the use of two horses; cf. *T'ieh Kuei* 114.1; *Yin Ch'ien Pien* 7.5.3. The pictographs for "chariot" on the bones and early Chou bronzes vary, but all more or less resemble the form 車, found on the Yü Ting (*K'ê Lu* 4.13a; for similar bone form, see *T'ieh Kuei*, 114.1). The chariot is depicted as seen from above, with the wheels conventionally shown as if in the horizontal plane. The pole and crossbar are plain, but the significance of the two v-shaped figures attached to the crossbar has long been debated. Some have supposed that they were merely trestles, used to keep the bar off the ground while the chariot was not in use. It has been my own opinion that these v-shaped figures were a sort of yoke, going over the necks of the horses, and this has now been proved to be the correct explanation. In excavating the early Chou tombs at Hsün Hsien, northern Honan, Mr. Kuo

Pao-chün found a great many chariots in situ, and was able to take out the bronze and even some of the wooden parts of early Chou chariots and to determine their place and function in the whole. Among the pieces recovered are several of these v-shaped yokes. Mr. Kuo very kindly showed and explained these to me in Kaifêng on May 4, 1935.

But since the character for "chariot" does not show anything but the shaft and the yokes which were probably more or less permanently affixed to it, the possibility that two other horses were also hitched on loose traces, even in Shang times, is still open. Nor does it seem possible to determine the size of the Shang team by the number of horses buried together. At Hsün Hsien, in one pit which was apparently used for a horse sacrifice, twelve chariots and seventy-two horses were found (verbal communication from Mr. Kuo, May 6, 1935). This is surprising, for I know of no mention of a six-horse team in any of the early literature. But at Anyang the largest number of horses found buried together in one place was thirty-eight (verbal communication from Liang Ssŭ-yung, July 2, 1935). Since this number is not divisible by four, six, or eight, it might be supposed to indicate two-horse teams, but the evidence is greatly weakened by the fact that no chariots were found buried in the same pit. At Hsün Hsien, as few as two horses were sometimes found buried together, indicating that the two-horse team was probably still used, on occasion, in early Chou times.

From the literature we would suppose that the usual Chou team consisted of four horses (cf. *Shih* 247, 260, 281, 285, etc.). A common word for team was 駟, made up of "horse" and "four" (cf. *Shih* 436 etc.). But in this team there were apparently two horses yoked by traces, not hitched directly to shafts, for we read:

"Of the four yellow horses of each chariot,
 The two outsiders inclined not to either side." (*Shih* 290).
And:
"The two insides are the finest possible animals,
 And the two outsides follow them regularly as in a flying
  flock of wild geese . . .
 His two insides have their heads in a line,
 And the two outsides come after like arms". (*Shih* 130).

From these passages we can see clearly that the two outside horses were a little back of the insides, so that the whole team was spread out fanwise, and that the outsides were apparently hitched by more or less loose traces, so that if not well trained and well handled they might have "inclined to either side".

The phrase used in the *Shih* to denote the two outside horses is 兩驂 *liang ts'an*, "the two *ts'an*". *Ts'an* is made up of "horse" and 參 *ts'an*; despite the statement of the *Shuo Wên* that *ts'an* is merely phonetic in the combination, it probably has the meaning of "three".

shown by the juxtaposition of the characters for "horse" and "chariot", but also by the phrase "drive the king's chariot". The character for "drive" here is an unusual form, composed of a pictograph of a horse and a human hand, evidently depicting the controlling of it[79]. Since the Shangs were driving horses to

In any case, just as 駟 *ssŭ* means "a team of four horses," so the *Shuo Wên* defines 驂 *ts'an* as "three horses hitched together".

But where *ts'an* is used to refer to each of two of the horses of a four-horse team, it obviously cannot mean "three horses". Instead, I suggest, it means "a third horse". From this character, I believe, we can see what was very probably the history of the Chinese four-horse chariot. At first only two horses were used. But sometimes, perhaps when the wheels became mired down, it became necessary to add a third horse, and this was naturally done on a loose trace since the positions beside the single shaft were already occupied. This third horse may have been added at one side or, perhaps more probably, it may have been put on long traces out in front of the other two, as an extra draft animal on long traces is put out in front of Peking carts at the present day. This extra pulling power must have been found a great advantage, especially on difficult roads. In time still another extra animal was added, and it was found convenient to attach the two outside of and a little behind the two horses of the original team. Finally these two extra horses came to be a part of the regular team, not merely added in emergencies but always hitched so. But because of this history the two outside horses continued to be called "the two third horses". This is, of course, merely theory, but it seems plausible.

This does not enable us, however, to be sure how many horses were hitched to the Shang chariot. Apparently the form of the shafts, etc., did not change much when the two outside horses were added. And if it did, this did not alter the form of the character for "chariot", for that shows little or no sign of four horses in the forms found on bronzes (cf. *Chin Wên Pien* 14.6b–7a). It appears from the *Shih* (p. 436) that four-horse teams were used by the Chous in their conquest, but the character *ch'ê* as we find it on the *Mao Kung Ting*, which is dated well after the Chou conquest, is almost identical with that character as we find it on the Shang oracle bones; cf. *K'ê Lu* 4.4a and *T'ieh Kuei* 114.1. They might, then, have used chariots with four horses in Shang times without leaving any trace of this in the bone inscriptions. On the other hand the use of the character *ts'an* as well as the method of harnessing appears clearly to indicate that the chariot was originally driven with only two horses.

79. *Yin Ching Hua* 1. So far as I know this is the only occurrence

chariots in the time of Wu Ting it is probable that they had the horse as a domestic animal at the time of their move to Anyang.

It is true that among the bones found by Andersson in one site of "early Yang Shao" age "About 40 bones of cattle certainly belong to tame animals, and the same is probably true of sheep and goats"[80]. But this site is far to the west, near Kuei Tê in eastern Chinghai (Kokonor), "situated quite close to the high Tibetan plateau"[81]. The site is known as Lo Han T'ang. It evidently represented a culture quite different from the pig-and-dog-raising, agricultural economy of the ordinary north Chinese Neolithic peoples. Andersson says that "The paucity of pigs' bones and, on the other hand, the abundance of remains of game ruminants and rodents shows that the inhabitants of this dwelling-place were predominantly hunters and cattle-raising nomads... We may with justice say that Lo Han T'ang even to this day is on the boundary between the pastoral and the hunting regions on the Tibetan borderland[82]".

Since Andersson dates Lo Han T'ang somewhere between his earliest, Ch'i Chia stage, and the next, or Yang Shao[83], it appears that domestic cattle must have been kept by nearby contemporaries of very nearly the earliest Neolithic people we know in north China. But apparently the practice was very slow to spread eastward. We have seen that according to Bishop in the previously known Neolithic sites in north China among domestic animals "it is only the dog and the pig which certainly go back to Neolithic times". Indeed even the bones of wild species of the horse and ox have not been found in any great numbers in the previously known Neolithic sites, in so far as my information goes[84]. On the other hand the Shang people, when they first

---

of the character referred to in this form, but Sun (*Chia Pien* 2.24a) and others have so interpreted it, and the context leaves little room for doubt of its meaning.

80. *Children of the Yellow Earth*, 242.
81. Ibid. 243.
82. Loc. cit.
83. Ibid. 241–2.
84. It is to be regretted that records of excavations in this region

come within our field of vision, graze cattle and sheep in large numbers and keep and drive horses. Here we have a definite hiatus.

Once again the black pottery culture of Ch'êng Tzŭ Yai seems to function as the "missing link" between the older Neolithic cultures and Shang culture. For among the bones found at Ch'êng Tzŭ Yai, Dr. C. C. Young of the Geological Survey of China has identified those of the horse, ox, and sheep[85]. Whether or not these animals were domestic is not yet completely certain. Dr. Young kindly showed me the skeletal material in his care and discussed his conclusions concerning it on April 22, 1935. That the dog and pig were domesticated at Ch'êng Tzŭ Yai he considers most probable, because the great number of milk dentitions in the material indicate that these animals were killed while young. He believes that the ox may well have been domestic, but is not certain of this. The species, significantly, is probably the same as that of the cattle of the Shang people, which we know were domesticated. Whether or not the horses found were domesticated is not revealed by the skeletal material.

A distinct possibility that both ox and horse were domesticated at Ch'êng Tzŭ Yai is raised by the fact that, according to the excavators, their bones were relatively numerous in the finds, next in frequency to those of the pig and dog[86].

---

do not give us more of specific, qualitative and quantitative information concerning the animal bones excavated. It is very important, of course, to have many books written on the styles of painted pottery, etc., and these things are invaluable. In this pioneering stage of archeology in China we must, of course, be grateful for any information. But it would be a boon greatly appreciated by some of us if excavators, both Chinese and western, would give us more of definite and even statistical information concerning the objects, bones, etc., actually found.

85. *Ch'êng-tzŭ-yai* 90–91. The species are *Equus sp.*, *Bos cf. exiguus*, and *Ovis changi* Teilhard and Young. *Ch'êng-tzŭ-yai* 91 reads "*Bos cf. exignus*", but this is evidently a typographical error; my information was obtained from Dr. Young on April 22, 1935.

86. *Ch'êng-tzŭ-yai* 91. Exact information on these points is unfortunately not yet available, as a complete statistical analysis of the bones found has not yet been published. The difficulty is increased

Another aspect of the culture found at Ch'êng Tzŭ Yai which shows it to be related to Shang culture is its pottery. The culture is known as a black pottery culture because of a type of very fine, highly polished black ware, wheel-made and sometimes no more than a single millimeter in thickness, which is typical of this culture and no other known[87]. This ware is found, of course, in the same culture in Hou Kang (II) at Anyang, but not in the Shang culture stratum there, although a black pottery somewhat resembling it was made by the Shang people[88]. The finest ware of the Shang people was not of this sort, but a kind of white pottery made of the same clay from which porcelain is made[89]. This "white pottery" of the Shangs was used to make ceremonial vessels, which were decorated with designs much like and in some cases identical with those found on Shang bronzes. Probably the finest of these ever recovered was excavated from a Shang tomb by the National Research Institute in the autumn of 1934[90]. Such designs as are found on this pottery have not been found at Ch'êng Tzŭ Yai, of course. But a small proportion of the pottery found there was also a white ware made from porcelain clay[91]; such ware has not been found, in so far as I know, in any other Neolithic culture in China.

---

by the fact that in certain respects the report treats of the materials from the upper, Bronze Age stratum, and the lower stratum together. But in response to my query on this point Mr. Liang Ssŭ-yung assured me that horse and cattle bones were relatively not infrequent in the lower as well as the upper stratum (verbal communication of May 2, 1935).

87. Cf. *Ch'êng-tzŭ-yai*, English Summary 12.
88. Verbal communication from Liang Ssŭ-yung, March 8, 1935.
89. Verbal communication from Liang Ssŭ-yung, March 8, 1935. Dr. John C. Ferguson considers this ware to be a kind of porcelain (verbal communication of March 4, 1935).
90. It is unfortunately broken, and not all of the pieces were recovered. It has not yet been published, but I examined it in Peiping on February 18, 1935. It is better than any of the many fine pieces published by Umehara in *Yin Kyo Shutsudo Hakushoku Doki No Kenkyu* 殷墟出土白色土器の研究 *Etude sur la Poterie Blanche Fouillee dans la Ruine de l'Ancienne Capitale des Yin* (Kyoto, 1932).
91. Cf. *Ch'êng-tzŭ-yai* 41.

It is not so much in its materials as in its forms, however, that the pottery found at Ch'êng Tzǔ Yai resembles that found in the Shang remains. Here the correspondences are so close that Liang Ssǔ-yung, who is a specialist on pottery and has spent a great deal of time in the minute analysis of these forms, goes so far as to state flatly that, while there are differences, the pottery technique of the Shang capital is quite definitely "a continuation" of the pottery technique of Ch'êng Tzǔ Yai[92]. It is to be noted that his dictum is not based on mere common possession of certain types such as the *li* and the *hsien*, by these two cultures, but rather on careful and even statistical comparisons of the form and measurements of thousands of lips, handles, necks, bases, etc.[93].

We have seen that there are four outstanding aspects of Shang culture which are shared by the black pottery culture of Ch'êng Tzǔ Yai and, in so far as is known, by no other Neolithic culture in the North China area. These are: the use of bones, prepared and burned in a distinctive manner, for divination; the building of structures from pounded earth with the use of a distinctive technique; the occurrence of the bones of the horse and probably the same species of ox in the remains of both cultures; the making of "white pottery" from the same clay which is used in the manufacture of porcelain, and the manufacture of pottery generally in forms so similar that the Shang technique is declared to be "a continuation" of the pottery technique of Ch'êng Tzǔ Yai.

These resemblances must be explained in one of three ways. Either these aspects of the two cultures were developed in each case independently, or they were derived independently from one or more outside sources, or they were borrowed by one culture from the other. We must examine each of these possibilities in connection with each of these four criteria.

The divination bone seems to be a definite link between these

92. *Ts'ai Anniv. Vol.* 561.
93. Some idea of Mr. Liang's method may be gained from his paper entitled *New Stone Age Pottery from the Prehistoric Site at Hsi-yin Tsun, Shansi, China; Mem. of the American Anthropological Association,* No. 37, 1930.

two cultures. It was not only found at Ch'êng Tzŭ Yai, but also in Hou Kang (II) at Anyang[94]. Since stratification shows the black pottery culture at Hou Kang to have been earlier than the Shang culture there, and since the divination bone associated with the black pottery culture is prepared by a method which is similar even to details but more primitive than the Shang method, and finally since no bone of this sort has been found elsewhere than in sites of these two cultures, it is more than probable that the Shang technique of bone divination was a development out of the technique of the black pottery people.

The pounded earth technique is not found exclusively in China, but it apparently has not been found in any Chinese Neolithic sites except those of the black pottery culture. It might have been obtained from an outside source by both the Shang people and the black pottery people, independently. But since the wall built at Hou Kang by this technique seems definitely to belong to Hou Kang (II), it is quite possible that the technique was obtained by the Shangs through the medium of the black pottery people; this is to leave out of discussion its ultimate place of origin.

The bones of the horse and the ox found at Ch'êng Tzŭ Yai are an unsatisfactory criterion, in our present state of knowledge. As domestic animals, they are generally considered to have been introduced from a region to the west of China[95]. Andersson's discovery of a very early Neolithic people who had the domestic ox, located on the western border of the north Chinese area, coupled with the fact that the ox as a domestic animal was apparently unknown even in the western parts of the north Chinese Neolithic area proper until very late, certainly bears this out[96]. The question is, then, whether the black pottery people obtained the ox and the horse first and passed them to the Shangs, or the Shangs obtained them first and passed them to the black pottery people, or both peoples obtained them, independently,

94. *Ts'ai Anniv. Vol.* 558.
95. Cf. Bishop, "The Beginnings of North and South in China", 305, 325.
96. Cf. *Children of the Yellow Earth* 242.

from outside sources. Such meager evidence as is now available leaves open the possibility that they obtained them independently.

For reasons which have been stated it appears that the horse and especially the ox were well known to the Shang people before the time at which they are supposed to have moved to Anyang. We cannot, therefore, say that the black pottery culture was in every respect anterior to Shang culture merely because Hou Kang (III) lies on top of Hou Kang (II). In Hou Kang (II), the black pottery culture at Anyang, the ox was present, but the horse is said to have been very rare[97]. It is among the possibilities, then, that the Shang people had the ox and the horse, in an earlier habitat, as early as or even earlier than the black pottery people had them, and they might even have passed them on to the Ch'êng Tzŭ Yai people. We may expect further light on this subject from the excavation of the many other black pottery sites known to exist.

Pottery forms are more certain. These were not mere importations from the outside world, and forms like those of the Shangs are found alike at Ch'êng Tzŭ Yai and in Hou Kang (II). If Shang pottery is "a continuation" of the technique of the Ch'êng Tzŭ Yai Neolithic potters, then the two cultures must, to some extent, have had a common background.

More than thirty sites of the black pottery culture are now known in the several districts around Anyang[98]. Two of them, near Hsün Hsien, were excavated by the Honan Archeological Research Association in 1932[99]. A large number of sites have been found in Shantung, some on the very seacoast[100]. From present information it appears that this culture flourished chiefly in the plains region centering about Honan and Shantung, though one site of it may have been discovered as far west as Hsian in Shensi[101]. It is to be noted that this is in general the same

97. Communication in a letter from Liang Ssŭ-yung, April 9, 1935.
98. Verbal communication from Mr. Liang Ssŭ-yung, March 8, 1935.
99. See *Ch'êng Li San Chou Nien Kung Tso Kai K'uang Chi Ti Êrh Tz'ŭ Chan Lan Hui Chan P'in Shuo Ming* (Kaifêng, 1935), 2, 4, 6.
100. Verbal communication from Dr. Fu Ssŭ-nien, April 5, 1935.
101. Verbal communication from Mr. Liang Ssŭ-yung, March 8, 1935.

region in which tradition places the various Shang capitals prior to the move to Anyang. In view, then, of such evidence as is now available it is distinctly possible that Shang culture was a branch of this same black pottery culture upon which was grafted the technique of making bronze and certain other culture traits. Whether the Shang people and the black pottery people were racially akin it is not possible to say at present, since no datable skeletal material was found in association with the black pottery remains at Ch'êng Tzŭ Yai[102], nor, I believe, in Hou Kang (II).

A Northeastern Culture Area

In any case, the black pottery culture has such relations with Shang culture that any investigation of the origins of Shang culture cannot but include some examination of the antecedents of the black pottery culture. While our knowledge of the latter is still in a most rudimentary stage, we are nevertheless justified in drawing the tentative conclusion that this culture was not merely the result of importing, wholesale, a culture from elsewhere and setting it down unchanged in north China. We may say tentatively that the black pottery culture was *a variety of Neolithic culture developed in and chiefly peculiar to northeastern China*. By the statement that it was a variety of Neolithic culture it is emphasized that it was a part of Neolithic culture generally. The statement that it was developed in and chiefly peculiar to northeastern China emphasizes the fact that the people who possessed this culture developed it into something in certain respects differing from Neolithic culture generally, imparting to it a distinctive character, and that they apparently invented certain of its distinctive criteria. The northeastern area here referred to appears to have been limited to what are now Honan and Shantung provinces, and southern Hopei; thus far, at least, the distinctive criteria of this culture have proved rare if not lacking in the extreme northeast. Actually, we can not be sure that this culture did not extend to the south, for

102. *Ch'êng-tzŭ-yai* 90.

excavations both in the east and the west have been confined chiefly to the north. But the great differences in culture between north and south China in historical times, which are based to a large extent on geography, make this somewhat doubtful.

The Bow and Arrow. The beginnings of a special culture area in northeastern China are not to be sought in the black pottery culture, however; they go back much earlier. One item in the evidence for this has to do with the bow and arrow.

These have played a very important part in Chinese culture right down to the time when they were finally displaced by Western firearms. Apparently they were the chief offensive weapon in the Chou period[1], and judging by the number of arrowheads found at Anyang they must have been very important to the Shangs. One of the reasons for the place which the bow has held among the Chinese is the fact that they used the very powerful composite, reflex bow, a far more formidable weapon than the English longbow and related types. The Shang people knew the reflex bow and probably had used it for some time before they moved to Anyang. For inscriptions which we can definitely date in the reign of Wu Ting show the reflex form[2], and in so far as I have observed all of the considerable number of representations of bows which we have on the oracle bones, even those of pellet bows, are of this type[3].

1. This is a point concerning which it is difficult to be quite certain. But we find in the *Shih* (619) a description of an attack on the Huai I which says: "How they draw their horn bows! [i.e., composite bows made partly of horn] How their arrows whiz forth!", and mentions no other weapons. We know from the large number of *kê* preserved to us that this weapon must have had some importance, but in even comparatively detailed descriptions of battles it is the bow and arrow which are chiefly mentioned; cf. *Tso Chuan* 340, etc.; *Shih* 513. I know of no passage describing the large scale use of *kê* in battle at this time. Laufer ("Some Fundamental Ideas of Chinese Culture" 166) apparently speaking of prehistoric times in China, says that "The offensive arm of that period was the composite bow".

2. Cf. for instance *Yin Ching Hua* 7. This piece of bone is dated by the occurrence on it of the names of two different diviners, either of which would be sufficient to date it from the time of Wu Ting.

3. Cf. *Chia Pien* 5.14ab, 12.19b–20a.

Whether or not the Neolithic peoples of north China knew the reflex bow is a point on which there seems to be no evidence. But we do know that whereas the bow was used a good deal by the northeastern Neolithic peoples, it was used very little indeed by those in the northwest. Arrowheads have been found in large numbers in Neolithic sites in northern Honan, at Yang Shao and elsewhere[4]. They have been found in a site which is ascribed to the Yang Shao culture at Hsi Yin Ts'un in Hsia Hsien, southwestern Shansi[5]. They occur in considerable numbers in the black pottery culture at Ch'êng Tzŭ Yai and Hou Kang (II)[6], as well as in the Shang remains[7]; an important type of Shang arrowhead is duplicated among the Ch'êng Tzŭ Yai artifacts[8].

But in speaking of the Yang Shao culture Andersson says, "A striking fact is that arrow points, which are quite common in Honan, and are there executed in several varied materials (slate, bone, mussel-shells) were exceedingly rare in Kansu"[9]. Li Chi says that the Yang Shao culture as it appears to the north, in Fengtien, is almost entirely lacking in arrowheads[10]. Speaking of the Chinese Neolithic generally, Bishop says that "the scarcity of weapons suggests that there was little warfare"[11]. But from the distribution of arrowheads it seems that the northeastern peoples (i.e., of the Honan-Shantung area) may have been somewhat more bellicose than their neighbors to the west, and the

4. Cf. *An Early Chinese Culture* 27; *Arch. Res. in Kansu* 12.
5. This site was excavated by Dr. Li Chi in 1926. For its dating, see his *Hsi Yin Ts'un Shih Ch'ien Ti I Ts'un (Ch'ing Hua Hsüeh Hsiao Yen Chiu Yuan Ts'ung Shu Ti San Chung*; Peking 1927) 29. The arrowheads are illustrated and discussed in *Ts'ai Anniv. Vol.* 77–79.
6. *Ch'êng-tzŭ-yai* 76, 80; *Ts'ai Anniv. Vol.* 558.
7. *Anyang Pao Kao* 574.
8. *Ts'ai Anniv. Vol.* 78–9. According to Li Chi this same type is also found in the supposedly Yang Shao site at Hsi Yin Ts'un, although not at Yang Shao itself; cf. loc. cit.
9. *Arch. Res. in Kansu* 12.
10. *Anyang Pao Kao* 339.
11. "The Rise of Civilization in China with Reference to its Geographical Aspects" 619.

fact that the black pottery people built high walls around their settlements, at Ch'êng Tzǔ Yai and apparently at Hou Kang (II), looks as if they had continued this tradition, since the defensive wall was not found by Andersson in Kansu save in his most recent, Iron Age, sites[12].

Divination Bones. The divination bones found in the black pottery sites are a peculiar feature of the greatest importance. It is true that the number found at Ch'êng Tzǔ Yai was very small. But the bones of this type found in the Shang remains were found in caches, where they had been buried together, and if they had not been disposed of in this way we might know comparatively few of the Shang oracle bones. We can not suppose that such a definite technique as is illustrated by the six bones found at Ch'êng Tzǔ Yai was developed to produce these and no more. The fact that such bones are found only in the black pottery and Shang culture indicates that they were a peculiar feature of the culture of the northeastern region—a feature of which the rôle, in Shang culture at least, was predominant.

The Li Tripod. Perhaps the most strikingly peculiar feature of the northeastern culture area was the 鬲 *li* tripod. Andersson has said, "It is tempting to think that the Li was invented by merging three vessels with pointed bottom in order to form a household utensil which could stand by itself, while at the same time it offered a very large contact surface to the fire when used for cooking"[13], and this theory has found very general favor. He also says, "As far as I know, *the Li is a ceramic type confined to the proto-Chinese and historically Chinese cultures*"[14]. This peculiar, bulbous-legged tripod and its related forms have played a very important part in Chinese culture; we find vessels made in such shapes even today. A very large number of vessels called by various names are really modifications of the *li*, some with beaks, etc. Many bronze vessels called 鼎 *ting* are really highly modified *li*. Their bottoms are not smooth and round,

12. Cf. *Arch. Res. in Kansu* 5.
13. *Arch. Res. in Kansu* 46–47.
14. Ibid. 47.

as those of a ting should be; instead they bulge slightly toward each leg, showing by this vestigial character that they have developed from the hollow legs of the *li*[15].

The 甗 *hsien*, sometimes called "steamer" is a *li* in which water is placed to produce steam, surmounted by another vessel in which the articles to be cooked are placed, the two being separated by a perforated partition. It is made sometimes in one piece, sometimes with the upper part removable[16]. This vessel was used for the offering of sacrifices, and as early as Shang times the pictograph of the vessel was used as a verb, "to sacrifice"[17]. The use of the name of this vessel in this manner, as well as the fact that Shang sacrificial vessels were very commonly made in this form, show that the peculiar *li* shape had its roots deep in Shang culture.

The *li* form is not merely a distinctive characteristic of Chinese culture, or of cultures in China—in so far as our present evidence goes, it was developed in and was perhaps the earliest distinctive peculiarity of the northeast China culture area. We have already observed that the painted pottery technique is considered to have come from the west, and to have affinities with Neolithic cultures as far away as the Near East[18]. That it was not developed in northeastern China is indicated by the relatively brief duration of the use of the painted pottery technique in that area. It has been found, as has been mentioned, at Hsi Yin Ts'un in southwestern Shansi, at Yang Shao in northwestern Honan, and in Hou Kang (I) at Anyang (but in a decidedly undeveloped form)[19]. Andersson also mentions "certain Yang Shao dwelling

15. Such a *ting* is illustrated in "On Shang Bronze," Plate II. See also *Sen-oku Sei-shô, The Collection of Old Bronzes of Baron Sumitomo* (rev. ed., Kyoto, 1934), Plate I (from its decoration this is probably a Shang piece). The *chia* of Plate XXVII is a modified *li*.

16. A *hsien* in two sections is shown in ibid. (hereafter referred to as *Sumitomo Collection*) 37.

17. See pages 207–218, below.

18. Cf. *Arch. Res. in Kansu* 10.

19. Cf. the illustrations of the painted pottery pot and sherds found at Anyang, in *Anyang Pao Kao* following 626, Plate 3, and the complicated and splendid designs on the pots found at Yang Shao and in

places in Eastern Honan, in the Ho Yin district, where painted pottery has been developed with especial splendor"[20]. The Honan Archeological Research Association[21] has excavated five painted pottery sites in Honan, during the last three years, at T'a P'o, Kung Hsien (near the confluence of the Lo with the Yellow River), at Ch'ên Kou and at Ch'ing T'ai[22] in Kuang Wu Hsien (about fifteen miles northwest of Chêngchow), and at Liu Chuang and Ta Chi Tien near Hsün Hsien (about fifty miles north of Kaifêng)[23]. When these northeastern Neolithic people did make painted pottery, they turned out vessels among the most beautiful which have ever been found anywhere in the world[24], but the technique was evidently an imported one and it did not persist. In so far as I am aware no painted pottery sites have been found in the northeastern area of any cultural stage much earlier or much later than the Yang Shao. As op-

---

Kansu, in "An Early Chinese Culture", Plates IX, X, XI, XII, and *Arch. Res. in Kansu*, Plates I, II, III, IV, VI, VII, VIII, IX.
20. *Children of the Yellow Earth* 184.
21. 河南古蹟研究會. This institution was formed by cooperation between the Honan Provincial Government and the National Research Institute. Its organization and work are described in a publication entitled *Ch'êng Li San Chou Nien Kung Tso Kai K'uang Chi Ti Êrh Tz'ŭ Chan Lan Hui Chan P'in Shuo Ming* (referred to hereafter as *Ch'êng Li Shuo Ming*) (Kaifêng, 1935).
22. This site is especially interesting. Mr. Kuo Pao-chün showed and explained to me the materials from this and other sites, at Kaifêng on May 4, 1935. The painted pottery designs from Ch'ing T'ai are quite elaborate, rather more so, I believe from superficial observation, than those which Andersson has published from Yang Shao.
   The most interesting find on this spot, however, was the remains of a house, apparently of painted pottery date, of a type not previously known, about two meters by three meters in size. Its walls, partially underground, were formed of a frame of reeds or wattles upon which mud was smeared. I have observed this type of wall in use in northern China at the present day. But in this case the mud walls had been fired, producing something resembling a brick house in one piece. This may be the earliest forerunner of Chinese brick and tile, neither of which have yet been found in the Shang materials.
23. For an account of these finds see *Ch'êng Li Shuo Ming* 3-6.

posed to this Andersson has found many sites in Kansu which he divides into six cultural stages, one of which he identifies as the Yang Shao stage and four of which are later. A very small amount of painted pottery was found even in the first, pre-Yang Shao stage[25], and the technique persisted through stages typified by magnificent examples of this art, even down to the most recent Iron Age stage which yielded a few vessels "covered with very exquisite painted designs, the main features of which are vertical triangles and horizontal zones of bird figures"[26]. Apparently, then, the painted pottery technique arrived later in the northeastern area than in Kansu, and disappeared very much earlier, leaving not even a great deal of influence on later Chinese art[27].

Even the Neolithic culture at Yang Shao does not appear to have been an imported one. Instead, it seems to have been a type of Neolithic culture which had previously existed in the same region, characterized by peculiar northeastern characteristics, upon which had been imposed as an intrusive technique the making of painted pottery and possibly other factors which went with it. A few sites found by Andersson in Honan show us what that culture, to which the painted pottery technique was added, was like. The type site of this variety of Neolithic culture is at Pu Chao Chai, a few miles west of Yang Shao.

24. Andersson says, "we should remember that such thin-walled, exquisitely shaped and beautifully decorated vessels as the P'an Shan urns and such graceful and in surface treatment perfect ceramic products as the painted dishes at Yang Shao Tsun are scarcely to be found in any other area of painted ceramics of the latest Stone age and incipient Metal ages."—*Children of the Yellow Earth*, 334.
25. Cf. *Arch. Res. in Kansu*, Plate V, 1b.
26. Ibid. 19, cf. Plate XI, 1 and 2.
27. This is not to say that it left no influence. Andersson illustrates, in *Arch. Res. in Kansu* 16, a continuous angular meander pattern found on Hsin Tien urns, and designs found both on Chinese bronzes and a Greek vase which show some relation to it. Mr. Orvar Karlbeck also showed me another pattern of diamond-shaped figures on a Kansu urn, which is found on Shang bronzes. But in general the painted pottery designs differ radically, in spirit as well as in detail, from Shang and later Chinese art.

This type of culture has no painted pottery whatever, but its monochrome vessels are very similar to those of Yang Shao. Andersson considers this culture to be the predecessor of the Yang Shao stage[28].

A culture of presumably similar age, slightly earlier than the Yang Shao, was also found in Kansu; it is called the Ch'i Chia stage. The difference between northeast and northwest in China was evidently considerable even before it was intensified by the coming of painted pottery, for these two pre-Yang Shao cultures are said to have little in common[29]. But it is important to notice that whereas in the northwest the coming of painted pottery was already heralded by a small amount of such ware, it was entirely lacking in the northeast. And while neither the *ting* nor the *li* tripod were present in the northwest, both of these vessels were even at this time characteristic of the northeast, and the *li* was already a highly developed form[30].

Thus in the Pu Chao Chai culture, the earliest known Neolithic culture in northeastern China, we also find our earliest evidence of the existence of a distinctive culture area in this region.

Even back in this culture we pick up the *li* tripod, which is to run like a tracer bullet through every period of culture in this area down to and including that of the Chinese Republic. Even in the Pu Chao Chai sites it was already well developed. Painted pottery did not eliminate it; along with their magnificent polychrome vessels, the potters of Yang Shao continued to make the *li*, so that it is "a very common feature in the Yang Shao deposit"[31]. Such a highly specialized development of the *li* form as the *hsien* "steamer" was made, apparently even as early as the Pu Chao Chai stage[32].

28. *Children of the Yellow Earth* 334; cf. also *Arch. Res. in Kansu* 37.
29. *Arch. Res. in Kansu* 38.
30. Loc. cit.
31. "An Early Chinese Culture", 33 and Plate XIV.6.
32. Andersson's statements on this point are not fully clear. In "An Early Chinese Culture", 60–61, he discusses, and in Plate XV.1 he illustrates what is almost certainly the removable upper portion of a

It is possible that there was a certain amount of conflict, and tendency to mutual exclusion, between the *li* as an eastern culture trait and painted pottery as a western importation. Mr. Kuo Pao-chün, of the Honan Archeological Research Association, says that in the five painted pottery sites which he has excavated neither the *li* nor the *hsien* was ever once found associated with the painted ware in the same culture stratum. He goes so far as to suggest that the *li* which Andersson found at Yang Shao were probably in a stratum separate from that of the painted pottery[33]. It seems quite possible, however, that the two might have mixed at certain points and remained separate at others.

In the black pottery culture the *li* tripod is one of the most common of all pottery forms, and the *hsien* and other sorts of vessels derived from the *li* are found at Ch'êng Tzŭ Yai and in Hou Kang (II)[34].

But although the *li* and even the *hsien* were known in the extreme west of the northeastern area, at Pu Chao Chai, before the painted pottery had arrived, no vessels of the *li* type have been found, in remains of supposedly equivalent period, to the west of this point. Andersson says, "In the earliest three stages, Ch'i Chia[35], Yang Shao and Ma Chang, there are very few or practically no traces of the Li, while at the same time the Ting tripod[36] is very rare or missing in Kansu. The only specimen

---

pottery *hsien*, excavated at Pu Chao Chai. And in *Children of the Yellow Earth* 222 he says that "In the Yang Shao dwelling-sites at Honan we made acquaintance with" the *hsien*. Apparently more than one was found, and they were found in Yang Shao proper as well as the Pu Chao Chai site, but it is not possible to be quite sure.

33. Verbal communication of May 6, 1935.
34. Cf. *Ts'ai Anniv. Vol.* 558; *Ch'êng-tzŭ-yai* 62–63, Plates XIII.2–7, XIX.7–8, XXII.1–3, 5, XXVIII. The *ting* type also occurs, cf. *Ts'ai Anniv. Vol.* 558; *Ch'êng-tzŭ-yai* 62, Plates XXI.5–6, XXII.6, XXIV.3, XXVI.1–2.
35. I have supplied commas here after "stages" and "Chia" which are not present in the original, because their absence might be confusing to readers not accustomed to these names of periods.
36. Little has been said up to this point concerning the 鼎 *ting*. It seems, as a matter of fact, to be an index of the northeastern culture

of the Li-tripod which I have recorded in my field notes from Kansu is a small fragment of a leg from one of the sites of the Yang Shao stage. It is only in the fourth stage of the prehistory of Kansu (the Hsin Tien stage) that we meet more abundant

area almost if not quite as good as the *li*, but I refrain from using it because of doubt which has been expressed as to its place of origin. Arne, in *Painted Stone Age Pottery from the Province of Honan, China*, 32–33, says: "I find no reason for moving the Chinese finds nearer our own times owing to the appearance of tripod vessels and their resemblance to later Chinese types of bronze. Tripod vessels turn up as early as in the oldest Troy (Town I). They are spoken of as kettle-like vessels with three tall feet and a broad vertical handle. They chiefly call to mind tripods of the *Ting* type. Thus the Chinese tripods may possibly proceed from a model imported from the west . . . Thus judging from the perhaps unsufficient archeological material known to me there is but very little distinctively Chinese in the Honan culture, although many of the elements introduced have survived in the fully developed Chinese civilization."

The foregoing contains an error in logic. The reasoning is that tripods like the *ting* have been found in the West, the *ting* is a Chinese tripod, therefore the Chinese tripod may have come from the West. As a middle term in this syllogism Arne has substituted, for the *ting* tripod, "the Chinese tripod" which includes both the *ting* and the *li*, a very different thing; his conclusion is therefore a non sequitur.

The *li* is a vessel of definitely peculiar type, unlikely to have been independently invented many times in human history. The *ting* is neither of these. It is essentially a round bowl standing on three legs. The round bowl is one of the most common and widespread of vessels, and there are various reasons, including the desire to straddle it over a fire, which might lead to the attachment of legs to it. The smallest number of legs practicable is three; economy of effort therefore makes the invention of the *ting* probable in such a case. It is quite possible, therefore, that the *ting* may have been invented not once but several times, quite independently.

But actually, as Andersson points out in the above passage, the *ting* appears to have been limited, in the early Neolithic sites known to us in China, to the same northeastern area which was the home of the *li*, and appears to the west much later than it does in the east. It is therefore more probable, in the light of our existing information, that the *ting* as found in China was an invention made in the northeastern area, than that it was imported from the far west.

remains of the Li, and in the fifth and sixth stages (Ssu Wa and Sha Ching) special types of Li are quite common"[37].

The "small fragment of a leg" mentioned here does not, of course, necessarily mean anything. It might be quite intrusive, or the result of trade or the spoils of war. It is of no more importance as evidence than the single isolated sherd of Yang Shao painted pottery which was found in the Shang culture stratum at Anyang[38]. The Hsin Tien, like the two later stages, was characterized by the occurrence of articles made of metal[39], so that apparently neither the *li* nor the *ting* became a part of the culture pattern in Kansu until after the end of the Neolithic period proper.

Andersson says, "Everything goes to show that the earliest known history of the Li centers in the area which has been by tradition marked down as the cradle of the Chinese civilization, the lower Huang Ho valley on the Shensi-Shansi-Honan borders. The presence or not of the Li in Kansu in the early premetallic stages is so far not quite settled, at any rate it was exceedingly rare in those early times, and only during the three later stages of Kansu prehistory did the Li ceramic family become richly represented by some peculiar local Kansu species. It then seems fairly probably that the Li tripod from its early home on the Shansi-Honan border slowly spread N.W.-ward to central Kansu[40]."

When these conclusions were published, in 1925, they were eminently reasonable. On the basis of more recent discoveries they are hardly tenable. Andersson supposed that "the Li centers in the area which has been by tradition marked down as the cradle of the Chinese civilization, the lower Huang Ho valley on the Shensi-Shansi-Honan borders." This is the region in which the Hsia dynasty is supposed to have flourished. One tradition places the first capital of that dynasty in the district in southwestern Shansi which still bears the name of Hsia

37. *Arch. Res. in Kansu* 47–8.
38. *Anyang Pao Kao* 337.
39. *Arch. Res. in Kansu* 21.
40. *Arch. Res. in Kansu* 48.

Hsien[41]. In 1926 Dr. Li Chi excavated a Neolithic site at Hsi Yin in this very district, finding tens of thousands of painted potsherds showing advanced Yang Shao technique. Both the ting and li tripods were entirely absent from these finds[42]. This is a fact of the first importance. It will be remembered that at Pu Chao Chai, a few miles west of the Yang Shao site, there was found a culture which, lacking painted pottery, "represents ... a real predecessor of the Yang Shao age"[43], but in which even the *hsien* was found and in which *li* of very fine quality were common[44]. The site at Hsi Yin, characterized by Yang Shao painted ware of high quality, is less than forty miles northwest of Pu Chao Chai. Between the dates of Pu Chao Chai and Hsi Yin there must have been time enough for the painted pottery technique not merely to enter but to allow the artisans at Hsi Yin to become thoroughly at home in their skill. Even if one holds that the inhabitants of Hsi Yin were invaders of the area, they must have occupied the site a very long time to leave such an enormous deposit of potsherds. But all of this time was not time enough, apparently, for the *li* form to travel forty miles to the northwest. Meager though our total evidence on the point still is, this is a most powerful indication that the region of the Shensi-Shansi-Honan borders was not in the center but on the very periphery of the early distribution of the *li*. And the fact that this form apparently did not reach Kansu until after the end of the Neolithic period goes far to corroborate this.

As to whether or not the *li* form occurred to the south of the Honan-Shantung area in Yang Shao times or earlier, I know of no information. It has not, I believe, been certainly identified, for that period, as an integral part of the culture of the areas represented by the modern provinces of Shensi, Shansi, Chahar, Jehol, or the Three Eastern Provinces[45]. Andersson did, how-

41. Cf. *Shih Chi* 2.19a. The Chi Chieh commentary quotes Huang-Fu Mi who says that one tradition places this capital at An I.
42. *Hsi Yin Ts'un Shih Ch'ien Ti I Ts'un* 29.
43. *Children of the Yellow Earth* 334.
44. *Arch. Res. in Kansu* 38.
45. In a letter of April 9, 1935, Mr. Liang Ssŭ-yung informed me

ever, find two pottery fragments which he identifies as almost certainly legs of the *li* in the deposit in the Sha Kuo T'un cave in the extreme southwest of Fêngtien Province[46]. But these by themselves do not constitute much evidence, and the very dating of this cave deposit as of Yang Shao age is not certain, as Andersson himself agrees[47]. The occurrence of the *li* in Fêngtien in this period is still subject to question[48].

It is a principle of archeology that, other things being equal, the place of origin of such a form is to be sought in the center of the area over which it is distributed. We still have too little information concerning relatively early Neolithic sites in northeast China. But such evidence as we have places the center of distribution of the *li* form to the eastward, probably in northeastern Honan somewhat south of Anyang. All of the evidence which we possess indicates that the *li* and its related forms are ceramic types typical of, and so far as we know originated in, northeastern China.

The *li* is still another factor, and probably the most important one, which indicates that the black pottery culture had roots, at least, deep in the culture of the northeastern area, rather than being an intrusive culture. The *ting* was "a very common type" at Ch'êng Tzǔ Yai[49], but the li was "even more common"[50].

---

that in so far as he is aware this is the case, adding "But it is still too early to draw any conclusion from this negative evidence".

46. *The Cave-deposit at Sha Kuo T'un in Fengtien* 30.
47. Ibid. 42. It is noteworthy that in the summary of the evidence which Andersson gives here, the artifacts which the two areas have in common are extremely rare either in one region or the other, weakening the force of the argument.
48. Andersson says (ibid. 41–42), with regard to "Torii's collections from S Manchuria and E Mongolia", that "It is rather surprising that he has never found fragments of the characteristic tripod Li which is preserved in such fine specimens in Honan and of which we have two legs in the small Fengtien cave collection. One feels almost inclined to wonder whether a tripod leg cannot possibly hide under some of Torii's 'anses de poteries', many of which have a shape very much reminding one of the Li legs."
49. *Ch'êng-tzǔ-yai, English Summary* 19.
50. Loc. cit.

The *hsien* also occurred in this deposit, and even more significant is the fact that the potters at Ch'êng Tzŭ Yai used the *li* form as a basis for the making of vessels of various types, indicating that it was not a newly acquired and slavishly imitated pattern [51].

Although we cannot, at present, discuss such questions save on a purely tentative basis, it does not seem possible to divorce the origins of Shang culture entirely from northeastern China, nor from the black pottery culture. But were the Shangs originally native to the northeastern area, or were they invaders who took over certain culture traits which were there before them? Were they a group of the black pottery culture people who learned to make bronze and developed a still more complex culture, or were they enemies of the black pottery people, possibly conquerors of them? We cannot tell. We may get some information on these points after the skeletons recently excavated at Anyang have been thoroughly measured and studied, especially if some of the black pottery sites yield skeletons which can be proved to belong to that culture. But this belongs to the future.

But even if investigation should ultimately prove that the Shang people were intruders into the northeastern region, this would not alter the fact that there were profound relations between Shang culture and the culture which existed in that area from a very early date. One of the most fundamental evidences of this is the part played by the *li* tripod in Shang religion. Mention has already been made of the fact that many Shang sacrificial vessels were cast in forms based on this shape; a number of those which are commonly classified as *ting* really show the rudimentary characteristics of the *li*, and from a historic point of view must be considered as highly modified specimens of the *li*. Even more important than this is the fact that the *li* form had become so thoroughly integrated into the religion of the Shang people that a simple pictograph of a *hsien* was used as a verb meaning "to sacrifice". This fact has not, to my knowledge, been pointed out previously; its demonstration must therefore be given in full.

The *hsien* "steamer" is, as has been said, a *li* surmounted by

51. See ibid., Plates XIX 7–8, XXII 1–3, 5, XXVIII.

another vessel having a perforated bottom to allow the passage of vapor generated in the *li*; sometimes the whole thing is cast in one piece. The modern character standing for this vessel is 甗 *hsien*. The left-hand side of this modern character shows plainly that the *li* is a component part of the vessel, for it is composed of the character *li* surmounted by *hu*, an abbreviated pictograph of a tiger[52].

虜 is a character in its own right, pronounced *küan* (Wade system, *chüan*) according to Karlgren[53] and the *K'ang Hsi Dictionary*. But the ancient pronunciation given for this character by Karlgren is very similar to that which he gives for *hsien*[54], and it was apparently used in one bronze inscription[55]

52. The *Shuo Wên* says that 虎 *hu* is a pictograph of "the markings of the tiger". But if we compare even the small seal form of the *Shuo Wên* with the forms of the character 虎 *hu* found on bronzes (cf. *Chin Pien* 5.8a) we can see that this is rather a garbled representation of the form of the whole tiger than an attempt to portray his markings. It is probably because this form had so far lost all semblance of the original pictograph, that two legs were added to form the modern character 虎 *hu* (many editions of the *Shuo Wên* show the late portion of this character as a man stooped over and resting on his hands and feet, as seen from the side; Tuan Yü-ts'ai says that this is a mistaken form, and that the *Shuo Wên's* character originally had only two legs like those of a man here. Cf. *Shuo Wên Lin* 2106b–2107a).

None the less, the element which surmounts *li* in the character *hsien* is an abbreviated form in relation to the modern character *hu* "tiger", and as such it represents accurately the ancient form of the character *hsien*. For on bronzes the "tiger" element surmounting *li* is most commonly, though not universally, an abbreviated pictograph of a tiger (cf. *Chin Pien* 10.2, 12.20a).

53. Bernhard Karlgren, *Analytic Dictionary of Chinese and Sino-Japanese* (Paris, 1923; referred to hereafter as *Analytic Dict.*), no. 497.

54. Cf. loc. cit.

55. See *Chi Ku Chai Chung Ting I Ch'i K'uan Shih* (1804; referred to hereafter as *Chi Ku Chai*) 7.18a, and *Chün Chin Wên* 2(2).10b. Whether the right-hand side of this character is *hu*, or is *ch'üan* "dog" and an abbreviated *hu* is not absolutely certain. Both Yüan Yüan, in the first reference above, and Jung Kêng in *Chin Pien* 10.2b give this character in a form which makes it appear to be *hu*. The *Chün Chin Wên* shows a break in one line which makes the right-hand side appear to be two elements, but this is probably due to mutilation of the inscription.

and twice in the oracle bones[56] as a variant form of *hsien*. The fact that the former character appeared on a bronze which is recorded as itself a *hsien*, and the context of its inscription, fixes its meaning; for the two characters on the bones the context is unfortunately insufficient.

It is a curious fact that the three forms just mentioned, and a majority of the bronze forms given in the *Chin Pien*[57] are composed with a pictograph, not of a *li* but of a *ting*. I do not think that this necessarily implies that any of these vessels were actually made with a *ting* as the lower part. Instead, the pictograph *ting* here seems to represent "a three-legged vessel" in general terms.[58]. *Hu* is said by the *Shuo Wên* to be phonetic in 虧 *chüan*; Karlgren says that this character represents a *li* "in tiger shape or with tiger ornaments"[59]. Neither of these explanations is wholly convincing. It may be that there was some symbolical connection between the tiger and the *hsien*, which is now lost to us; I know of no tradition of sacrifices either of or to the tiger in ancient times. But at any rate there was some connection, and when we find a character composed of pictographs of a *ting* and a tiger it means, sometimes at least, "the three legged vessel qualified by the tiger", i.e., *hsien*[60]. When we come to the characters of the *Shuo Wên* and later, scholars have been more meticulous and composed both 鬳 *hsien* and 獻 *hsien* with *li*, indicating its shape more exactly.

56. *Yin Hou Pien* 2.23.2; 2.38.5. Sun does not attempt to read these characters, placing them in the appendix to his *Chia Pien*, 69a. They are quite clearly composed, however, of a *ting* on the left-hand side and a tiger on the right. For the substitution of the *ting* for the *li* here, see further discussion.

57. 10.2ab.

58. That this is possible is indicated by an occurrence of the character *li* which is made up of *ting* and *li* written together; cf. *Chên I Wên* 4.14a. The character functions in the inscription as the name of the vessel itself, and the vessel is recorded as a *li*. Therefore it must be *li*.

59. *Analytic Dict.* no. 497.

60. The tiger obviously had an important function in the compound, whether merely phonetic or symbolic. For we even find two occurrences of the character *hsien* which have no pictograph of a vessel at all, the whole left-hand side of the character consisting solely of a pictograph of a tiger; cf. *Chin Pien* 10.2b.

The modern character for the vessel, 甗 hsien, has as its right-hand side the character wa, "pottery", as a determinative to distinguish it from the character composed with the ch'üan determinative, which now means "to sacrifice, present", etc. But this form with wa came into existence quite late; while it is found in the Shuo Wên and the Tso Chuan⁽⁶¹⁾ it does not occur, in so far as I am aware, in any bronze inscription. But the character 獻 hsien, with ch'üan, "dog", as determinative, was used on bronzes regularly as the name for the vessel. The dog was, of course, one of the principal domestic animals of the Neolithic inhabitants of north China, second in importance only to the pig. Dog bones in considerable numbers were found in the Shang remains at Anyang, and we know from the bone inscriptions that dogs were sacrificed frequently by the Shangs⁽⁶²⁾. In Chou times the dog was a very usual sacrificial victim⁽⁶³⁾. It is for this reason, no doubt, that ch'üan appears here⁽⁶⁴⁾. In this compound character we have a hsien on the left and a dog on the right, giving us a picture of a sacrifice in process. Thus the character is now used exclusively, I believe, in its verbal sense⁽⁶⁵⁾, and as early as the Shih and the Shu we find it used to mean "to sacrifice" and even "to present to a [human] superior"⁽⁶⁶⁾.

The pictograph of the sacrifice by means of the hsien was often used, then, to denote the vessel. Was the pictograph of the vessel alone ever used as a verb meaning "to sacrifice"? In Shang times both hsien as the name of the vessel and the verb hsien meaning "to sacrifice" were regularly represented, I believe, by a simple pictograph of the vessel itself, without the

61. *Tso Chuan* 174.9, 340.17.
62. Cf. *Yin Ch'ien Pien* 1.26.2, 1.46.1, 1.46.3, 3.23.6, etc.
63. Cf. *SSC I Li* 8.9b, 10.10a; *Chou Li* 36.10ab; *Li Chi* 5.19b–20a.
64. In a long list of special sacrificial names given to various kinds of offerings in the *Li Chi*, it is only the dog which is spoken of as a *hsien*, "sacrifice". This may well have its root in the etymology of the character. See *SSC Li Chi* 5.19b.
65. I.e., it may be used as a verbal noun meaning "offering, contribution", but this sense is derived from the meaning "to sacrifice", rather than throwing back to "a sacrificial vessel".
66. *Shih* 375, 618–20, etc.; *Shu* 437.

addition of either "tiger" or "dog"[67]. Twelve occurrences of such a pictograph on the oracle bones are listed by Sun in his *Chia Pien*[68]. All of the authorities known to me list them as forms of the character 甗 *hsien*, standing for the vessel itself[69]. But if due consideration is given to their contexts, it does not appear certain that a single one of these characters is the noun *hsien*, "a steamer". On the other hand there are cases in which the inscription makes sense if, and only if, we interpret it as *hsien* "to sacrifice".

In the case of six of these twelve characters the context is either totally lacking or insufficient to shed any light on their significance; they will not be included in this discussion[70]. Of the remaining six, three are somewhat doubtful in meaning. One reads: 丙寅卜賓貞子甗[?]... *ping yin pu Pin chên tzŭ hsien* [?]...[71]. Tung Tso-pin holds that *Tzŭ Hsien* is a proper name here, the name in fact of one of the sons of King Wu Ting[72], but his whole theory on this point is subject to some question. It is possible, in the context, that *hsien* here functions

67. Sun, in his *Chia Pien*, lists one form under the character 獻 *hsien*; it occurs in *Yin Ch'ien Pien* 8.11.2. But the form of the left-hand side of the character here is most unusual if, indeed, it is this character at all, and the context is so scanty as to give little aid in fixing its meaning.
68. 12.19b. As a matter of fact, not all of these are clearly *hsien*. The forms found on *Yin Ch'ien Pien* 5.3.5, *Yin Hou Pien* 1.27.10 (twice) and 2.17.6 do not certainly stand for a double or compound vessel. The legs, however, are depicted as marked off from the body, and it would be very difficult to determine precisely in such cases where the vessel ceases to be a *li* and becomes clearly a *hsien*, without examining the vessel itself.
69. Cf. *Chia Pien* 12.19b; *Chia Ku Hsüeh, Wên Tzŭ Pien* 12.9b; *Yin Hsü Wên Tzŭ Lei Pien* 12.11; *Yin K'ao Shih*, chung 38b.
70. These inscriptions are: *T'ieh Kuei* 235.1; *Yin Ch'ien Pien* 5.3.5, 5.4.1, 7.37.1; *Yin Hou Pien* 2.7.15, 2.7.16.
71. *Yin Hou Pien* 2.8.1. Tung Tso-pin translates this inscription in *Ts'ai Anniv. Vol.* 385. His rendering of the character left untranslated here seems doubtful. *Hsien* he renders as *li*, but this is surely mistaken, for the pictograph is very clearly that of a *hsien*.
72. Loc. cit.

as a verb, "to sacrifice", but it is not certain. On one piece of bone we find twice the succession of characters 尊鼎·*tsun hsien*⁽⁷³⁾. On the oracle bones as in the first form given by the *Shuo Wên*, *tsun* is composed of two hands lifting up a goblet of wine, and means "to sacrifice wine". Used in a double expression of this sort, the words almost certainly denote a double sacrifice of wine and something else. It is almost impossible to interpret *hsien* as meaning the vessel here. Still, we can not say that it quite certainly means "to sacrifice".

The three remaining occurrences are less equivocal. One reads: 乙卯卜賓貞㕰龜 ... *i mao pu Pin chên hsien kuei* ...⁽⁷⁴⁾ *Hsien kuei* must mean "sacrifice a tortoise"⁽⁷⁵⁾; if we interpret *hsien* as the name of the vessel it is scarcely possible to translate the inscription. The second contains the characters *ming hsien*, "command *hsien*"⁽⁷⁶⁾. One cannot command a bronze or pottery vessel, but one may issue the command "to sacrifice", and I believe that that is what is meant in this inscription. In the third and last we have *ming* and *hsien* in the same order separated by a character which is not clear⁽⁷⁷⁾. This middle character is probably a proper name, the whole passage meaning "command so-and-so to sacrifice". On the other hand, it might be possible to interpret *hsien*, in these last two inscriptions, as a proper name, so that this is not quite certain.

73. *Yin Hou Pien* 1.27.10. As was mentioned before, the pictograph here may denote a *li* instead of a *hsien*.

74. *Yin Ch'ien Pien* 7.5.2.

75. For other instances of the sacrifice of the tortoise, called by terms more usual in the bone inscriptions, cf. *Yin Hou Pien* 1.19.6; *Yin Hsü Shu Ch'i Hsü Pien* 6.21.8; *Anyang Pao Kao* 179, no. 381.

76. *Yin Ch'ien Pien* 5.4.3. One strange fact about this inscription is that it has the characters *chên pu* in this order, which I do not recall having seen elsewhere. Unusual arrangements do constantly crop up in the inscriptions, however, and I do not believe that this is sufficient reason to throw out the inscription as forged. Nor does it, as might seem at first, indicate the characters *ming* and *hsien* to belong to two different inscriptions, for such separation makes more problems regarding the inscription as a whole than it solves. Furthermore, the sequence *ming hsien* has a precedent in 5.4.2.

77. *Yin Ch'ien Pien* 5.4.2.

Further evidence that the simple pictograph of a *hsien* was used in Shang times as a verb meaning "to sacrifice" is supplied by two very remarkable weapons. The first of these I have examined carefully on several occasions, and had photographed[78]. It is a broad-bladed bronze ax-head, seven and one-quarter inches wide and nine and three-eighths inches high. Except for the inscriptions, which differ on the two sides, it has identical decoration on each side; this decoration is typical of Shang bronzes, as is the patination and the general shape of the weapon. The two characters it bears show great similarity, in one case virtual identity, with forms found on the oracle bones. There is little room for doubt that it is a Shang production. Three months after first seeing the ax just mentioned and recognizing the great significance of its inscriptions, I was both surprised and delighted to find the same set of inscriptions, this time on a bronze *kê*. I have not seen this weapon itself, but only the pictures and rubbings of its inscriptions published in a work issued by Mr. Huang Chün, proprietor of the Tsun Ku Chai and one of the leading dealers in antiquities in Peiping[79]. Unfortunately this *kê* is very plain, having little of decoration by which it can be dated. But since it is a *kê* of typical Shang form, and since its two characters are almost identical even to details with those found on the ax mentioned above, I think that it is certainly a Shang weapon.

The character on one side of these weapons is 伐 *fa*. The *Shuo Wên* said that this character was composed of "a man holding a *kê*", and later authorities have followed this. This has always been one of the explanations hard for beginners to understand, and with good reason. The oracle bones, as well as bronze inscriptions and the stone classics[80], make it quite clear that

78. I first encountered this ax in the shop of a Peiping antique dealer, who consented to let me have it photographed. It was later acquired by the William Rockhill Nelson Memorial Gallery of Art of Kansas City, and is now in its collections.

79. *Yeh Chung P'ien Yü* (Peiping, 1935) 50ab. This work consists of pictures and rubbings of objects, nearly all from Anyang, which have passed through Mr. Huang's hands.

80. Cf. *Chin Pien* 8.4a and *Shuo Wên Lin* 3606a.

the man is not holding the *kê* at all, but rather is being struck by it[81]. Both on the oracle bones and on bronzes the man in the character is seen from the side and is being struck by the *kê* from behind and, almost without exception, in the neck. This is important.

The character *fa* is used in two ways on the oracle bones. It is used to mean "to attack", in the sense of launching a military expedition against enemies[82]. It is also used to mean "to slay a human victim as a sacrifice"; possibly its meaning could be made still more specific, "to behead a human victim as a sacrifice". We find it used in this sense, repeatedly and unmistakably, in the inscriptions[83].

81. A character composed of a man as seen from the front, who is holding a *kê*, 㐰, is included by Mr. Sun in his *Chia Pien* along with the forms listed under *fa*. This is an error, despite the statement of the *Shuo Wên*.

This character is listed as appearing on four pieces of bone, as follows: (1) *T'ieh Kuei* 209.4. (2) Ibid. 254.2 (twice). (3) *T'ieh Yün Ts'ang Kuei Chih Yü* (referred to hereafter as *T'ieh Yü*) 4.1 (twice). (4) *Yin Hou Pien* 1.22.6 (twice). Since (2) and (4) are duplicate rubbings of the same bone, the latter need not be considered, so that we are dealing with only five real occurrences of this character.

In every case it is preceded by the character 子 *tzǔ*. One need not accept all of Tung Tso-pin's conclusions in order to admit, what is abundantly evident, that the inscriptions which he has assembled in *Ts'ai Anniv. Vol.* 380–386 show that there were proper names beginning with *tzǔ* in Shang times. In each of the five cases under consideration it is obviously as the latter half of such a name that the character we are discussing functioned; this is proved by the fact that in (3) it is twice preceded by the character *hu*, "command", implying that what follows is the name of a person. This character is not a form of *fa*, for it differs in use as well as in form from that character as we find it both on bones and bronzes.

82. Cf. *Yin Ch'ien Pien* 3.29.7, 4.31.3, 4.39.4, etc., etc.

83. Cf. for instance *Yin Ch'ien Pien* 1.18.4, which divines concerning a sacrifice, by the king, to Wên Wu Ting (T'ai Ting), consisting of ten men, six oxen, and six *yu* of wine. The characters referring to the human sacrifice are 伐十人 *fa shih jên*. There are three other inscriptions on this same piece of bone, all calling for human sacrifice and using the term *fa* to denote it.

The expression "*fa* so many men" is relatively rare, however. More

Many scholars, especially among the Chinese, have strongly resisted the conclusion that human sacrifice was practiced in Shang times. Complete data on this point must be reserved for a later paper, which will deal with human sacrifice exclusively. But any doubt which might have existed previously was finally removed by the excavation, in the Shang grave field at Anyang excavated by the National Research Institute in the fall of 1934 and the spring of 1935, of more than a thousand headless skeletons, and a corresponding number of skulls buried separately[84]. From the manner in which they were buried, there can be no doubt that they were sacrificial victims. Ten headless skeletons, neither more nor less, were buried together in an oblong pit. In some cases the wrists were crossed together behind the back, indicating that the hands were tied in this position before decapitation[85]. Near this rectangular pit is a square pit, containing ten skulls, standing upright in regular rows, and all facing north. I have seen a number of these skulls and skeletons in situ, in the process of excavation. That the burials are always of ten individuals together is significant in connection with the fact that the numbers of human beings mentioned as being sacrificed, in the oracle bone inscriptions, is commonly divisible by ten. The number ten apparently had some religious significance, but what it was is uncertain[86]. Along with the skeletons are found various small objects, such as bronze knives and ax-heads, small grinding-stones, etc., always in sets of ten[87], as if there was one for each victim. Possibly these were a part of some ritual equipment or ceremonial garb with which the victims were accoutered

---

frequent is the expression "*fa* so many 羌 *ch'iang*"; see *Ts'ai Anniv. Vol.* opp. 423, no. 2.2.0202. The meaning of *ch'iang* in such cases has been much debated. It quite certainly means men, in such contexts human sacrificial victims. Complete evidence for this will be detailed in a later paper on human sacrifice.

84. Verbal communication from Liang Ssŭ-yung, July 1, 1935.
85. None of the skeletons which I personally saw showed this clearly, but it was evident in a photograph of such skeletons in situ which Liang Ssŭ-yung showed me on February 18, 1935.
86. Cf. *SSC Tso Chuan* 9.12b.
87. Verbal communication from Liang Ssŭ-yung, Feb. 18, 1935.

before being slain. A hundred or more victims, of which only the skulls have been found, were apparently slain at the closing of another tomb excavated on the Hou Kang site at Anyang in the spring of 1934, but its date has not yet been determined to be Shang beyond question[88]. But there can be no question that the Shangs practiced human sacrifice by beheading the victims, just as the oracle bones had led us to suppose. The character *fa*, then, which appears on one side of each of the two bronze weapons under discussion[89], is a verb meaning "to sacrifice a

88. This tomb was 7.2 meters long, 6.2 meters wide, and 9.5 meters deep. It had approaches only on the north and south, in this resembling the Chou tombs at Hsün Hsien, rather than the great Shang tombs near Hou Chia Chuang which have approaches on four sides. The whole was filled with pounded earth, but the center was dug out by grave robbers in very early times. More than thirty skulls, crushed in the process of pounding the earth, were recovered by the excavators from the remaining undisturbed earth around the sides, and from this they calculate that there must originally have been more than a hundred of them. These were apparently freshly decapitated heads, not old heads taken on the battlefield, because several of the cervical vertebrae were still attached to them, and these would drop off quickly due to decomposition. This tomb was shown and explained to me at Anyang on April 25, 1934, by Mr. Tung Tso-pin.

89. This character, as it appears on these two weapons, is rather more pictographic than any occurrence of it known to me on the bones or in any other bronze inscription. The victim is more unmistakably a human being, and the hand of the executioner holding the *kê* is clear. But except for this hand the character is only a more pictorial form of what we find regularly in the inscriptions, easily recognizable as such.

Already in inscriptions on late oracle bones *fa* has developed to a form almost identical with the modern character, as 伐 which is found on *Yin Ch'ien Pien* 1.18.4 (this inscription is proved very late by the occurrence of the name of Wên Wu Ting, i.e. T'ai Ting, second from the last of the Shang kings). It will be noted that in this form, as in some others on the bones, the vertical line in the right-hand half of the character, i.e., the *kê*, is not a smooth curve as it is in the modern character and even in bronze inscriptions. Instead, it is composed of two straight lines, forming an obtuse angle just above the lower short line which crosses it. The lower portion of the quasi-vertical line with the short line crossing it forms a hand. The human hand is regularly so represented in combinations on the bones; cf. the character 受 *shou*, *Chia Pien* 4.24–6.

human being". In the corresponding position on the other side of each of these two weapons we find virtually identical pictorial representations of a *hsien* "steamer"[90]. Their resemblance to all the forms of the character *hsien* found on the oracle bones is considerable, and the resemblance to five forms on the bones is

---

The etymology of the form 戈 *kê* has never, in my opinion, been properly explained. As a pictograph of a dagger-ax with a long straight handle it is incomprehensible. The form 丁 which we find most commonly on the bones is perfectly straight forward, but has little obvious connection with the later forms. The "solution" of the *Shuo Wên* only complicates matters with further fallacies, as contemporary scholars agree. Lin I Kuang, in his *Wên Yüan* 2.12b, says that the short line at the bottom represents a sort of stand for holding the *kê* erect, but this does not explain the apparent curve to the right of the lower part of the handle of the weapon in the bronze and modern forms. In so far as I am aware, there is only one instance of this character by itself on the bones which resembles the later form. It is 㦰, in *Yin Hou Pien* 1.10.11. But in this case the quasi-vertical line is not a single curve, but is obviously composed of two straight lines, the upper vertical one representing the shaft of the weapon and the lower slanting one a part of the hand. The representation of the shaft has been foreshortened to facilitate writing. This inscription is proved, by the forms of its characters and especially of *wang* "king", to be quite late, perhaps from the reign of the next to the last Shang king. While I know of only this one instance of this form of *kê* alone, its occurrence in this same form in late instances of *fa* provides ample corroboration. Further conventionalization for easy writing converted the two straight lines into a single curve, and the modern character *kê* was the result.

Further corroboration of this etymology is given by the history of the characters 戊 *mou* and 戌 *hsü* in Shang times as shown on the chart opposite 410, *Ts'ai Anniv. Vol.* In the case of both these characters the handle of the weapon is straight down to the period of the next to the last king, at which time the hand is added just as was done at about the same time to *kê* and *fa*.

When this history is understood it will be seen that the characters occurring on the two bronze weapons under discussion are nothing more than pictorial forms of the character *fa*.

90. In fact, they are identical save for the addition of a straight line across the top of the one published by Huang, forming a narrow band around the lip, and the fact that the "ears" or handles are moved a little closer together in that on the ax of the Nelson Gallery. The latter is very slightly broader, in proportion to its height, than the former; otherwise the form is quite identical.

so close as to be very striking[91]. Since this pictograph of a *hsien* occupies a position corresponding to that on the other side of *fa*, which means "to sacrifice", it is altogether probable that *hsien* here is used as a verb meaning "to sacrifice" also. These two cases provide still further evidence that the simple pictograph of a *hsien* was used as such a verb in Shang times.

Religion is normally among the most conservative aspects of any culture. Chinese culture, and Chinese religion, have been at least normally conservative in historic times. If the Shangs used a pictograph of the *hsien*, which has a *li* as its base, as a verb meaning "to sacrifice", then the *li* form must have been very well integrated into Shang culture. They not only did use it thus, but did so in at least one bone inscription which is demonstrably from the time of Wu Ting[92], only a few decades after the probable date of their move to Anyang. This, together with the fact that a considerable proportion of the Shang sacrificial vessels were based on the *li* form, shows that the most striking characteristic of the northeastern culture area had an important place in Shang culture and, conversely, that some at least of the roots of Shang culture were set firmly in the peculiar culture of the northeastern district.

In discussing the problem of the origins of Shang culture we must distinguish clearly between those elements which are shared by Shang culture and by previous Neolithic culture, and those elements in Shang culture which, in so far as we can tell, were not shared by previous Neolithic culture. It is important to emphasize the word "previous", because as we have seen it is possible that the Neolithic people at Ch'êng Tzǔ Yai may not have had the horse and ox, for instance, any earlier than the possibly bronze-using ancestors of the Shang people at Anyang had them.

The Manufacture of Bronze

There are, as we have seen, certain elements in Shang culture which were demonstrably present in the Neolithic culture existing

---

91. I.e., *T'ieh Kuei* 235.1; *Yin Ch'ien Pien* 5.4.2, 7.5.2, 7.37.1; *Yin Hou Pien* 2.8.1.

92. *Yin Ch'ien Pien* 7.5.2. This inscription is dated by the name of the diviner Pin.

in northeastern China prior to the time at which the Shangs appear on our horizon. On the other hand, there are some elements of Shang culture which have not been reported, thus far, from any previous culture in this area. One of these is the wheeled vehicle[1]. The most important is the technique of

1. It seems quite possible, however, that the wheeled vehicle might have been known to the black pottery people at Ch'êng Tzŭ Yai, although it has apparently not been found there; it must be remembered that we could hardly be certain that the Shang people had wheeled vehicles if we did not have the inscribed bones. If the horse at Ch'êng Tzŭ Yai was domesticated, this would almost seem to imply some type of vehicle, since it is agreed that horseback riding was not practiced in China till well into Chou times; cf. Bishop in *Pacific Affairs* 7.314. It might be held that the people at Ch'êng Tzŭ Yai raised horses for their meat. But if so this practice did not come down, for I know of no record of extensive eating of horse-flesh by the early Chinese; the paucity of sacrifices of horses mentioned on the Shang oracle bones also militates against this possibility.

The wheel, in the form of the potter's wheel, was apparently used in China well before the Bronze Age, though it seems not to have been used in the earliest Neolithic cultures in China which we know, prior to the introduction of painted pottery. Both Andersson ("An Early Chinese Culture" 28) and Arne (*Painted Stone Age Pottery from the Province of Honan, China,* 11) have made the definite assertion that some at least of the painted pottery of Yang Shao age was made on the potter's wheel. They based this statement on the occurrence of fine parallel lines on the inside and outside of the vessels, and the thinness and fineness of the ware itself. But Palmgren, after a study probably more detailed and exhaustive than that of either Andersson or Arne, reached quite a different conclusion; see his *Kansu Mortuary Urns of the Pan Shan and Ma Chang Groups.* The Pan Shan urns have been set down as a Kansu phase of the Yang Shao culture, while the Ma Chang is considered a little later (ibid. 4). Concerning these vessels Palmgren states flatly that they were not made with the potter's wheel; the striation remarked by others he assigns to the use of the "ring" method in their manufacture, the use of modelling discs to form the neck, and the turning of the pot by hand but without the use of a wheel in the effort to obliterate the traces of the rings (ibid. 1, 3, 89). In fact Dr. Palmgren says that no one of the very great number of pieces of Chinese Neolithic pottery of an age approximately equivalent to Yang Shao which he has examined ever bore what appeared to be definite traces of the use of the potter's wheel (verbal communication from Dr. Palmgren, June 14, 1935). Mr. Liang Ssŭ-yung does not find

making and casting bronze, the proper criterion of the Bronze Age.

Since certain of these elements in Shang culture, which are not found in Neolithic cultures, are found in Bronze Age cultures farther west, particularly in the Near East, it has been customary to declare out of hand that they must have been imported from the Near East, or elsewhere, to China[2]. This is of a piece with the general tendency of Occidental scholarship in this field to look for the origins of the Chinese people, the Chinese writing system[3], etc., almost anywhere but in China. In seeking to

---

Dr. Palmgren's evidence altogether convincing, however. He points out that modern Chinese pots, turned on a high-speed wheel, are very frequently so deformed in the process of removal from the wheel, and reworked by hand so much afterward to overcome this, that every trace of wheel work is removed (verbal communication of July 1, 1935). This question is very important in connection with Arne's statement, in discussing such wares in Asia and southeast Europe generally, that "It is ... only the Susa pottery that, like that of Honan, was prepared at a very early age with the help of the potter's wheel" (op. cit. 31). It also has some bearing on Andersson's tendency to ascribe a late date to the Yang Shao culture because of the supposed occurrence of the potter's wheel ("An Early Chinese Culture" 31).

But whether it was used in the Yang Shao culture or not, there seems no doubt that the potter's wheel was used by the people of the black pottery Neolithic culture which preceded the Shang. If there were no other proof it is evident that perfectly regular pottery less than one millimeter in thickness could hardly have been made without it (cf. *Ch'êng-tzŭ-yai* 114). Spiral markings on the bottoms also show its use (ibid. 45, Plate X.7–10). The potter's wheel was of course used regularly by the Shang people.

2. Legge based his belief to this effect on different grounds. He wrote (*Chinese Classics*, Vol. III, *Prolegomena* 189): "Believing that we have in the 10th chapter of the Book of Genesis some hints, not to be called in question, of the way in which the whole earth was overspread by the families of the sons of Noah, I suppose that the family, or collection of families,—the tribe,—which has since grown into the most numerous of the nations, began to move eastwards, from the regions between the Black and Caspian seas, not long after the confusion of tongues."

3. Cf. "An Early Chinese Culture" 30–31.

prove that Chinese culture was imported into China some scholars have not hesitated to employ proofs of the most forced and dubious character. And even in serious scholarly productions of recent date we still find it said that the hypothesis that the Chinese were immigrants from the west is supported by Chinese traditions[4]. But more than twenty years ago Dr. Laufer pointed out that "In the earliest records of the Chinese we meet no tradition pointing to an immigration from abroad"[5]. And I am now able to reaffirm this, on the basis of an examination not only of all the available early literature but also of many thousands of inscriptions on bone and bronze which were not completely available when Dr. Laufer wrote. It would seem that what have been termed early traditions of an immigration from the west would better be termed speculations of questionable value and comparatively late date. In regard to this whole question we should be willing to recognize that a priori, in advance of all examination of evidence, it would be equally possible for any or all aspects of the Bronze Age civilization to have originated in eastern Asia and travelled west. It is solely a question of the weight of evidence with regard to each individual culture trait or complex.

It is almost universally agreed that the technique of making and casting bronze must have been imported into China from some western point. It is frequently said that this must be true for two reasons, first because the technique of casting bronze appears considerably later in China than in the west, and secondly because the technique appears in China in a highly developed form, no evidence of the earlier stages in the perfection of the process having been found in China. But at the present time our evidence is hardly sufficient to provide a sound basis for either of these positions.

We can not prove that bronze appeared much later in China than in the west merely by the comparatively late date of the site at Anyang. We cannot assign even approximately accurate

4. See, for instance, Arne, *Painted Stone Age Pottery from the Province of Honan, China* 34.
5. "Some Fundamental Ideas of Chinese Culture" 161.

dates to the latest Neolithic sites, unless to that of Hou Kang (II)—elsewhere there are no real criteria, in so far as I am aware. Until about 1920 it was doubted that Stone Age men had lived in China at all[6]. When large numbers of Neolithic sites were found it was said "Yes, but we have no Paleolithic". Paleolithic remains were found in the Ordos in 1923[7], and it was said, "Yes, but not in China proper". In 1928 traces of Paleolithic man were found in the valley of the Yellow River between Shensi and Shansi[8], and now we have skeletons from the very region of Peking. What may yet be found in China only a bold man would predict.

The argument that crude bronzes, showing earlier stages in the technique of casting, have not been found in China, is not necessarily very telling. Very few indeed are the places in China where bronzes have been "excavated" rather than merely dug up surreptitiously by ignorant peasants or, at best, by the agency of dealers in antiquities. Unless they have been excavated scientifically, so that they can be dated by associated objects, bronzes must be dated by one or both of two criteria—inscription or style. If we should find bronzes from a period much earlier than that represented by Anyang, there is good reason to believe that they would be uninscribed. Inscriptions on Shang bronzes are very brief as compared with those of Chou times, and there is some evidence that the casting of any inscription at all was a practice which did not become general until late in Shang times[9]. Nor would style be much help if—as is thor-

6. Cf. "An Early Chinese Culture", 11.
7. Teilhard de Chardin and Licent, "On the Discovery of a Paleolithic Industry in Northern China", *Bull. of the Geol. Soc. of China*, 1924, 3.1.45–50.
8. See *Mem. of the Geol. Surv. of China*, Series A, No. 8, pp. 34–5.
9. In *Ts'ai Anniv. Vol.* opp. 410, Tung has given a table of the various forms of the cyclical "stems" and "branches" found on the oracle bones of various periods. I have compared these characters as found on a number of supposedly Shang bronzes with this table, and also analyzed the inscriptions as to the forms of other characters. In every case those inscriptions I have examined seemed, where dating was possible, to date from the last four reigns of the Shang period. These

oughly possible—early and comparatively crude bronzes were excavated. For the criterion of style is applicable only when a large number of dated pieces of a particular type have been found, making it possible thereafter to assign similar date to similar pieces. This is obviously impossible for the older, at present unknown and possibly nonexistent periods. More primitive bronzes would probably be undecorated—not a few plain, undecorated pieces were made even by the Shang people. If early, crude, undecorated pieces were dug up at random by peasants and sold to antique dealers they would probably be set down as late pieces—possibly Han—of poor quality. This may have happened already. For some time in Peiping we have been surprised by being shown, by dealers, small bronze vessels from Anyang made in a shape considered typical of the late Chou or Han period [10]. Sometimes they were undecorated and uninscribed, in which case they presented no difficulty since later objects as well as Shang things are found at Anyang. But sometimes they had typical Shang decoration and inscriptions so similar to those of the oracle bones that they could hardly be placed much later than the Shang period. One famous authority stated flatly that they could not have been made at the same time as the other Shang things, because "the criterion of style is infallible". But late in 1934 the National Research Institute excavated just such a vessel from a Shang grave along with many other typical Shang bronzes and artifacts [11]. We are still very far from having a definitive table of styles for Chinese bronzes, even for the historic periods [12].

---

results are not definitive, however, as I have not a large enough body of inscriptions which I can be sure are Shang for comparison. But they are at least suggestive.

10. See "On Shang Bronze", Plate IIIA.

11. I examined this vessel in Peiping on February 18, 1935. Its exterior is almost covered with the so-called "cloud pattern"; it is uninscribed, in so far as my examination revealed.

12. Another evidence of this fact is the Shang bronze knife, with its handle terminating in a ring, such as is illustrated in *Ts'ai Anniv. Vol.* 90–91 and "On Shang Bronze", Plate VI. Before the Anyang excavations such knives were often described as "late Chou", "Han", or "Scythian".

As a matter of fact I have seen a large number of Shang bronzes which were very crude as compared with the finest work of the Shang craftsmen. Cast ridges are frequently present [13], and ridges and "faults", due to imperfect alignment of the parts of a mold, are not rare, even in pieces of elaborate design and otherwise flawless workmanship [14]. It has sometimes been said that ancient Chinese bronzes were not reworked after casting, but came perfect from the mold. But I have seen a number of pieces, which there is good reason to assign to Shang date, which had quite evidently been smoothed with some abrasive substance after the casting. I have published an enlarged photograph of a portion of the surface of one such vessel [15]. It would seem that a great many centuries must have been required to make the transition from the technique which produced the poorest to that evidenced by the best even of the Shang bronzes we know. Yet there is some reason to suppose that the exquisite and the crude were produced side by side at Anyang, for people of varying prestige or economic status [16]. This whole subject is so fraught with problems, and is one on which so little light is available and so much is promised, that it does not encourage generalization at the present time.

From the excavations at Hou Kang, however, we get sound evidence which provides important corroboration of the theory that the fundament of the process of making and casting bronze was probably not originated in China, but was a technique brought in from elsewhere. It will be remembered that in the

13. See "On Shang Bronze", Plate IVA.
14. As has already been said, the question of whether the molds mentioned were used to cast the bronze itself directly, or only to cast a wax model which was then used in the *cire perdue* process, is one which is still sub judice.
15. "On Shang Bronze", Plate IVB. All of the surfaces on this vessel which are not covered by heavy patination show such marks of filing or smoothing. The scratches continue under the patination showing that they were made in ancient times rather than recently.
16. Since some of even the crude bronzes are inscribed, and the practice of casting inscriptions may have become widespread only at a comparatively late date.

important excavation on this site three distinct cultures were found. The first, called an "early Yang Shao" Neolithic culture, occurred in a stratum of "deep gray" earth about two meters thick [17]. Above this was a stratum of hard brown soil, a meter in thickness, in which a few relics of the culture just mentioned were found, but they were "extremely scarce" [18]; this apparently represents an intermediate period of relative inoccupancy. Above this was a stratum varying up to nearly two meters in thickness, of so-called "green earth", characterized by the remains of the black pottery Neolithic culture. Above this was a stratum one meter in thickness in which the soil and the artifacts characteristic of the Shang and the black pottery culture were "mixed together without any clear line of discrimination" [19]. Above this is a stratum, about two meters thick, containing the earth and the artifacts including corroded bronze which are typical of the Shang culture stratum.

It does not appear, then, that there was any great period of time between the end of the black pottery period at Hou Kang and the coming of Shang culture [20]. But neither in the black pottery culture of Hou Kang (II), nor in the black pottery stratum at Ch'êng Tzǔ Yai was any metal whatever found.

Certainly the superlative technique of Shang bronze casting [21] must have represented the end point of a course of evolution, from the first discovery of the process, requiring many centuries if not millenia. If all of that development had taken place in China it is highly probable, to say the least, that we should

17. Cf. *Ts'ai Anniv. Vol.* 556.
18. Loc. cit.; *Anyang Pao Kao* 614.
19. Loc. cit.
20. In fact some of the excavators have considered the theory that the black pottery people were in possession of the site right up to the time when the Shangs took it over (verbal communication from Mr. Tung Tso-pin, April 25, 1934).
21. Mr. Laurence C. S. Sickman, Curator of Far Eastern Art in the Nelson Gallery of Art, Kansas City, tells me that the finest of the Shang casting is equal, not only to any casting which ever has been done in the world, but to the very best which can be done today, with all the resources of modern science.

find at least a few bronze arrowheads or weapons captured from their enemies among the remains of the black pottery culture known to us. Since these have not been found, this must be entered as a most important factor in the evidence indicating that the casting of bronze did not originate in China but entered relatively late and as a relatively developed technique.

Another question which must be answered sooner or later is whether or not the Shang people, when we first know them at Anyang, had only recently learned to make bronze. Perhaps a better statement of the question would be whether the technique of making bronze had only recently been introduced into the northeastern area at that time. There are certain indications which justify us in supposing that, on the contrary, bronze had been made in this area for a considerable period prior to the time when the Shangs moved to Anyang. The fact that vessels of various sorts based on the *li* tripod form were cast quite commonly is one of these. The complicated technique of casting had not only been mastered, but had been widely applied to the execution of vessels of peculiar local forms, a process which would probably have required a period considerably longer than that of the residence at Anyang.

Another factor of importance in this connection is the *kê*. This weapon has been discussed previously. It was a battle-ax with a pointed blade, like a dagger, a "dagger-ax". It was fitted with a wooden haft [22], in Shang times about the height of a man or possibly a little shorter [23]. There are two types of weapons of this sort, distinguished chiefly by the method of attaching the head to the haft. One type is hafted like our common ax, with the wood passing through a hole in the metal head; this, according to Li Chi, should be called a 瞿 *ch'ü* [24].

22. This is proved not only by deduction but also by the plain traces of wood still present on some of the weapons excavated.
23. The character *fa* on the oracle bones shows a man and a *kê* side by side, and from more than a hundred instances of this character known it is possible to draw this inference. It is corroborated by an undeciphered proper name which shows a man holding and brandishing a *kê*. For both of these see *Chia Pien* 8.4–6.
24. *Ts'ai Anniv. Vol.* 82–3.

No very close parallels to this weapon from other areas are known to me, but axes having some resemblance to it are more or less common in Bronze Age sites elsewhere [25].

The true *kê* is hafted by passing the tang of the ax itself through an opening in the wood of the shaft. This weapon seems to be peculiar to China [26]. In fact, it is barely possible that in the Shang period it was peculiar to the northeastern area, since it has not been reported, I believe, from the large series of sites excavated by Andersson in Kansu, of which he dates the latest as probably from 600–100 B.C. [27]. On the other hand it apparently did not develop out of Neolithic culture. No examples of this weapon in stone have been reported as actually excavated in Neolithic sites [28], and it is perhaps impossible for

25. W. M. Flinders Petrie, in *Tools and Weapons* (London, 1917), Plate XI, has illustrated a number of them from various Bronze Age sites. He has included two Chinese weapons of this type (which almost exactly resemble several Shang examples I have seen), but it is to be noted that hardly any of the others illustrated is so nearly pointed as the Chinese specimens. His statement on page 13 that a certain "Minussinsk axe... seems to be a probable source for the Chinese forms", is unconvincing on the basis of his illustrations.

26. This is the conclusion of Dr. Li Chi after a considerable investigation of the subject; cf. *Ts'ai Anniv. Vol.* 82–4. Andersson, in *Children of the Yellow Earth*, 213, discusses the evolution of this weapon in China, but mentions no outside parallels. In "An Early Chinese Culture" 10, he wrote "I am inclined to think that the Chinese Ko might be an autochtonous (sic!) type. Schetelig... is of the opinion that the Chinese and the Western haches poignards are probably of common origin. Unfortunately I have not access to the descriptions of the Mycenean and Babylonian haches poignards referred to by Schetelig, but I am familiar with the hache poignard of Italy and northern Europe, not only from the Ligurian rock engravings referred to but from illustrations of several specimens which evidently belong to a type of weapon widely different from the Chinese Ko."

27. *BMFEA* 1.153.

28. Andersson, in "An Early Chinese Culture", 10, describes "The fortunate discovery in Northern Chihli, of an undoubted Ko made in stone, and representing a type much more primitive than any of the known bronze Ko of the early dynasties". But he does not say that it was excavated with other Neolithic artifacts; apparently it merely "turned up", like most Chinese antiques. At first it did not occur to

this type of weapon to be made successfully of stone. It must be made of a material of high tensile strength, which stone does not possess, in order that the tang may be thin and yet strong. If the tang is not thin, then the wooden shaft must be of great diameter in order to permit a large enough hole to be made in it to receive the tang. But a shaft of great diameter and some five or six feet long would make a weapon so clumsy as to be ineffective.

It appears, then, that the *kê* was a type which must have been developed during the period of the possession of the bronze technique. Since it seems to have no exact parallels elsewhere, that development may well have taken place in the general region of northeastern China. But early in the residence of the Shangs at Anyang this weapon occupied a most important place in their culture [29]. This is a further indication that the

---

me to question that this stone example might be the prototype of the metal *kê*. But in a letter of Dec. 18, 1934, Mr. Bishop wrote me saying, "Andersson's stone *ko* is pretty obviously a stone reproduction of a metal form, and is moreover not necessarily a *ko* of any form". I believe he is right. Stone objects were made for ceremonial use long after the advent of bronze, and were sometimes copied after bronze forms. A type of ceremonial *kê* not uncommon at Anyang has a bronze tang and socket for the blade, while the blade itself is made of stone which is sometimes described as jade. *Kê* made entirely of stone are also found at Anyang. For illustrations of sixteen weapons of stone and stone combined with bronze, from Anyang and supposedly Shang, see *Yeh Chung P'ien Yü* 2.12–18.

But all of the stone bladed *kê* from Anyang which I have examined were so thin and delicate that they could not possibly have been used for anything but ceremonial purposes; they would have shattered in the first shock of battle. And the fact that no stone *kê* are reported from the many Neolithic sites which have been excavated militates strongly against the theory that this important type had a Neolithic background. Indeed, a true *kê* of stone is perhaps impossible; see text further.

29. In bone inscriptions demonstrably from the time of Wu Ting we find the pictograph *kê* very frequently, both by itself and as part of the important character *fa*. Its meaning when used independently is not easy to determine; possibly it was a proper name (cf. *Kuei Tzŭ* 1.3.2, 1.6.3). *Fa*, even at this early date was the regular verb used to express "to attack [the enemy]"; cf. *Yin Ch'ien Pien* 6.30.2, 7.35.1, *Yin Hou Pien* 1.17.1, etc., etc. Since this is the case, it is improbable that weapons of this type were a very recent invention or importation.

Shang people, when we first encounter them at Anyang, were not novices in the manipulation of bronze, but on the contrary carried on a Bronze Age technique which had existed in the Chinese area for some centuries.

Most surprising of all the most recent finds at Anyang is the discovery, in May, 1935, of between seventy and eighty bronze helmets. Most of them were damaged, but two were in almost perfect condition [30]. That they were Shang is unquestionable; not only were they found in one of the great Shang tombs, but some of them even bore typical Shang decoration [31]. On the top was a short open tube, evidently for the insertion of some sort of decoration; this is very interesting in view of the fact that several pictographs of warriors on the oracle bones

---

On the other hand, it must be granted that we can not determine, from these pictographs alone, whether the weapons depicted were true kê, with the tang passing through the handle, or ch'ü, with the wood passing through an opening in the bronze. But according to my observation of the weapons passing through Peiping shops in the last two years, the number of kê which come from the Shang ruins is much greater than that of ch'ü. It may be questioned whether a new invention could have gained such great popularity in the few centuries of probable Shang residence at Anyang.

The fact that ceremonial replicas of these weapons are made of stone, or stone combined with bronze, and the fact that a great number of the kê found are too thin and impractical for anything but ceremonial use, shows that this can hardly have been a recent invention, for innovations are seldom used in this manner. Even more important is the fact that in one of the great, presumably royal tombs excavated at Anyang in May, 1935, a large number of such weapons, estimated at well over a hundred, were found (verbal communication of June 5, 1935, from Mr. Liu Chieh, who saw these objects being excavated). Considering the usual conservatism practiced in the selection of articles for burial with the dead, this provides further evidence that the kê had been established for some time.

30. Verbal communication from Liang Ssŭ-yung, July 1, 1935.

31. Two helmets of this type, from Anyang, plain but practically perfect, were offered on the Peiping antique market in 1934, and were acquired by the Nelson Gallery of Art, Kansas City. In view of the recent finds these helmets may undoubtedly be set down as Shang.

show them wearing some sort of tall headdress, as in the form 👤.[32] It has been stated categorically that metal was never used in the manufacture of Chinese armor in antiquity. This was rendered dubious even before these finds by a Western Chou bronze inscription which seems pretty clearly to mention it[33], and now there can be no question that it was used, for helmets at least, even in the Shang period. This, together with the hundreds of pieces of bronze chariot fittings[34], bronze decorations for harness[35], and other objects of the sort, show that the Shang people were thoroughly habituated to bronze and had probably been using it for a long time.

The recently discovered Shang sculptures seem to presuppose a long acquaintance with metal. It might be possible to carve marble statues, of the size and excellence of those found at Anyang, with only stone tools. But it is altogether improbable that

32. *Yin Ch'ien Pien* 6.20.3. The meaning of this character is uncertain—it may be a proper name—but from the fact that the man in the character is holding a *kê* there is no doubt that he is a warrior.

33. See *K'ê Lu* 13.8. The expression 介金 *chieh chin* probably means "armor metal", i.e., "metal armor". *Chieh* is Kuo Mo-jo's reading of this character (*Liang Chou Hsi* 62) and is shown to be probably correct by the very similar form of the earliest character given on the Wei stone classics (*Shuo Wên Lin* 498b). See also Kuo's further discussion, *Liang Chou Hsi* 70.

One of the early forms of *chieh*—the one from which the modern character developed—consists of a pictograph of a man, with a line on either side of his body evidently representing a protective covering; this is evident, for instance, in the form given in the *Shuo Wên*, as well as in the second form given by the Wei stone classics. The original meaning of this character, therefore, was probably "armor". And it is used in this sense several times in the *Tso Chuan* (205.11, 340.3, 613.10). Indeed, it would seem from one form discussed by Kuo (*Liang Chou Hsi* 69-70) that even chain mail may have been used in the Western Chou period, but I know of no archeological support for this.

34. More than four hundred pieces of bronze chariot fittings (not including harness decorations) were excavated from one pit at Anyang (verbal communication from Liang Ssŭ-yung, May 2, 1935).

35. I have seen a number of horses' skulls, excavated at Anyang, each of which had dozens of decorated bronze bridle ornaments still in place, in lines corresponding to the straps of the bridle. Some of those which come into the antique market are inlaid with turquoise.

sculpture, under such conditions, would have become the highly developed art which produced these examples.

An additional fact which points to the same conclusion is the form of the Shang bronze arrowhead. The type is remarkably fixed[36] and highly sophisticated. It is of the flat type, but has such a definite rib in the middle that the effect is that of two "wings" fitted to a central column of bronze[37]. This column is not round but, in specimens I have examined, octagonal[38]; it is continued by a long tapering tang. The outer edges of the "wings" are not straight but slightly convex. The arrows are barbed, and in the more acute examples the points of these barbs are extremely sharp; after three thousand years in the ground they will still prick one's fingers if handled carelessly. The line between the point of the barb and the column is not straight but slightly curved, so that the two of these curves together appear to form an arch corresponding to the more acute curve of the outer edges of the "wings". There is nothing in the slightest degree crude about these arrowheads. Their surfaces still show a gleaming smoothness where they are not eaten into by patination. Their tapering octagonal center column gives the effect of being fluted. The curves and proportions are perfectly balanced, so that the whole is a truly artistic production. It would be very difficult to improve this design either from an aesthetic or utilitarian standpoint.

W. M. Flinders Petrie, in his *Tools and Weapons*[39], gives drawings and photographs of two hundred fifty-six types of arrowheads and darts from various parts of the world and various periods, some of them as late as Medieval Europe. If one may judge from these illustrations, not one of them was the equal in design or in execution, and few of them can even be compared

36. It is illustrated in *Anyang Pao Kao* 242, III.3.*ting* (cf. "On Shang Bronze", Plate VC and E). On page 243 Li Chi writes: "Nearly all of the bronze arrowheads from the Yin ruins are of this form". All of the actual specimens which I have examined, totalling a considerable number, have been of this type, varying only in length and breadth.

37. These "wings" are thinner, in specimens I have examined, than in that illustrated in *Anyang Pao Kao* 242, III.3.*ting*.

38. But see *Ts'ai Anniv. Vol.* 76, where it is almost square.

39. Plates XLI, XLII.

with the typical Shang bronze arrowhead. Dr. Li Chi has pointed out that Petrie says, "Ribbed blades are not of early date. The oldest here is that from Mykenae, 38 (1100 B.C.?)"[40]. The head to which he refers has a plain, rounded bottom, without barbs and quite primitive in appearance—yet the date to which he tentatively assigns it is roughly contemporary with the fall of the Shangs, who had well before that been making arrowheads both ribbed and barbed, and brought them, in fact, to something close to perfection.

Premature though it would be to draw conclusions in the present inadequate state of our knowledge, there are many indications which make it evident that whatever the history of bronze making may have been, the Shang people and their ancestors, when they made objects of bronze, stamped them with something of their own culture; they had done more with the bronze technique than merely to take it over wholesale and slavishly imitate an imported procedure. If this were not the case, it would be difficult to understand the results of Andersson's excavations in Kansu. Most authorities consider the bronze technique to have come, with other aspects of the Bronze Age civilization, along the northern steppe route which comes down through Kansu as if through the neck of a funnel, to reach the northeastern plains of China[41]. This being the case, we ought normally to expect in Kansu a bronze industry at an earlier date, and producing objects of finer quality, than is found farther east, if the bronze technique of the Shang craftsmen was merely a repetition of what they had acquired through this route. As has been mentioned, Andersson found a number of sites in Kansu which he groups as three Neolithic[42] and three which are now called Bronze Age and Early Iron Age. He has published drawings of some copper objects found, which are in geometric shapes of almost childlike simplicity[43]. But concerning bronze

40. *Tools and Weapons* 34.
41. Cf. Bishop, the "Rise of Civilization in China", 625, and map on 620; *Arch. Res. in Kansu* 30–31.
42. I.e., Aeneolithic and Late Neolithic; *Arch. Res. in Kansu* 23.
43. Ibid. 18.

objects found he has said very little. In the actual description of materials even from his most recent stage, in his preliminary report, he did not mention bronze at all[44], although he did speak of "a sequence of cultural stages, marked by the growing use of copper and bronze"[45]. The situation which this reflects, in Kansu, stands in the sharpest contrast to that at Anyang where bronze molds, slag and charcoal[46], arrowheads, spearheads, *kê, ch'ü*, knives, axes, adzes, etc., have been encountered in connection with dwelling sites, and bronze weapons or vessels or both in almost every grave, making the fact that a great bronze industry flourished on this spot one which must smite any excavator with inescapable force. The reason for the difference in Kansu can hardly be ascribed solely to lack of excavation or to the type of places excavated, for those of the most recent stage in Kansu are described as "a number of sites . . . Both burial sites and dwelling places"[47].

In 1929 Andersson wrote: "Zusammen mit diesen Graburnen kommen bei Sha Ching . . . verschiedene Gegenstände aus Stein und Knochen vor, darunter die typischen rechteckigen Messer, aber auch kleine Gegenstände aus Bronze, hauptsächlich Knöpfe und Zierate für das Gewand des Toten"[48]. In the same article he ascribed the approximate date of 600-100 B.C. to this latest, and presumably richest in bronze[49] of the Kansu stages.

Chinese bronze vessels are equal to the finest objects of the sort ever produced anywhere by man. Shang bronze vessels, as a group, are probably the finest of Chinese bronzes. Among the Shang bronzes excavated by the National Research Institute in 1934 and 1935 are complicated vessels which show a genius of design and a complete mastery of technique such as to take the breath of a hardened connoisseur. Corresponding to these we have, even at a much later date, in Kansu, the region through

44. Ibid. 18–19.
45. Ibid. 3.
46. Cf. *Anyang Pao Kao* 681.
47. *Arch. Res. in Kansu* 18.
48. *BMFEA* 1.152.
49. Since he speaks of a "growing use of copper and bronze"; *Arch. Res. in Kansu* 3.

which this technique is supposed to have come to the Shangs, "small bronze objects, chiefly buttons and ornaments for the dead"[50].

In so far, at least, as present evidence will carry us, we may certainly draw the conclusion that the Shang people and their cultural ancestors in China tremendously improved and elaborated the technique of casting bronze—they did not rest content with merely continuing a borrowed craft.

Shang Decorative Art

Inseparable from this whole problem is the question of the origin of the characteristic designs of Shang art. These are found on bronze vessels, weapons and tools, on the white pottery, on carved bones which are sometimes inlaid with turquoise, and in the sculpture. They were sometimes carved and sometimes painted on the walls of the wooden chambers constructed at the bottom of the great tombs[1]. In so far as I know virtually nothing has been found in any Neolithic sites, either of the black pottery or the painted pottery types, which can be considered ancestral to these motifs. A meander pattern found in Kansu has been mentioned, and a pattern of "diamond-shaped" parallelograms found on a few Shang bronzes has been found on a Kansu urn by Karlbeck[2]. I have observed something resembling the same thing, and also a pattern of small circles bordered by straight lines which occasionally occurs on Shang bronzes, on two potsherds from Ch'êng Tzŭ Yai[3]. But these will go a very short distance to explain Shang decorative art. The emergence

50. Dr. Nils Palmgren confirms that recent study of the Kansu materials has yielded nothing which can be compared in any sense to the Shang vessels or decoration, the most complicated bronzes from that area being small representations of animals (verbal communication of June 30, 1935).
1. On May 2, 1935, I saw some of this painting, presumably lacquer, and some of the carving still preserved in the decomposed wood, at Anyang. The painting was in three colors, red, black, and white.
2. See page 200, above, note 27.
3. *Ch'êng-tzŭ-yai*, Plate X.28, 30. These sherds are, of course, from the lower, Neolithic stratum; see ibid. 45.

of this distinctive, unmistakable, highly developed decorative art, without known Neolithic antecedents, presents a very interesting problem.

Attempts have naturally been made to link up this art with western models. Concerning the ubiquitous so-called *t'ao t'ieh*, or "ogre mask", Rostovtzeff says, "I have not the slightest doubt that what is meant is a horned lion-griffon, the most popular animal in the Persian art"[4]. He further says, "In my book on the *Iranians and Greeks* I was inclined to accept a common origin, from which both the Chinese and the Scythian animal style were derived. I must say that I was wrong. The real Scythian style as described above is different if compared with the early Chinese animal style of the Chou period. It is more primitive, more realistic, less conventionalized. It does not operate with fantastic animals. The fantastic animals entered the repertory of the Scythian animal style in South Russia late, probably not before the fifth to the fourth centuries B.C. Some features, of course, are common to the Chinese and the Scythian animal style: the use of beaks and eyes as ornaments, the treatment of extremities in a conventional way, the filling of surface on the animals' bodies with other animals, the animal palmettes. However, it seems as if all these features, which are common to the Scythian and to the Chinese animal style, appeared in the Chinese art comparatively late"[5]. He places their advent into Chinese art almost as late as the Han period.

On the contrary, at least three of these supposedly late features, namely "the use of . . . eyes as ornaments, the treatment of extremities in a conventional way, the filling of surface on the animals' bodies with figures of other animals" are among the most common characteristics of Shang decorative art, possibly more typical of the Shang than of later Chinese art. The Shang period ended about the eleventh century B.C. But dated examples of Scythian art, according to Rostovtzeff, hardly go back of the seventh century B.C.[6], at about which time there were evidently trade relations between the Chinese and its

4. *The Animal Style in South Russia and China*, 70.
5. Ibid. 73–74.
6. Ibid. 24.

possessors[7]. If there was any borrowing between the two styles of art, this leaves distinctly open the possibility that the influence went from east to west rather than vice versa[8].

Bishop, on the other hand, considers the Shang art to be in large measure a continuation of an art which had long existed in this same general region[9]. Very little in the way of specific antecedents to the Shang art in this region is known, at present, to me. But it is quite certain that between the designs on Shang bronzes, white pottery, and carved bones, and the Shang culture revealed by the oracle inscriptions, there are relationships which are neither superficial nor fortuitous.

Probably the most characteristic single property of Shang design is the so-called *lei wên*, "thunder pattern", and *yün wên*, "cloud pattern." The method of distinguishing between these two does not seem to be universally agreed upon. Fundamentally, however, they consist of series of spirals, often very fine but sometimes made up of heavy lines. These spirals are sometimes round, sometimes squared; the former are commonly called *yün wên*, the latter *lei wên*. But there are intermediate forms

7. Ibid. 66.
8. An interesting illustration of a "standard top" is published by Rostovtzeff, ibid. Plate VI, 1 and 2. On pages 26–27, he says, "Such standard tops are one of the peculiarities of the Scythian life and burial ritual". But this particular one is dominated by a large, typical example of the eye of Chinese art, with its corner drawn down by the Mongoloid eyelid and the iris conventionally enlarged, exactly like the eyes which are found by hundreds on Shang bronzes, and very similar to those found on Shang sculpture (cf. *Anyang Pao Kao* opp. 250) and the oracle bones (cf. *Chia Pien* 4.1–2a).
9. *Pacific Affairs* 7.310. He says, "The art of the Shangs seems in large part to have been taken over from the indigenous peoples, for its designs have comparatively little in common with those of the West, their affinities being rather with what has been called 'Oceanic' art". In a footnote he continues, "This name is not altogether a happy one, for the so-called 'Oceanic' style of art must have originated somewhere in continental Asia before it invaded the Pacific area". I personally prefer not to speak of Shang art having been "taken over from the indigenous peoples" because there is no evidence, as far as I am aware, to prove that the Shang people were not as indigenous to the general region in which we find them as any other people there.

which are hard to place; in actual practice the two terms are applied to a series of patterns which blend imperceptibly into one another. In bronze vessels of the first quality the whole surfaces, even including the bodies of animals in relief, may be covered with such spirals, almost incredibly fine and sharp. On the white pottery they are commonly more heavy. If we had, as evidence, nothing more than the form of the cloud in Chinese art, the definite impression of swirling vapors which these designs convey, and the fact that we frequently find them associated in Shang art with the dragon, we might be justified in conjecturing that they had some connection with the phenomena of rain. Fortunately we can carry our research much deeper than this. Two ancient forms of the character *lei*, "thunder", quoted by the *Shuo Wên*, include exact replicas of the squared spiral which is the thunder pattern of Shang design. And even on the Shang oracle bones we find a symbol which has great resemblance to the so-called cloud pattern used, unmistakably in connection with rain, possibly as a pictograph of a cloud [10] possibly as representing lightning.

Another motif of great importance in Shang design is the dragon. The *Chia Pien* lists forty-one characters, appearing on the oracle bones, which are considered to be forms of *lung*, "dragon", and there are still others not listed there. In none of these inscriptions, nor in any other known to me, is there any context which links the dragon unmistakably with water and rain. But the forms on the bones are unmistakably reptilian,

10. The character in which it occurs, , is interpreted as *tien* "lightning" in *Yin Lei Pien* 11.10b, and as *pao* "hail" (after Yeh Yü-shên) in *Chia Pien* 11.13a (the reference to *Yin Ch'ien Pien* 7.24.4 is apparently erroneous, since there is no such inscription).
It is not possible to define the character with certainty by means of this material. Only four of the citations in the *Chia Pien* have contexts, i.e. *Yin Ch'ien Pien* 3.19.2, 3.22.1; *Yin Hou Pien* 2.1.12, 2.42.7. In the first and the third of these inscriptions the character in question follows the character *yü* "rain" in a manner showing that it relates to allied phenomena. This same symbol, minus its dots or circles, apparently compounded with *yü*, makes up what is interpreted as the character *tien*, "lightning", in a bronze inscription; cf. *Chin Pien* 11.5b. It is quite clear that this basic pictograph had to do with rain, but whether as a representation of a cloud or of lightning is difficult to say.

if not snakelike[11], and there is good reason to suppose that at least a part of the origin of the dragon came from some aquatic animal[12]. That it was closely associated with water from a very early period is unquestionable. I do not know of any passage in the earliest literature which connects it with the production of rain, but there can be little doubt that this association also is quite ancient. The *Wên Yen,* one of the *Ten Wings* of the *I Ching* says "Clouds follow the dragon"[13]. In the *Lü Shih Ch'un Ch'iu*[14] we read 以龍致雨 "Rain is produced by means of the dragon". This is probably a reference to ceremonies for making rain involving sympathetic magic; there is every reason to suppose that such practices may go back even to the Shang period.

The "thunder" and "cloud" patterns almost certainly, and the dragon very possibly, were associated with rain. This coincides precisely with the fact that two of the most frequent questions encountered on the oracle bones are whether or not it will rain[15],

11. The dragon is constantly associated with the snake in ancient literature; see for instance *SSC I Ching* 8.10a.
12. The *Tso Chuan,* 729.12, says "The dragon is a creature of the water". The explanation of the first line of the first hexagram of the *I Ching* is: 潛龍勿用 *ch'ien lung wu yung* (also quoted in *Tso Chuan* 729.12). The *Shuo Wên* says that *ch'ien* means "to pass through water" or "to hide, secrete". Giles (*Chinese-English Dictionary*, rev. ed., 1912; No. 1739) defines it as "to lie hid at the bottom of water".

In the *Shih* (138) we read:
"In the marshes is the spreading water-polygonum". The name of this plant in the original is 游龍 *yu lung,* "wandering dragon". It is so called because it is an aquatic plant and because of "the way in which its branches and leaves spread themselves out" (Legge's note, *Shih* 138).

Mencius (279) tells us, "In the time of *Yâo,* the waters, flowing out of their channels, inundated the Middle Kingdom. Snakes and dragons occupied it". Likewise the *Chung Yung* (*Chinese Classics*, Vol. I, 421): "The water now before us appears but a ladleful; yet extending our view to its unfathomable depths, the largest tortoises, iguanas, iguanadons, dragons, fishes, and turtles are produced in them."

13. *SSC I Ching* 1.15a. For a similar statement see *Ch'u Tz'ŭ* (Chin Ling Shu Chü, 1872) 13.23a.
14. 20.10b.
15. Not all of the questions concerning rain have agricultural significance. Sometimes it is desired to know whether rain will interfere with hunting; cf. *Yin Ch'ien Pien* 2.35.3. But there are other cases,

and whether there will be a good harvest[16]. That such designs are widely used to decorate Shang sacrificial bronzes is just what we should expect, since prayers and sacrifices for rain and for a good crop are among the most important aspects of the religion revealed by the oracle inscriptions[17].

What has been called the 饕餮 *t'ao t'ieh*, literally "glutton", sometimes called "the ogre mask", is almost universal on the

---

like ibid. 3.29.3 and 4.53.4 where the anxiety concerning rain is specified to be on account of the harvest. From this we may be sure that a not inconsiderable proportion of the hundreds of questions concerning rain which appear in the published inscriptions alone had to do with agriculture.

16. Cf. *Yin Ch'ien Pien* 3.29.4–3.30.6, etc. The character 年 *nien*, which has later been used to mean "year", meant "harvest" in the Shang bone inscriptions. Sometimes the query is simply as to whether the harvest in general will be good, as in ibid. 3.30.4. But we also find specific questions such as 我受黍年 *wo shou shu nien*, "will I receive a harvest of millet?", and the same asked concerning other agricultural products, so that we know that *nien* must refer to the yield or harvest rather than to the period of time. This is also shown by the fact that when the bone inscriptions are dated as to day, month, and (rarely) the year of the king's reign, "year" is expressed by 祀 *ssŭ*, "sacrifice", rather than by *nien*; cf. ibid. 3.28.4.

Tung Tso-pin has pointed out (cf. *Anyang Pao Kao 519–20*) that *nien* on the bones is composed of 禾 *hê*, "growing grain", and 人 *jên*, "man". The former is of course signific, while the latter apparently functions solely as phonetic. Tung points out that certain of the bronze forms have 壬 *jên* as phonetic instead; cf. *Chin Pien* 7.11–12. According to Karlgren's reconstruction of the ancient sounds, either of these would seem to be possible phonetics for the character *nien*; cf. *Analytic Dictionary* nos. 669, 930, and 934. The *Shuo Wên* gives 千 *ch'ien* as the phonetic, which does not seem very probable on the basis of *Analytic Dictionary* no. 1076. Karlgren rejects this explanation, and explains the seal form as "千 the thousand grains". But if we examine the older forms it appears that the *ch'ien* of the seal form is merely a corruption of the lower line of the *hê* and the *jên*, misinterpreted by late scribes because "one thousand" on both bones and bronzes was represented by a pictograph of a man crossed by a horizontal line; cf. *Chia Pien* 3.2a, *Chin Pien* 3.2a. Fundamentally, then, the seal form and even the modern form are composed of *hê* and *jên* "man", much corrupted.

17. Cf. *Yin Ch'ien Pien* 1.50.1, 7.5.2; *Yin Hou Pien* 2.33.5, etc.

more elaborate Shang bronzes. A great deal has been written about the origin and identity of this motif, or class of motifs. Rostovtzeff says: "It has the form of an animal mask, consisting of a pair of eyes, a pair of ears, two horns and a crest. The animal certainly belongs to the family of felines. I have not the slightest doubt that what is meant is a horned lion-griffon, the most popular animal in the Persian art"[18]. Others have supposed this motif to be fundamentally bovine; still others have considered it a highly grotesque version of the human face.

Since designs which are grouped together under this name are almost universal on the most elaborate of Shang and early Chou bronze vessels, one should be justified in concluding that a creature known as *t'ao t'ieh* was an important factor in the culture, probably in the religion, of these periods. If so, we should expect to find it mentioned frequently in the literature of time. There is no mention of any such being on any of the oracle bone inscriptions known to me, and I believe that it does not occur in them. I have never encountered it in any bronze inscription. In so far as I am able to ascertain the name *t'ao t'ieh* occurs once, and once only, in the whole of the thirteen classics. We find it in the following passage in the *Tso Chuan:*
縉雲氏有不才子貪于飲食冒于貨賄・・・天下之民以比三凶謂之饕
饕舜臣堯賓于四門流四凶族渾敦窮奇檮杌饕餮投諸四裔以禦魑魅
Legge translates: "[The officer] Tsin-yun [In the time of Hwang-te] had a descendant who was devoid of ability and virtue. He was greedy of eating and drinking, craving for money and property.... All the people under heaven likened him to the three other wicked ones, and called him [*t'ao t'ieh*, i.e.] Glutton. When Shun became Yaou's minister, he received the nobles from the four quarters of the empire, and banished these four wicked ones, Chaos, Monster, Block, and Glutton, casting them out into the four distant regions, to meet the spite of the sprites and evil things."[19] There is nothing in this to indicate that the individual stigmatized by the characters

18. *The Animal Style in South Russia and China* 70.
19. *Tso Chuan* 280.12–13, and 283.

t'ao t'ieh possessed an importance which would explain the wide occurrence of what is supposed to be his image on ritual bronzes. If there had been a widely current legend or myth about this creature the commentators on this passage should have explained it, since this is apparently the only passage in the classics which mentions him. But neither the Chin nor the T'ang commentator has a word to say on the subject; apparently they knew nothing[20]. The *Yao Tien*[21] of the *Shu* also says that Shun banished four malefactors, but the list is a different one from which the name *t'ao t'ieh* is significantly omitted[22]. The same is true of a large number of other works which recount this tradition, all without any mention of *t'ao t'ieh*[23].

The *Yao Tien* of the *Shu* is, of course, quite late[24]. And the passage from the *Tso Chuan*, quoted above, belongs to a pattern of legend which does not appear in the literature until rather late in Chou times; how early the passage itself was written it would be difficult to say. There is not, so far as I know, any other occurrence of the expression *t'ao t'ieh* in any work which can be considered at all early, until we come to the *Lü Shih Ch'un Ch'iu* of Ch'in date. There we read: 周鼎著饕餮有首無身食人未咽害及其身 "On a Chou *ting* there is figured a *t'ao t'ieh*. It has a head but no body. *This creature was in the very act of devouring a man, but had not yet swallowed when disaster overtook its body.*"[25] This story apparently has nothing to do with the tradition related by the *Tso Chuan*. It evidently originated in a period when the characters *t'ao t'ieh* had come to be merely a conventional name for this type of decoration, and when this type of decoration had come to consist only of a head. The Shang heads of this type very frequently have bodies attached,

20. *SSC Tso Chuan* 20.19b.
21. In the *chin wên* text. In the *ku wên* this passage occurs in the *Shun Tien*. The latter text divides the *Yao Tien* of the former into two parts, of which the second part, prefaced by twenty-eight added characters, is called the *Shun Tien*.
22. *Shu* 39–40.
23. Cf. the many passages of this sort quoted by *Chin Wên Shu K'ao*, 1 hsia, 23–26.
24. See page 97, above, notes 1 and 2.
25. *Lü Shih Ch'un Ch'iu* 16.3b.

but when this was less and less the case in later times, this ingenious story of man-eating and its punishment was probably invented to explain the omission.

In fine, there is nothing in Chinese literature to justify the conclusion that in ancient times there was a creature, or a class of creatures, denoted by the characters *t'ao t'ieh*, of enough importance to warrant the widespread reproduction of its image on ritual vessels[26]. Giles states a current theory when he says that the *t'ao t'ieh* was "Represented on old bronze and other vessels .. in all cases as a warning against gluttony"[27]. But this explanation is totally inadequate. It might carry some weight as referring to the usages of some of the puritanical literati, but the early Chous, and the Shangs from what we know of them, were hard-drinking, heavy-eating fighters, whose religion was directed toward practical ends. We may be sure that any motif which is found so widely on their sacrificial vessels had something to do with the practical objects of their cult.

On the one hand, we find no creature called *t'ao t'ieh* which seems suitable as the model for all these forms. On the other, if we turn to the designs themselves, we shall quickly see that they are much too various to have been representations of a single type of creature. Under this name we find lumped together representations of beings of the most divergent sorts. Sometimes they wear horns which are distinctly bovine, and give the general impression of the head of an ox[28]. Others have unmistakably the great curved horns of the ram[29], while yet others wear the characteristic "bottle horn" which is frequent on the dragons of Shang art[30]. In my opinion the name *t'ao t'ieh* cannot be supposed to stand for a type of creature represented;

26. There is, of course, a varied mythology built around this name in works of Han and later date. But this paper is concerned with origins, and especially with the Shang period, so that such late mythology has little relevance in the present connection.
27. *Chinese-English Dictionary*, No. 11,159.
28. Cf. for instance *Yeh Chung P'ien Yü*, shang 17.
29. Cf. ibid. 18.
30. This variation would seem to constitute a fatal weakness in Karlgren's theory. He says: "The *t'ao-t'ie* is, in my opinion, nothing but a dragon mask. The dragon (*yang*, male) is, as we have seen, a

it rather denotes a style of treatment, especially the splitting to be discussed in the next section, to which various animal forms were subjected in the production of designs for this art.

The ox and the sheep are very important among the animals which have supplied these motifs, and this is significant in connection with the fact that these animals were important among those sacrificed by the Shang people, as we know from the oracle bones[31].

Eyes are among the most ubiquitous of Shang motifs, and a very large proportion of them are of one peculiar type. They appear in *t'ao t'ieh*, and on the heads of dragons and other animals difficult to name. And they appear in isolation, in odd places on

---

regular fecundity-fertility symbol, and as such the *t'ao-t'ie* regularly occurs on the bronzes of the ancestral temple."—*BMFEA* 2.41.

31. Cf. *Yin Ch'ien Pien* 1.24.3, 1.29.1, 1.45.5, 3.23.6, 4.17.5, 4.52.4, etc., etc.

In so far as we know no agricultural products save liquor were sacrificed by the Shang people. But this does not necessarily mean that we must conclude, as many Chinese scholars do, that they were a primarily pastoral people simply because they sacrificed sheep and cattle. They also sacrificed large numbers of pigs (cf. ibid. 3.23.6, 4.17.5, 7.3.3, 7.29.2, etc.), and pig bones, with those of the ox, were most numerous among those excavated in the Shang remains at Anyang (*Anyang Pao Kao* 574). The raising of large numbers of pigs is considered incompatible with nomadic life; rather it is a concomitant of a settled economy depending to a considerable extent on agriculture (cf. *Arch. Res. in Kansu* 50). And it is to be remembered that swine were among the prime factors in every culture which we know in northeast China, from the very earliest Neolithic down to and including the Shang. Even the most ardent advocates of the theory that the Shangs were a pastoral people grant that there is very little reflection of a pastoral economy in the oracle inscriptions. We find repeated divinations as to the harvest, but none, they admit, asking about the increase of flocks and herds. One of them meets this very neatly by holding that this is because the increase of flocks and herds is comprehended in divinations concerning the *nien*,. "the produce of the year"; cf. Kuo Mo-jo, *Chung Kuo Ku Tai Shê Hui Yen Chiu* (Shanghai, 1932), 243–4. But this theory meets serious obstacles in two facts. First, as was shown above, the character *nien* has as its signific a pictograph of growing grain. Second, when the specific nature of the *nien*, "produce", divined about is stated it is always, in every case I have seen and even in those quoted by Kuo, agricultural, never livestock.

bronzes, on the bodies of sculptured stone figures[32], etc., where they have a decorative and probably magical function. If the white of the eye is figured at all, these eyes are almost universally human, Mongoloid eyes, showing the conformation caused by the unusual attachment of the eyelid in the Mongoloid peoples. This is the case even with eyes which appear in the head of a long scaly dragon, or a head wearing the horns of the ox or the sheep. The dipping down of the inner corner of the eye is frequently exaggerated, conventionalized into a varitable downward hook.

Another extremely common Shang motif is the cicada. Its function, aside from the decorative, is uncertain[33]. But for the origin of such a motif we hardly need look outside of north China, where the buzz of these insects during the summer season is at times almost deafening.

What was the origin of the Shang decorative art we are not in position to state definitely at this time. But we can say that it was a sort of art which could perfectly well have been developed by a Mongoloid people living in northeastern China, practising an agricultural economy in which the ox and the sheep figured prominently—i.e., by the Shang people and their cultural ancestors.

From our present evidence it would appear that, whatever the mode of their coming, sheep and cattle as domestic animals were grafted on to an economy depending chiefly on agriculture, swine, and dogs, which had existed in northeast China from the earliest Neolithic times we know, rather than coming in the form of a pastoral nomadic economy which completely replaced the Neolithic way of life. Since religion is normally conservative, and the ox and sheep were important sacrificial animals for the Shangs, they had probably had them a long time. But it is to be noted that these animals were apparently used in sacrifices which had as one of their most important ends the assistance of agriculture.

32. *Anyang Pao Kao* opp. 250 shows such eyes on the forearms of a sculptured human figure; they also occur on the bodies of sculptured animals.

33. Mention has already been made of the fact that certain scholars have supposed that a pictograph of the cicada is used on the oracle bones to mean "summer", but that this is improbable; see page 110 above.

Foreign Parallels To Shang Design

What of parallels or resemblances to this art in areas outside of northeastern China? To the west, they are hard to prove. Andersson has dated the latest of his numerous Kansu sites as much later than the end of the Shang period[1], yet he says, "we never found upon our small and plain bronze objects, in the Kansu sites, any decorative design resembling the rich ivory-carvings described from the capital of Yin or recalling that of archaic Chinese bronze vessels"[2]. Bishop says that the designs of Shang art "have comparatively little in common with those of the West, their affinities being rather with what has been called 'Oceanic' art"[3]. He says further, "This name is not altogether a happy one, for the so-called 'Oceanic' style must have originated somewhere in continental Asia before it invaded the Pacific area."[4]

I am not well enough acquainted with the art of the Pacific Islands to be able to make any observations in this connection. But I have had one experience so frequently that it is worth recording. Almost every time that I have gone over a series of Shang designs with a non-Chinese person to whom they were new, I have heard the exclamation, "How similar they are to the Aztec and other Middle American art!" Some of those who have said this have been persons with more than a superficial knowledge of Middle American design. Racial affinities between Chinese and American stocks have long been recognized. Recently it has been announced that affinities between certain linguistic stocks of eastern Asia and North America have been at least tentatively established[5]. Resemblances between the

1. *BMFEA*, 1929, 1.152–153.
2. *Arch. Res. in Kansu* 30.
3. *Pacific Affairs* 7.310.
4. Loc. cit., note 31.
5. Writing in Peiping, I have not at hand the specific references on which to base this statement. And while I know that it is true, I prefer not to ascribe the announcement to a particular scholar for fear of error.

mythology of these two areas have been pointed out[6]. If careful study by those well qualified to make such comparisons should prove that there are fundamental similarities in the art of these regions, this would be of great importance. But conclusions must wait for such careful research.

There is one area, however, in the art of which I have been able to observe certain definite, important resemblances to Shang art. But before these details are gone into, we must consider three factors in Shang culture which link it with a culture area which lies on the borders of the arctic zone and is described as more or less "circumpolar". One of these is the knife of rectangular or semi-lunar form. We have seen that such knives are not found in the Near East or in Europe, but were used by Neolithic men in China as well as by the Shangs[7]. Examples in stone have also been found in ancient sites of the Asiatic Chukchee and of the American Eskimo, while iron knives of this sort are still used by the same peoples[8]. Andersson has observed stone knives from prehistoric South America which he considers reminiscent of the rectangular knives of eastern Asia[9]. Another factor shared by the circumpolar culture area and Shang culture is the composite bow. The Shang bow must have been composite because, as has been shown, it was reflex[10], and this form is scarcely possible except in a composite bow. This is quite remarkable since most of the less cultured peoples of Asia use the simple bow to this day[11]. The third of these factors is the use of "tailored" clothing, with sleeves. This was by no means universal even among the cultured peoples of the world at an early date. But it is characteristic of the circumpolar area, and was used by the Shangs as we know from the fact that the character 衣 *i*, "coat", appears frequently in the bone

6. Cf. for instance Ed. Erkes, "Chinesisch-Amerikanische Mythenparallelen". *T'oung Pao* (1926), 24.32–53.
7. Cf. *Children of the Yellow Earth*, 208; *Anyang Pao Kao* 248–249.
8. "An Early Chinese Culture", 3.
9. *Children of the Yellow Earth*, 209.
10. See p. 195, above.
11. "Some Fundamental Ideas of Chinese Culture", 165.

Foreign Parallels 247

inscriptions as ⟨⟩, a pictograph of a garment with sleeves [12]. Neither the composite bow nor tailored clothing is confined, of course, to the Chinese and the circumpolar culture areas. And it is not the present purpose to contend that any of the three factors named was borrowed either by the northern area from the Chinese or vice versa. But it is desired to point out that common possession of these three distinctive properties indicates a strong probability that the way lay to some extent open for cultural interchange between the two areas. The importance of this lies in the fact that the circumpolar culture area forms a bridge, as it were, between Asia and North America.

12. It is apparently not used with this meaning in the bone inscriptions, however, at least not in any of the sixty-one inscriptions in which it occurs which have been examined by me (These are the inscriptions listed by the *Chia Pien* 8.10–11, with the exception of *T'ieh Kuei* 49.2; *Ch'ien Pien* 1.10.2, 1.16.4, 2.41.1, 8.12.4; and *Kuei Tzŭ* 2.6.2. In these six cases I find it impossible, for various reasons, to be sure that this character occurs). In many of these cases the context is too fragmentary or too ambiguous to allow us to ascertain even approximately the function of the character *i*. It is apparently used as a place name in twelve cases, as follows: *Ch'ien Pien* 2.7.3, 2.11.5 (twice), 2.12.2 (twice), 2.15.1 (twice), 2.28.5, 2.32.2, 2.32.3, 2.41.5, 2.43.1. It evidently functions as a verb, meaning "to sacrifice", in twenty-four cases, as follows: *T'ieh Kuei* 12.2, 23.3; *Yin Ch'ien Pien* 1.30.4, 2.24.6, 2.25.2, 2.25.4, 3.27.7, 3.28.1, 4.3.5, 4.6.3, 4.10.2, 6.33.7; *Yin Hou Pien* 1.20.1, 1.20.2, 1.20.3, 1.20.4, 1.20.5, 1.20.6, 1.20.7, 1.31.1, 2.34.1; *Kuei Tzŭ* 1.21.7, 1.27.4; *Chien Yin Tzŭ* 26.3.

Wang Kuo-wei (*I Shu*.II, *Yin Li Chêng Wên* 6b) and Lo Chên-yü (*Yin K'ao Shih* 3.56) agree that *i* as a verb meaning to sacrifice or as the name of a type of sacrifice is unknown in ancient Chinese literature. But Wang points out that in a very early Chou bronze inscription we find the passage: 王衣祀于王丕顯考文王 "The king made an *i* sacrifice to the king's greatly illustrious father, King Wên" (*K'ê Lu* 11.15b). The character so used here is identical with the character *i* as we find it in some of the bone inscriptions. Since King Wên is referred to as the *k'ao*, "father", of the reigning king, this vessel must be from the time of King Wu, i.e., from the very beginning of the Chou period. At this time, then, we should expect to find Shang usages still persisting, and this inscription serves as another piece of evidence that there was a sacrifice called *i* in Shang times.

All of this might be considered, however, as evidence that this

One of the most distinctive characteristics of Shang decorative art is a peculiar method by which animals were represented on flat or rounded surfaces. It is as if one took the animal and split it lengthwise, starting at the tip of the tail and carrying the operation almost, but not quite, to the tip of the nose [13]. Then the two halves are pulled apart and the bisected animal is laid out flat on the surface, the two halves joined only at the tip of the nose. The head still appears to be one head, for there is only one nose, and the two eyes appear to be looking more or less straight forward. There are two jaws, one on each side, but if one looks at the whole head together they seem merely to be the two sides of the mouth. But there are two necks, one on either side, and two bodies. If one cover either half of the strange double beast thus formed, he will find that either half, beginning from the middle of the shared nose, appears to be a complete beast as seen from the side. The Shang craftsmen went much further. In what is possibly their favorite design we find that the whole head appears to be that of an animal, possibly bovine, with two bodies, one stretching away on either side. If we cover one half of this creature the remaining half is a dragon, with tail held high. But if we look closely at the tail we see that it has a crest, and that its point is the beak of a bird of which even the

---

character did not have the meaning of "clothing" in the Shang period. But it is to be remembered that the range of the content of the divination inscriptions is narrow, and that a great many characters appear in them in extended usages and as proper names which never have their proper sense in these materials. The character *i* as we find it on the bones is a good pictograph of a coat, it has considerable resemblance even to the modern character, and it is identical with *i* as we find it on Chou bronzes with context which shows that it does mean "clothing" (cf. for instance *K'ê Lu* 4.13a). It is also identical with the same character as we find it even in the *Shuo Wên*. We also find what is apparently *ch'iu*, "fur clothing", on the bones in the very graphic form (*Yin Ch'ien Pien* 7.6.3, *Yin Hou Pien* 2.8.8), although the context unfortunately does not fix its meaning.

Altogether, there can be very little doubt that *i* was originally a pictograph of a tailored garment, even though we do not find it used with this significance in the bone inscriptions.

13. For an example, see "On Shang Bronze", Plate XIB.

eye may be present; from this aspect what was first the foot of the bovine animal and later of the dragon now appears to be the foot of the bird. Sometimes the artist went even further and made of each horn a little dragon in its own right [14].

In Scythian art the extremities of one animal may sometimes be worked into the body of another. But in so far as I know the technique of representing an animal by splitting its body up to the head and laying out the two halves on either side is not characteristic of Scythian art. And it is generally considered that the dated art of this type is considerably later than Shang times. More important still, the whole spirit of Scythian art is profoundly different from that of Shang design.

In studying Shang design I have constantly been aware of the feeling that this art had great resemblances, certainly in spirit and possibly in detail, to that of the group of Indians of the north Pacific coast of North America which are known to American anthropologists as the Northwest Coast Indians. I have been able to find very little material on this Northwest Coast art in Peiping, but what I have found has served to strengthen that impression and provide corroboration of certain important details, small in amount though that corroboration necessarily is. Certainly there is a great similarity of feeling. And I have found one incontrovertible case of a design simulating the splitting and spreading out of an animal, over the whole front of a house, in a manner quite like that of the Shangs [15]. In another case the head of an animal only was represented as if split and applied flat to the surface [16]; the chest on which it occurs is said to be "typical of carved and decorated wooden chests fashioned by the northwest Pacific coast Indian tribes" [17]. Such use of the split head only was also common with the Shang designers.

14. Cf. "On Shang Bronze", Plate XII.
15. *Annual Report of the Smithsonian Institution*, 1927, following 494, Plate 6; "An old painted house front of the Kwakiutl Indians at Alert Bay, Vancouver Island, British Columbia".
16. Ibid. 1930, following 556, Plate 17; a carved and painted wooden chest.
17. Loc. cit.

In so far as I know, this representation of the animal as if split and laid out flat is characteristic only of Chinese art and of that of the Northwest Coast Indians, but this does not mean, of course, that it may not exist elsewhere. The Northwest Coast Indians also make a great deal of use of extra heads, beaks, and eyes, added on the plain surfaces of larger animals, in a way reminiscent of, though not identical with, the Shang practice [18]. The many isolated eyes [19] used by the Northwest Coast designers recall most forcibly their similar use in Shang art, and cause one to wonder if there was some magical reason for this which was possessed by both peoples. It must be said, however, that in none of the cases available to me in Peiping is the eye of the Northwest Coast art a Mongoloid, "slanting" eye, like that common with the Shangs. But there is a distinct similarity in the fact that the Northwest Coast eye very frequently tends toward the rectangular in shape, while the pupil frequently and the whole eye occasionally has a like form in Shang design.

I have no intention of trying to explain these similarities at present. What has been stated is fact—as such, it must have some explanation. But what that is, I prefer to leave to those who are expert in the art and archeology of the various areas concerned, who may in the future be able to give us sound theory, at least, rather than mere conjecture. Here it is desired merely to point out that up to this time attempts to find the origins or affinities of Shang art to the west of its home in northeast China have for the most part proved abortive, ending in confessed failure or very ill-considered affirmation. This being the case it is worth while to direct our scrutiny to the north and south of this area and to the east, to the islands of the Pacific and to America. To North America particularly the way for cultural transmission seems to have been open to some degree. And preliminary reconnaissance of the art of these areas justifies the hope that careful research in these directions may not prove unfruitful.

18. Cf. the many plates in Franz Boas, *Primitive Art* (Oslo, 1927), 183–298.

19. Cf. ibid. 205. Here are given seven detailed drawings of the conventional tails, wings, and fins of birds and sea mammals; all appear to contain at least one eye, while most have several.

At least it is well worthy of the attention of experts in these matters.

Concerning the racial and geographical origins of the Shang people we can not yet go very far in drawing conclusions. We must wait for further data. But with regard to the origins of Shang culture we can be more definite, even though our evidence in this regard also is far from complete. There is much in Shang culture which appears to have come from points to the west, and there are elements which came from the south[20]. The technique of painted pottery came to northeast China, flourished, and disappeared. The potter's wheel, horses and cattle, and the technique of bronze manufacture came and remained. But they do not make the impression of having come as a culture which displaced that which was before them, even in a measure. Instead, they supplemented it. Bronze was used as a new and better medium for making vessels in forms which had been used by the Neolithic inhabitants of northeast China for a long, long time. The bow and arrow, long important in northeast China, continued as probably the most important weapon in warfare, although arrowheads were sometimes made of bronze. The

20. The water buffalo, and possibly rice, were factors of Shang culture which appear to derive from the south. Bones of the water buffalo were affirmed to occur in the Shang remains by Dr. Li Chi, in *Anyang Pao Kao* 576, but others have denied the validity of this identification. Even if we had no other evidence, I should be inclined to believe that the water buffalo was known to the Shang people for the reason that many of the bovine heads found on Shang bronzes have horns like those of the water buffalo rather than of the common domestic ox. Fortunately the skeletal material excavated leaves us in no doubt; Dr. Li's statement is unquestionably correct. On April 22, 1935, Dr. C. C. Young of the Geological Survey of China showed me the Anyang skeletal material in his care, and explained the factors which prove that it includes the water buffalo. Horn-cores excavated are of two types, one round, the other triangular in section; the latter is, of course, characteristic of the water buffalo. The bovine metacarpus also occurs in two forms, one slender, the other broad and flat; the latter form, according to Dr. Young, aids the water buffalo in walking through mud. The buffalo found at Anyang has been identified by Dr. Young as *Bubalus mephistropheles* Hopwoods.

economy continued to be a combination of agriculture and animal husbandry, as it had been in Neolithic times.

If we turn to the less material aspects of Shang culture we receive even more sharply the impression that here was a culture stamped strongly with the mark of an individual genius. The craft of bronze manufacture and casting was raised to a pitch of excellence which can hardly have been known to those who brought or transmitted the bronze technique to northeast China.[21] The Shang decorative art, strong yet subtle, complex and intricate but never florid, has no close parallels anywhere and no demonstrated parallels of any sort to the west. Shang religion, which we know fairly well from the oracle bones, was unlike that of any other important, cultured people in the world[22].

Summary

The Shang people apparently occupied the city at Anyang, as their capital, from about the time of Pan Kêng to shortly before, or possibly until the time of, the Chou conquest. The problem of this paper is to shed some light on their antecedents, racial, geographical, and cultural. Present evidence indicates that North China has been inhabited chiefly by a very similar type of Mongoloid men from Neolithic times, if not even earlier, to the present. The indications which we now possess lead us to expect that future research will show the Shangs to be of similar stock. As to the geographical origins of the Shang people we have nothing save tradition, and this can not be supposed to be very trustworthy. Tradition locates the numerous capitals of the Shangs chiefly in northeastern Honan, southern Hopei, and southwestern Shantung.

The problem of the origins of Shang culture is to a considerable extent the problem of the origins of Chinese culture. Some have tried to show that this was imported into China, almost ready-

---

21. My colleagues of the Oriental Institute of the University of Chicago profess themselves amazed at the excellence and the state of preservation of the Shang bronzes, which they say are unparalleled among their Near Eastern finds.

22. Several subsequent papers will be devoted to Shang religion.

made, from elsewhere. But recent discoveries show that even in the earliest Neolithic culture known in northeast China certain characteristic properties of Shang culture were present. Northeast China has apparently constituted a distinctive culture area from the earliest Neolithic times we know. Its culture was like Neolithic culture generally, of course, but with certain peculiarities of its own. Most important among these were the *li* tripod and its related forms, which were apparently unknown outside this area until late in Neolithic times. But they preceded the painted pottery in northeast China, were not driven out by it, and remained after the painted ceramics disappeared from this region. And they were important in the black pottery Neolithic culture which appears to be the closest Neolithic relative to Shang culture. Pottery forms, a peculiar method of scapulimancy, building with pounded earth, and other factors link this culture to that of the Shangs, which stratification proves to have succeeded it in time. It is barely possible that Shang culture was a branch of this black pottery culture upon which certain techniques associated with the Bronze Age were grafted.

The process of making and casting bronze was probably not invented in China, but brought in from some point to the west. But the best bronze casting of the Shangs is equal to the finest work of the sort ever done anywhere, up to and including the present. It appears that Shang craftsmen must have made great improvements on the work of their teachers in this respect. Shang decorative art is baffling in its almost complete lack of antecedents in our known materials. It resembles little in Neolithic art. Attempts have been made to show that it was borrowed from the West, but these have proved abortive. While we can not say with any certainty what were its origins, it appears to have been intimately related to the religion and the mode of life of the Shang people themselves as these are revealed in the oracle bones. Preliminary comparisons lead to the expectation that careful study may show relations between Shang art and some of the art found in America and in islands of the Pacific.

Chinese culture is unique in its continuity. Its most striking characteristic is a capacity for change without disruption. It would appear that that characteristic goes back even to the Neolithic cultures which preceded the Shang in northeast China. Shang culture, like all great cultures, was eclectic, fertilized by influences from many quarters. But these influences and techniques, when they were accepted, met the same fate which has overtaken every people, every religion, every philosophy which has invaded China. They were taken up, developed to accord with Chinese conditions, and transmuted into organic parts of a culture which remained fundamentally and characteristically Chinese.

BOOKS AND ARTICLES CITED

The following list is neither a bibliography of the subjects treated in these papers nor a complete list of the works used in their preparation. Chinese characters for proper names, if not given here, will be found in the index.

ANDERSSON, J. GUNNAR *The Cave-deposit at Sha Kuo T'un in Fengtien, Palaeontologia Sinica*, series D, vol. I, fasc. 1 (Peking, 1923)
   Children of the Yellow Earth: Studies in Prehistoric China. Translated from the Swedish by E. Classen (London, 1934)
   "An Early Chinese Culture," *Bulletin of the Geological Survey of China*, vol. V (1923), no. 1, pp. 1–68
   Preliminary Report on Archaeological Research in Kansu. With a note on the Physical Characters of the Prehistoric Kansu Race by J. Davidson Black. *Memoirs of the Geological Survey of China*, series A, no. 5 (Peking, 1925)
   "Der Weg über die Steppen, *BMFEA*, vol. I (1929), pp. 143–163
ARNE, T. J. *Painted Stone Age Pottery from the Province of Honan, China. Palaeontologia Sinica*, series D, vol. I, fasc. 2 (Peking, 1925)
BISHOP, CARL WHITING "The Beginnings of North and South in China," *Pacific Affairs*, vol. VII (1934), pp. 297–325
   "The Bronzes of Hsin-Cheng Hsien," *Chinese Social and Political Science Review*, vol. VIII (1924), no. 2, pp. 81–99
   "The Chronology of Ancient China," *JAOS*, vol. 52 (1932), pp. 232–247
   Man from the Farthest Past, Smithsonian Scientific Series, vol. 7 (Washington, 1930)
   "The Neolithic Age in Northern China," *Antiquity*, 1933, pp. 389–404
   "The Rise of Civilization in China with reference to its Geographical Aspects," *The Geographical Review*, vol. 22 (1932), pp. 617–631
BLACK, J. DAVIDSON *The Human Skeletal Remains from the Sha Kuo T'un Cave Deposit* in comparison with those from Shao Tsun and with recent North China Skeletal Material. *Palaeontologia Sinica*, series D, vol. I, fasc. 3 (Peking, 1925)
   "On the Discovery of a Paleolithic Industry in Northern China," with P. Teilhard de Chardin, *Bulletin of the Geological Society of China*, vol. III (1924), no. 1, pp. 45–50

"On a Presumably Pleistocene Tooth from the Sjara Osso Gol,"
with P. Licent and P. Teilhard de Chardin, *Bulletin of the Geological Society of China*, vol. V (1927), pp. 285–290
   Preliminary Report, etc. see under J. Gunnar Andersson
   A Study of Kansu and Honan Aeneolithic Skulls and Specimens from Later Kansu Prehistoric Sites in Comparison with North China and other Recent Crania. Part 1, On Measurement and Identification. *Palaeontologia Sinica*, series D, vol. VI, fasc. 1 (Peiping, 1928)

BOAS, FRANZ   *Primitive Art* (Oslo, 1927)
CH'ÊN CH'IAO-TS'UNG 陳喬樅   *Chin Wên Shang Shu Ching Shuo K'ao* 今文尚書經說攷. Huang Ch'ing Ching Chieh Hsü Pien 1079–1116
Ch'êng Li San Chou Nien Kung Tso Kai K'uang Chi Ti Êrh Tz'ǔ Chan Lan Hui Chan P'in Shuo Ming 成立三週年工作概況及第二次展覽會展品說明 (Kaifêng, 1935)
Ch'ien Han Shu 前漢書 (Chin Ling Shu Chü, 1869)
Ch'u Tz'u 楚辭 (Chin Ling Shu Chü, 1872)
CH'Ü JUN-MIN   *Yin Ch'i Pu Tz'ǔ* 殷契卜辭, with Jung Kêng, (Peiping, 1933)
CHANG KUO-KAN 張國淦, ed.   *Han Shih Ching Pei T'u* 漢石經碑圖 (Peiping, 1931)
CHI FO-T'O, ed.   *Chien Shou T'ang So Ts'ang Yin Hsü Wen Tzŭ* 戩壽堂所藏殷虛文字. *I Shu Ts'ung Pien* 藝術叢編 (1918)
CHIN LÜ-HSIANG 金履祥   *Chin Jên-shan Hsien Shêng Shang Shu Chu* 金仁山先生尚書注 (1879)
Chin Shu 晉書 (Chung Hua Shu Chü reprint, 1923, of palace edition of 1739)
CHU FANG-P'U   *Chia Ku Hsüeh, Wên Tzǔ Pien* 甲骨學, 文字編 (Shanghai, 1933)
Chu Shu Chi Nien T'ung Chien 竹書紀年統箋 (Chêkiang Shu Chü, 1877)
CHU YU-TSÊNG 朱右曾   *I Chou Shu Chi Hsün Chiao Shih* 逸周書集訓校釋. Huang Ch'ing Ching Chieh Hsü Pien, 1028–1037
CREEL, HERRLEE GLESSNER   "On the Origins of the Manufacture and Decoration of Bronze in the Shang Period," *Monumenta Serica*, vol. I (1935), no. 1, pp. 39–70
ERKES, EDUARD   "Chinesisch-Amerikanische Mythenparallelen," *T'oung Pao*, vol. XXIV (1926), pp. 32–53
FRASER, E. D. H., compiler *Index to the Tso Chuan*, revised by J. H. S. Lockhart (London, 1930)
GILES, H. A.   *A History of Chinese Literature* (New York and London, 1901, reprinted in 1931)
GOODRICH, LUTHER CARRINGTON   *The Literary Inquisition of Ch'ien-lung*. (Baltimore, 1935)

Books and Articles Cited

HAYASHI TAISUKE, ed. *Kuei Chia Shou Ku Wên Tzŭ* 龜甲獸骨文字 (1921)

Hou Han Shu 後漢書 (Chin Ling Shu Chü, 1869)

HSIEH SHANG-KUNG 薛尙功 *Li Tai Chung Ting I Ch'i K'uan Shih Fa T'ieh* 歷代鐘鼎彝器款識法帖. (Liu Shih ed. 1903)

HSÜ CHING-TS'AN *Yin Hsü Wên Tzŭ Ts'un Chên* 殷虛文字存眞. Vol. I (Kaifeng, 1933)

Hsün Tzŭ 荀子 (Chêkiang Shu Chü ed., 1876)

HUANG CHÜN, ed. *Yeh Chung P'ien Yü* 鄴中片羽. (Peiping, 1935)

JUNG KÊNG. *Chin Wên Pien* 金文編. (1925)

Yin Ch'i etc. see under Ch'ü Jun-min

KARLGREN, BERNHARD *Analytic Dictionary of Chinese and Sino-Japanese.* (Paris, 1923)

Philology and Ancient China. (Oslo, 1926)

K'Ê CH'ANG-CHI *Yin Hsü Shu Ch'i Pu Shih* 殷虛書契補釋, (1921)

KU CHIEH-KANG 顧頡剛 *Ku Shih Pien* 古史辨, 5 vols. (Peking, 1926-1935) Volume IV edited by Lo Kên-chai

KUO MO-JO 郭沫若 *Chin Wên Ts'ung K'ao* 金文叢攷. (Tokyo, 1932)

Chung Kuo Ku Tai Shê Hui Yen Chiu 中國古代社會硏究. (Shanghai, ed. of 1932; first publ. in 1929)

Liang Chou Chin Wên Tz'ŭ Ta Hsi 兩周金文辭大系. (Tokyo, 1932)

Pu Tz'ŭ T'ung Tsuan 卜辭通纂. (Tokyo, 1933)

Kuo Li Chung Yang Yen Chiu Yüan Li Shih Yü Yen Yen Chiu So Chi K'an 國立中央硏究院歷史語言硏究所集刊, Bulletin of the National Research Institute of History and Philology (Academia Sinica). (Canton, 1928; Peiping, 1930-1933; Shanghai, 1933)

Kuo Yü 國語 (T'ien Shêng Ming Tao Pên, reprint of 1800)

LAUFER, BERTHOLD "Some Fundamental Ideas of Chinese Culture," *Journal of Race Development*, vol. V (1914), pp. 160-174

LEGGE, JAMES, translator *Chinese Classics*
Vol. I, *Confucian Analects* 論語 (2nd ed. revised, Oxford, 1893)
Vol. II, *The Works of Mencius* 孟子 (2nd ed. revised, Oxford, 1895)
Vol. III, *The Shoo King* 書經. (London, 1865)
Vol. IV, *The She King* 詩經. (London, 1871)
Vol. V, *The Ch'un Ts'ew with the Tso Chuen* 春秋與左傳 (Hongkong and London, 1872)

LI CHI 李濟 *An Yang Fa Chüeh Pao Kao* 安陽發掘報告, Preliminary Reports of Excavations at An Yang, published by Nat. Res. Inst. Four volumes consecutively paged. Vols. I-II (Peiping, 1929); vol. III (Peiping, 1931); vol. IV (Shanghai, 1931).

Ch'êng-tzŭ-yai 城子崖, ed. with Liang Ssŭ-yung and Tung Tso-pin. *Archaeologia Sinica*, No. 1 (Nanking, 1935). Published in two editions of which one contains a summary in English.
 Hsi Yin Ts'un Shih Ch'ien Ti I Ts'un 西陰村史前的遺存. Ch'ing Hua Hsüeh Hsiao Yen Chiu Yuan Ts'ung Shu Ti San Chung (Peking, 1927)
 "Yin Hsü T'ung Ch'i Wu Chung Chi Ch'i Hsiang Kuan Chih Wên T'i 殷虛銅器五種及其相關之問題," *Ts'ai Anniv. Vol.*, pp. 73–104
LIANG SSŬ-YUNG *Ch'êng-tzŭ-yai*, see under Li Chi
 "Hsiao T'un Lung Shan Yü Yang Shao 小屯龍山與仰韶," *Ts'ai Anniv. Vol.*, pp. 555–568. Separately reprinted, 1933.
 New Stone Age Pottery from the Prehistoric Site at Hsi-yin Tsun, Shansi, China. Memoirs of the American Anthropological Association, No. 37 (Menasha, Wisc., 1930)
LICENT, PÈRE E. "On a Presumably Pleistocene etc." see under J. Davidson Black
LIN I-KUANG *Wên Yüan* 文源. (1920)
LIU CHIEH *Ch'u Ch'i T'u Shih* 楚器圖釋. (Peiping, 1935)
LIU Ê 劉鶚, ed. *T'ieh-yün Ts'ang Kuei* 鐵雲藏龜 (1903). Reprinted with transcriptions 釋文 by Pao Ting 鮑鼎 (1931)
LO CHÊN-YÜ *Chên Sung T'ang Chi Ku I Wên* 貞松堂集古遺文 (1931)
 T'ieh-yün Ts'ang Kuei Chih Yü 鐵雲藏龜之餘 (1915)
 Yin Hsü Ku Ch'i Wu T'u Lu 殷虛古器物圖錄 (1916)
 Yin Hsü Shu Ch'i Ch'ien Pien 殷虛書契前編 (1912)
 Yin Hsü Shu Ch'i Ching Hua 殷虛書契菁華 (1914)
 Yin Hsü Shu Ch'i Hou Pien 殷虛書契後編 (1916)
 Yin Hsü Shu Ch'i Hsü Pien 殷虛書契續編 (1933)
 Yin Hsü Shu Ch'i K'ao Shih 殷虛書契考釋 (1914; revised and enlarged 增訂 edition, 1927). All references are to the latter.
 Yin Hsü Shu Ch'i Tai Wên Pien 殷虛書契待問編 (1916)
 Yin Hsü Wên etc. see under Shang Ch'êng-tso
 Yin Shang Chên Pu Wên Tzŭ K'ao 殷商貞卜文字攷 (1910)
 Yin Wên Ts'un 殷文存 (1917)
LO KÊN-CHAI *Ku Shih Pien* see under Ku Chieh-kang
LOCKHART, J. H. S. *Index* to etc. see under E. D. H. Frazer
Lü Shih Ch'un Ch'iu 呂氏春秋 (Chêkiang Shu Chü, 1880)
MENZIES, JAMES MELLON *Oracle Records from the Waste of Yin*. (Shanghai, 1917)
 "Shang Tai Wên Hua 商代文化," *Ch'i Ta Chi K'an* 齊大季刊, vol. I (1932), pp. 1–7
PALMGREN, NILS *Kansu Mortuary Urns of the Pan Shan and Ma Chang Groups*. Palaeontologia Sinica, series D, vol. III, fasc. 1 (Peiping, 1934)

PAO TING *T'ieh-yün* etc. see under Liu Ê
PETRIE, W. M. FLINDERS *Tools and Weapons Illustrated by the Egyptian Collection in University College, London, and 2,000 Outlines from other Sources.* (London, 1917)
ROSTOVTZEFF, M. *The Animal Style in South Russia and China.* (Princeton, 1929)
Sen-oku Sei-sho 泉屋清賞, The Collection of Old Bronzes of Baron Sumitomo. (Rev. ed. Kyoto, 1934)
SHANG CH'ÊNG-TSO *Fu Shih So Ts'ang Chia Ku Wên Tzǔ* 福氏所藏甲骨文字. (Nanking, 1933)
  Yin Ch'i I Ts'un 殷契佚存. (Nanking, 1933)
  Yin Hsü Wên Tzǔ Lei Pien 殷虛文字類編, with explanations by Lo Chên-yü. (1923)
Shih Chi 史記 (Chin Ling Shu Chü, 1870)
Shih San Ching Chu Su 十三經注疏 (Kianghsi ed. 1815)
STEELE, JOHN, translator *The I-Li.* (London, 1917)
SUN HAI-PO *Chia Ku Wên Pien* 甲骨文編. (Peiping, 1934)
SUN I-JANG *Ch'i Wên Chü Li* 契文舉例 (1904)
TCHANG, PÈRE MATHIAS, S. J. *Synchronismes Chinois. Variétés Sinologiques,* no. 24. (Shanghai, 1905)
TEILHARD DE CHARDIN, PÈRE "On a Presumably Pleistocene etc." see under J. Davidson Black
  "On the Discovery etc." see under J. Davidson Black
  Preliminary Observations on the Pre-loessic and Post-Pontian Formations in Western Shansi and Northern Shensi, with C. C. Young. *Memoirs of the Geological Survey of China,* series A, no. 8 (Peiping, 1930), pp. 34–35
TING FU-PAO 丁福保, ed. *Shuo Wên Chieh Tzǔ Ku Lin* 說文解字詁林 (1928)
TSANG LI-HÊ 臧勵龢 et al. ed. *Chung Kuo Ku Chin Ti Ming Ta Tz'ǔ Tien* 中國古今地名大辭典. (Shanghai, 1930)
Ts'ai Yuan-p'ei, Studies presented to, on his Sixty-fifth Birthday, by Fellows and Assistants of the National Research Institute of History and Philology 慶祝蔡元培先生六十五歲論文集. Vol. I (Peiping, 1933); vol. II in preparation.
TUAN YÜ-TS'AI 段玉裁 *Shuo Wên Chieh Tzǔ Chu* 說文解字注. Huang Ch'ing Ching Chieh, 641–655
TUNG TSO-PIN 董作賓 *Ch'êng-tzǔ-yai,* see under Li Chi
  "Chia Ku Nien Piao 甲骨年表, A Chronological Table of the Discoveries of the Oracle Bones of Anyang," *Bull. Nat. Res. Inst.,* vol. II (1930), no. 2, pp. 241–260
  "Chia Ku Wên Tuan Ti Yen Chiu Li 甲骨文斷代研究例," *Ts'ai Anniv. Vol.,* pp. 323–424

"Yin Hsü Yen Kê 殷墟沿革," *Bull. Nat. Res. Inst.*, vol. II (1930), no. 2, pp. 224–240

UMEHARA SUEJI *Yin Kyo Shutsudo Hakushoku Doki no Kenkyu* 殷墟出土白色土器の研究 Étude sur la Poterie blanche fouillée dans la Ruine de l'Ancienne Capitale des Yin. (Kyoto, 1932)

WANG HSIANG *Fu Shih Yin Ch'i Chêng Wên* 簠室殷契徵文 (1925)
 Fu Shih Yin Ch'i Lei Tsuan 簠室殷契類纂 (1920)

WANG HSIEN-CH'IEN 王先謙 *Shang Shu K'ung Chuan Ts'an Chêng* 尚書孔傳參正 (1904)

WANG KUO-WEI 王國維 *Chien Shou T'ang So Ts'ang Yin Hsü Wên Tzŭ K'ao Shih* 戩壽堂所藏殷虛文字攷釋. *I Shu Ts'ung Pien* 藝術叢編 (1919)
 Chin Pên Chu Shu Chi Nien Su Chêng 今本竹書紀年疏證, Wang, *I Shu*, vol. III
 Kao Tsung Yung Jih Shuo 高宗肜日記, Wang, *I Shu*, vol. I, pt. 1, pp. 4–5
 Ku Pên Chu Shu Chi Nien Chi Chiao 古本竹書紀年輯校, Wang, *I Shu*, vol. III
 Shuo Kêng, 說耿, Wang, *I Shu*, vol. I, pt. 12, p. 4
 Shuo Po 說亳, Wang, *I Shu*, vol. I, pt. 12, pp. 2–4
 Shuo Shang 說商, Wang, *I Shu*, vol. I, pt. 12, pp. 1–2
 Shuo Shang Sung 說商頌, Wang, *I Shu*, vol. I, pt. 2, pp. 17–18
 Shuo Tzŭ Hsieh Chih Yü Ch'êng T'ang Pa Ch'ien 說自契至於成湯八遷, Wang, *I Shu*, vol. I, pt. 12, p. 1
 Shuo Yin 說殷, Wang, *I Shu*, vol. I, pt. 12, pp. 4–5
 Wang Chung-ch'io Kung I Shu 王忠愨公遺書, Collected works of Wang Kuo-wei (1927–1928)
 Yin Chou Chih Tu Lun 殷周制度論, Wang, *I Shu*, vol. 1, pt. 10.
 Yin Li Chêng Wên 殷禮徵文, Wang, *I Shu*, vol. II
 Yin Pu Tz'ŭ Chung So Chien Hsien Kung Hsien Wang K'ao 殷卜辭中所見先公先王考 and *Hsü K'ao* 續考, Wang, *I Shu*, vol. I, pt. 9

WU CH'I-CH'ANG *Chin Wên I Nien Piao* 金文疑年表. (Peiping, 1933; reprinted from *Kuo Li Peiping T'u Shu Kuan Kuan K'an*, vol. VI, 5–6)

WU SHIH-FÊN 吳式芬 *Chün Ku Lu Chin Wên* 攈古錄金文. (1895)

WU TA-CH'ÊNG 吳大澂 *K'ê.Chai Chi Ku Lu* 愙齋集古錄. (1896)
 Shuo Wên Ku Chou Pu 說文古籀補. (1898)

YEH YÜ-SHÊN 葉玉森 "Shuo Ch'i 說契," 學衡 *Critical Review*, no. 31 (1924). (Published together with "Yen Ch'i Chih T'an" as a separate volume, Peiping, 1929)
 T'ieh-yün Ts'ang Kuei Shih I 鐵雲藏龜拾遺. (1925)
 "Yen Ch'i Chih T'an, chuan chia 罕契枝譚,卷甲," 學衡

Critical Review, no. 31 (1924). (Published together with "Shuo Ch'i" as a separate volume, Peiping, 1929)
"Yin Ch'i Kou Ch'ên 殷契鉤沈," 學衡 Critical Review, no. 23, (1923). (Published separately, Peiping, 1929)
YOUNG, C. C. Preliminary Observations etc. see under Teilhard de Chardin
YÜAN YÜAN 阮元 Chi Ku Chai Chung Ting I Ch'i K'uan Shih 積古齋鐘鼎彝器款識. (1804)

BIBLIOGRAPHICAL ABBREVIATIONS

Analytic Dict.	KARLGREN, BERNHARD: Analytic Dictionary of Chinese and Sino-Japanese
Anyang Pao Kao	LI CHI: An Yang Fa Chüeh Pao Kao
Arch. Res. in Kansu	ANDERSSON, J. GUNNAR: Preliminary Report on Archaeological Research in Kansu
BMFEA	Bulletin of the Museum of Far Eastern Antiquities, Stockholm
Bull. Nat. Res. Inst.	Kuo Li Chung Yang Yen Chiu Yüan Li Shih Yü Yen Yen Chiu So Chi K'an
Chên I Wên	LO CHEN-YÜ: Chên Sung T'ang Chi Ku I Wên
Ch'êng Li Shuo Ming	Ch'êng Li San Chou Nien Kung Tso Kai K'uang Chi Ti Êrh Tz'ŭ Chan Lan Hui Chan P'in Shuo Ming
Chi Ku Chai	YÜAN YÜAN: Chi Ku Chai Chung Ting I Ch'i K'uan Shih
Ch'i Ts'un	SHANG CH'ÊNG-TSO: Yin Ch'i I Ts'un
Ch'i Tz'ŭ	CH'Ü JUN-MIN: Yin Ch'i Pu Tz'ŭ
Chia Pien	SUN HAI-PO: Chia Ku Wên Pien
Chien Yin Tzŭ	WANG KUO-WEI: Chien Shou T'ang So Ts'ang Yin Hsü Wên Tzŭ
Chin Nien Piao	WU CH'I-CH'ANG: Chin Wên I Nien Piao
Chin Pien	JUNG KÊNG: Chin Wên Pien
Chin Wên Shu K'ao	CH'ÊN CH'IAO-TS'UNG: Chin Wên Shang Shu Ching Shuo K'ao
Chu Shu	Chu Shu Chi Nien T'ung Chien
Chün Chin Wên	WU SHIH-FÊN: Chün Ku Lu Chin Wên
JAOS	Journal of the American Oriental Society, New Haven
JRAS	Journal of the Royal Asiatic Society, London
K'ê Lu	WU TA-CH'ÊNG: K'ê Chai Chi Ku Lu
Ku Chu Shu	WANG KUO-WEI: Ku Pên Chu Shu Chi Nien Chi Chiao

Kuei Tzŭ	HAYASHI TAISUKE: *Kuei Chia Shou Ku Wên Tzŭ*
Li Tai T'ieh	HSIEH SHANG-KUNG: *Li Tai Chung Ting I Ch'i K'uan Shih Fa T'ieh*
Liang Chou Hsi	KUO MO-JO: *Liang Chou Chin Wên Tz'ŭ Ta Hsi*
Lun Yü	LEGGE, JAMES: *Confucian Analects*
Mencius	LEGGE, JAMES: *The Works of Mencius*
On Shang Bronze	CREEL, HERRLEE GLESSNER: "On the Origins, etc."
Shih	LEGGE, JAMES: *The She King*
Shu	LEGGE, JAMES: *The Shoo King*
Shuo Wên Chu	TUAN YÜ-TS'AI: *Shuo Wên Chieh Tzŭ Chu*
Shuo Wên Lin	TING FU-PAO: *Shuo Wên Chieh Tzŭ Ku Lin*
SSC	*Shih San Ching Chu Su*
Sumitomo Collection	*Sen-oku Sei-shô*
Ti Ming Tien	TSANG LI-HÊ, et al.: *Chung Kuo Ku Chin Ti Ming Ta Tz'ŭ Tien*
T'ieh I	YEH YÜ-SHÊN: *T'ieh-yün Ts'ang Kuei Shih I*
T'ieh Kuei	LIU Ê: *T'ieh-yün Ts'ang Kuei*
T'ieh Yü	LO CHÊN-YÜ: *T'ieh yün Ts'ang Kuei Chih Yü*
Ts'ai Anniv. Vol.	Ts'ai Yuan-p'ei, Studies presented to, etc.
Tso Chuan	LEGGE, JAMES: *The Ch'un Tsew with the Tso Chuen*
Wang, I Shu	WANG KUO-WEI: *Wang Chung-ch'io Kung I Shu*
Yin Ch'ien Pien	LO CHÊN-YÜ: *Yin Hsü Shu Ch'i Ch'ien Pien*
Yin Ching Hua	LO CHÊN-YÜ: *Yin Hsü Shu Ch'i Ching Hua*
Yin Hou Pien	LO CHÊN-YÜ: *Yin Hsü Shu Ch'i Hou Pien*
Yin Hsü Pien	LO CHÊN-YÜ: *Yin Hsü Shu Ch'i Hsü Pien*
Yin K'ao Shih	LO CHÊN-YÜ: *Yin Hsü Shu Ch'i K'ao Shih*

INDEX

Andersson, J. Gunnar, 34n., 35n., 125, 126, 153n., 156, 174, 180, 188, 192, 196, 197 198, 199n., 200, 200n., 201, 201n., 202, 203n., 204, 206, 219n., 228n., 232, 233, 245, 246.
Anyang as the Shang capital, 64–65, 132–140.
Armor, metal, 229n., 230n.
Arne, T. J., 34n., 203n., 219n., 220n., 221n.
Arrowheads, bronze, 226, 231–232, 233, 251.

Bamboo as material for books, 24n., 42.
Bamboo Books, xvii–xxii, 25n. authenticity of current text, xxi, xxii.
Bishop, Carl Whiting, xvii, 24n., 33n., 64n., 118n., 142n., 153n., 155n., 157, 166n., 168, 169, 179, 182, 183n., 192n., 196, 228n., 232n., 236, 245.
Black, Davidson, 149, 155n., 166n.
Boas, Franz, 250n.
Books, Shang, 41–48.
Bow, composite, 195–196, 246–247.
Bow and arrow, 195–196, 251.
Bronze, 19, 144–148, 168–169, 218–234, 224n., 225n., 251, 252, 253.
Buildings, Shang, 182n.

Capitals of the Hsia dynasty, traditional locations of, 120–128.
Capitals of the Shang dynasty, traditional locations of, 157–168.
Ch'ao Kê 朝歌, 12n.

Characters found in the Shang inscriptions, type of, 38–39.
Chariot, 185–188.
Chariot fittings, bronze, 230.
ch'ê 習, 38.
ch'ê 車, 185n.
Ch'êng Tzŭ Yai, 156n., 172, 172n., 174, 176–194, 197, 202, 225.
Chi Fo-t'o 姬佛陀, 8.
chih 之 in Chou documents, 67–68.
Chou propaganda, 51–52, 57–63, 80–93, 105–106, 112.
Chronology, xvi–xxii.
Chu Fang-p'u 朱芳圃, 13.
Chu Hsia 諸夏, 113–115, 116.
ch'ü 瞿, 144n., 226, 229n., 233.
Ch'ü Jun-min 瞿潤緡, 13.
Chün Shih, 106n.
Cicada, 108, 110, 244.
Cire perdue process, 168–169, 224n.
Clothing, tailored, 246–247, 248n.
Coffin, not found in early Chinese graves, 142–143.

Dating criteria for oracle bones, 10–13.
Decree of Heaven, 56, 60–62, 105.
Dog, 182–183, 188–189, 210, 244n.
Dragon, 237–238, 243.
Duke of Chou, 58, 61, 86, 89, 92, 106.

Erkes, Ed., 246n.
Eye motif, 243–244, 250.

fa 伐, 213–214, 216n., 216–218, 226n., 228n.

263

Index

Fan Wei-ch'ing 范維卿, 2.
fang 方, 59n.
Ferguson, John C., 13, 190n.
Feudal system, 54(2), 102–104.
Forged oracle bones, 2.
Freer Gallery of Art, 10, 16.
Fu Shêng 伏生, 29, 30.
Fu Ssŭ-nien, 傅斯年, 193n.

Goodrich, Luther Carrington, 90.

Hayashi, Taisuke 林泰輔, 8.
Hê Chien Hsien Wang 河間獻王, 29.
Helmets, bronze, 229.
History, emphasis on, 32–33.
Horse, 183, 185–189, 191, 192–193, 219n., 251.
Hou Kang, 170–172, 174, 180, 181, 192–193, 194, 197, 202, 222, 224–225.
Hsi Po K'an Li, 48, 76–81, 89.
hsia 夏, 100–101, 106–113.
hsien 甗, 191, 198, 201, 201n., 202, 205, 207, 207–218.
Hsü Ching-ts'an 許敬參, 13.
Hsü Chung-shu 徐中舒, 127(2), 128.
Huang Chün 黃濬, 213.
Human skeletal material, Neolithic, 149–150.
Human skeletal material, Shang, 140–149, 150–153.

Irrigation, 175.

Jung Kêng 容庚, 13, 208n.

Kan Shih, 97n., 99n.
Kao Tsung Yung Jih, 48, 69–76.
Kao Yao Mo, 97n.
Karlgren, Bernhard, 7, 23n., 73, 74, 208, 209, 239n., 242n.
kê 戈, 144, 144n., 195n., 213–214, 217n., 226–229, 233.
K'ê Ch'ang-chi 柯昌濟, 8.

Knife, semilunar and rectangular, 173–174, 246.
Ku Chieh-kang 顧頡剛, 63, 68, 99n.(2).
K'ung An-kuo 孔安國, 29, 163n.
Kuo Mo-jo 郭沫若, 13–14, 67, 71n., 84n., 101n., 104n., 112, 230n.
Kuo Pao-chün 郭寶鈞, 142n., 185n., 199n., 202.

Lacquer, 234n.
Laufer, Berthold, 118n., 168, 221.
lei wên 雷紋, 236–239.
li 鬲, 175, 191, 197–198, 201–218, 226.
li 禮, 117.
Li Chi 李濟, 16, 144n., 174, 196, 196n., 205, 226, 227n., 231n., 251n.
Liang Ssŭ-yung 梁思永, 16, 141, 142n., 145n., 146, 152, 171, 172, 174, 179n., 190n., 191, 191n., 193n.(3), 205n., 215n.(3), 219n., 229n., 230n.
Licent, Emile, 154, 155n., 222n.
Lin I-kuang 林義光, 101n., 107.
Literary style, not identical with colloquial in Western Chou period, 23n.
Liu Chieh 劉節, 119n., 229n.
Liu Ê 劉鶚, 3.
Lo Chên-yü 羅振玉, 4(2), 5, 9, 13, 134n.

Menzies, James Mellon, 3, 5, 6, 13, 74, 74n.
Messages written to spirits, 36–38.
mu 牧, 183.

Northeastern culture area, a, 194–218.

Oracle bones, Shang, xviii, 1–16, 137–138, 139, 192, 238, 239, 240, 243n.

Index

Oracle bones, Neolithic, 176–177, 191, 191–192, 197.
Oral transmission of literature, 22–32.
Ox, 182–185, 188–189, 191, 192–193, 218, 242, 243, 243n., 244n., 251.

Pacific culture area, 245–250.
Paleolithic remains, 154–155, 222.
Palmgren, Nils, 170n., 219n., 234n.
Pan Kêng, 48, 63–69.
Pao Ting 鮑鼎, 10.
Peking man, 153.
Petrie, W. M. Flinders, 227n., 231–232.
Phallic cult, 73–74.
Pig, 182, 183, 188, 243n., 244n.
Pottery, black, 171–172, 179–180, 190, 192, 193–194, 225.
Pottery, painted, 171, 175, 198–202, 219n., 251.
Pottery, white, 190, 191, 234.
Pounded earth, 178–182, 191, 192.
Prone burial, 141–142, 147.

Quipu, 33n.

Rice, 175, 251n.
Rostovtzeff, M., 179n., 235n., 236n., 240.

Sacrifice, 243, 243n.
Sacrifice, human, 214–218.
Sculpture, 18, 230–231, 234, 244.
Shang Ch'êng-tso 商承祚, 9, 13(2).
Shang Shu 尚書, 21n.
Shang Sung, 21, 48–54, 103.
Sheep, 183f., 189, 242, 243, 243n., 244n.
Shu, early and genuine books of, 111, 111n.
shu 書, 43–44.
Sickman Laurence, C. S., 225n.
Split animal motif, 248–250.

Sun Hai-po 孫海波, 14, 43n., 73n., 110, 211, 211n., 214n.
Sun I-jang 孫詒讓, 4.
Suppression of literature, 90–93.

t'ai 台, 76–77, 77n.
T'ang Shih, 48, 55–63.
t'ao t'ieh 饕餮, 235, 239–243.
Tchang, Mathias, xvi.
Teilhard de Chardin, P., 154, 154n., 155n., 222n.
tien 典, etymology, 42. See also 24n.
T'ien 天, 50, 56–57, 65n., 97n.
ting, 鼎 201, 202, 202n., 204, 205, 206, 207, 209.
Tombs, probably royal, 18, 137.
Treaties, 37.
ts'an 驂, 186n.
tsu 祖, etymology, 73–74, 73n.
Tu Lin 杜林, 29.
Tuan Fang 端方, 2.
Tung Tso-pin 董作賓, 8, 10(2), 10–13, 40n.(2), 42n., 43, 45, 45n., 47, 71n., 101n., 108, 109, 109n., 110n., 112n., 142n., 171n., 211, 211n., 214n., 216n., 222n., 225n., 239n.

Umehara, Sueji 梅原末治, 190n.

Wang Hsiang 王襄, 8, 9.
Wang I-jung 王懿榮, 2.
wang jo yüeh 王若曰, 58n., 85–88.
Wang Kuo-wei 王國維, xvii, 8(2), 9, 25n., 49–50, 72, 73, 74, 78n., 80, 135n., 158, 159–163, 164, 165.
Water buffalo, 251n.
Wei Tzǔ, 48, 76, 81–89.
Wên Hou Chih Ming 文侯之命, 26.
Wheel, 219n., 251.
Writing, 21, 33–47.
Writing-brush, 25, 42–46.
Wu Ch'i-ch'ang 吳其昌, 84n.

Yang Shao culture, 170–175, 188, 196, 198–201, 202, 202n., 203–205, 219n., 225.
Yao Tien, 97n.(2), 98n.
Yeh Yü-shên 葉玉森, 9, 108, 109.
Yetts, W. Percival, 136n., 167.
Yin 殷, 1n., 50, 64–66, 135.

Yin hsü 殷虛, 6–8, 136.
Young, C. C. 楊鍾健, 154n., 189, 251n.
yü 聿, etymology, 43.
Yü Kung, 97n., 98n.
yün wên 雲紋, 236–237, 238.